ISLAM IN PRISON
Finding Faith, Freedom and Fraternity

Matthew Wilkinson
Lamia Irfan
Muzammil Quraishi
Mallory Schneuwly Purdie

With a foreword by
Sir David Calvert-Smith and Eoin McLennan-Murray

P

First published in Great Britain in 2023 by

Policy Press, an imprint of
Bristol University Press
University of Bristol
1–9 Old Park Hill
Bristol
BS2 8BB
UK
t: +44 (0)117 374 6645
e: bup-info@bristol.ac.uk

Details of international sales and distribution partners are available at
policy.bristoluniversitypress.co.uk

British Library Cataloguing in Publication Data
A catalogue record for this book is available from the British Library

ISBN 978-1-4473-6360-6 paperback
ISBN 978-1-4473-6361-3 ePub
ISBN 978-1-4473-6362-0 ePdf

Cover design: Robin Hawes
Front cover image: iStock/MoreISO
Bristol University Press and Policy Press use environmentally responsible
print partners.
Printed and bound in Great Britain by CMP, Poole

In grateful memory of Professor James A. Beckford:
scholar, pioneer, mentor and friend.

Contents

List of figures, infographics, images and tables

Figures

Infographics

Images

Tables

List of abbreviations

BAME	Black, Asian and Minority Ethnic
CE	Common Era, refers to the same time span as *Anno Domini*, that is after the death of Christ
HMP	Her/His Majesty's Prison[1]
HMPPS	Her/His Majesty's Prison & Probation Service
PSI	Prison Service Instruction
POELT	Prison Officer Entry-Level Training
PRIMO	Prison-based Interventions for Muslim Offenders
TACT	Terrorism Act
UCIP	Understanding Conversion to Islam in Prison

---

[1] This book was researched and written from March 2019 to early September 2022 in the reign of Her Majesty Queen Elizabeth II. It is published in the reign of His Majesty King Charles III.

About the authors

Matthew Wilkinson is Professor of Religion in Public Life at Cardiff University and Principal Investigator of *Prison-based Interventions for Muslim Offenders* (PRIMO). He has been instructed as an expert witness in Islamic theology in 32 terrorism and hate crime cases, most recently by the Manchester Arena Inquiry. He is author of numerous widely read publications on contemporary Islam, including *The Genealogy of Terror: How to Distinguish Between Islam, Islamism and Islamist Extremism* (Routledge, 2019) and *A Fresh Look at Islam in a Multi-faith World: a Philosophy for Success through Education* (Routledge, 2015).

Lamia Irfan at the time of writing was Research Fellow in Contemporary Islam at the School of Oriental & African Studies (SOAS), University of London. Her PhD and subsequent publications from it have made an original contribution to understanding the situation and needs of Muslim offenders immediately post release and to critical realist theory. She is currently Senior Management Consultant at Capco.

Muzammil Quraishi is Professor of Criminology & Criminal Justice, University of Salford and Co-investigator of PRIMO. He has pioneered empirical research into Muslims in criminal justice settings for the past 20 years with an eye to issues of social justice and reform. His latest book is *Towards a Malaysian Criminology* (Palgrave, 2020).

Mallory Schneuwly Purdie is Senior Researcher at the Swiss Centre for Islam and Society, University of Fribourg. She has researched religion in society and prison chaplaincy in prison for the past 15 years and, as well as publishing widely, leads prison staff training on understanding Muslims in prison.

Acknowledgements

Islam in Prison is the outcome of the research project *Understanding Conversion to Islam in Prison* based at SOAS, University of London in partnership with the University of Salford and the University of Fribourg, Switzerland.

Understanding Conversion to Islam in Prison required multiple sources of support, advice and encouragement to complete before and during the challenging period of the Covid-19 pandemic. The following individuals at different times and in different ways all made significant contributions to the successful accomplishment of our research. The authors are indebted to all of them.

Professor Anna Sapir Abulafia
University of Oxford
Professor of the Study of the Abrahamic Religions

Maqsood Ahmed OBE
Former and first Muslim Advisor, HMPPS

Batool Al-Toma
Founder Director, Convert Muslim Foundation

Mohammed Amin MBE
Co-Chair, The Muslim Jewish Forum of Greater Manchester

Professor Irene Becci
Institute of Social Sciences of Religions
Université de Lausanne, Switzerland
Professor of Emerging Religions & New Spiritualities

The late Professor James Beckford
University of Warwick
Professor Emeritus, Department of Sociology

Professor Nigel Biggar
University of Oxford
Regius Professor of Moral and Pastoral Theology

Professor Ben Bradford
UCL
Professor of Global City Policing

Sir David Calvert-Smith QC
Parole Board of England and Wales, former Director of Public Prosecutions

Sir Anthony Figgis KCVO CMG
Former Marshall of the Queen's Diplomatic Corps

Professor Sophie Gilliat-Ray OBE
University of Cardiff
Professor in Religious and Theological Studies
Director, Centre for the Study of Islam in the UK (Islam-UK)

Jane Haberlin
Balint Consultancy, Psychoanalytic Psychotherapist

Professor Alison Liebling
University of Cambridge
Professor of Criminology & Criminal Justice

Eoin McLennan-Murray
Former Chair, Howard League for Penal Reform
Former President, Prison Governors' Association

Chris Thew
Director, Orbital Design

Baljit Ubhey OBE
Crown Prosecution Service
Director, Prosecution Policy & Inclusion

Our funders, the Dawes Trust, not only financed *Understanding Conversion to Islam in Prison*, but the Dawes Trustees and their advisers were also sources of moral support and sound advice at a number of critical junctures in the research.

We would also like to acknowledge the trust placed in us by Her Majesty's Prison and Probation Service, UK and the Prison Services of Switzerland and France by granting us access to prisons to conduct our research.

In particular, Rory Stewart OBE, UK Minister of State for Prisons (2018–19), had the foresight to understand the need for this research and kindly and sensitively facilitated access to prisons.

We would also like to acknowledge the contributions of enlightened prison governors, prison chaplains, prison officers and prisoners from the ten prisons where we researched without whose friendly participation this research would not have happened but who, for reasons of research anonymity, must remain nameless.

Policy Press, in particular Commissioning Editor Rebecca Tomlinson and her team, were models of flexibility and understanding throughout the writing of this book.

The authors would also like to express their gratitude to their spouses and children whose love and patience sustained them throughout the research. In particular, Matthew Wilkinson would like to mention the significant contribution made by his beloved wife, Lucy Wilkinson, who, although not listed as an author, played an indispensable role in the organisation and execution of this research and the preparation of this book, and for the joy and mathematical support brought by his loving son, Gabriel.

Foreword

Sir David Calvert-Smith and Eoin McLennan-Murray

For most of those working in the criminal justice system since 9/11, the topic of Islam and Muslims in prison has been shrouded in mystery.

We know from our different experiences as a High Court Judge and Chair/member of the Parole Board on the one hand, and as a Number One Prison Governor on the other, that many convicted offenders are becoming Muslim in prison. We have also had some direct experience of the psychological and rehabilitative benefits, and the criminogenic risks, of that religious choice, and, on occasion, the difficulties currently involved in telling between them. We have never really known, or had the means to know, the extent of conversion and change into and within Islam in prison, the different types of Islamic Worldview held by prisoners, the extent of Islamist Extremism in prison, or how the experience of Islam affects the lives of prisoners on a daily basis.

Islam in Prison successfully plugs that gap in practical knowledge. It is, as its authors claim, a 'one-stop-shop' which comprehensively puts the reader, professional, academic or simply interested, in the picture about everything that they will need to know about Islam itself and Islam in prison. For example, it provides a concise, well-written and myth-busting short history of Islam, as well as a comprehensive and fascinating account of the Worldviews, and the experiences of conversion and rehabilitation, of Muslim prisoners.

Its practical and operational observations will assist prison officers, prison chaplains and prison governors to understand Islam and the Muslims in their custody and care, and help enormously to break down the barriers of mistrust and misunderstanding through which professional relationships in prison can so easily, and dangerously, turn sour.

The interest, utility and readability of the book derives in part from the quality of the research behind it. The research represents the largest and most detailed study on Islam in prison to date, carried out by researchers from a variety of disciplines, each of whom is a leader in their field.

The interest, utility and readability of the book also derive from the vivid voices of Muslim prisoners themselves. The prisoners' accounts of the experiences of their faith in prison are always interesting, usually hopeful, occasionally alarming and sometimes moving. Their core message is clear: if Islam and Muslims are properly understood, well taught and sensitively managed in prison, then this religious choice can be a powerful factor supporting successful rehabilitation and reintegration into free society.

In short, this book should be read by prison professionals and policymakers, lawyers, judges and members of the Parole Board, as well as by journalists, academics and students of criminology and contemporary Islam. It will broaden your understanding of Islam and, almost certainly, change the way that you think about Islam, Muslims and prisoners. We heartily recommend it.

Sir David Calvert-Smith
Member of the Parole Board, former High Court Judge,
former Director of Public Prosecutions for England and Wales

Eoin McLennan-Murray
Former Chair Howard League for Penal Reform,
former President Prison Governors' Association,
former prison governor HMP Coldingley and others

Introduction: A tale of three prisoners

Abdurrahman

At 11am on 29 November 2019, in a prison in the south of England, a convicted murderer and once-feared gang leader, Abdurrahman, now a Muslim mosque orderly, was knocking on the doors of the prison chaplains in the multi-faith chaplaincy area of Her Majesty's Prison (HMP) Cherwell (Category C Prison) asking if anyone would like a cup of tea.

As he prepared the tea, Abdurrahman reflected on the prospect of his upcoming marriage to a Muslim woman whom he had befriended on prison visits, authorised exceptionally by the managing chaplain. He ran through the short guest list of family and friends and was amazed at the quantum shift in his attitude to women since his conviction, inspired by the example of the Prophet Muhammad's (may the peace and blessings of God be upon him)[1] respectful marriage to Khadija (may God be pleased with her).[2]

Although Abdurrahman knew that he and his wife would not be able to consummate their marriage for years, he wanted to ensure that they could chat at close quarters and hold hands during prison visits in a religiously permitted (halal) way. After attending to the needs of the Muslim, Anglican, Catholic, Jewish and Hindu prison chaplains, Abdurrahman moved onto the purpose-designed prison mosque to vacuum clean it for the Friday Congregational Prayer.

That afternoon, Abdurrahman was scheduled to attend a Qur'an recitation class with the Muslim prison chaplain. Abdurrahman was a designated Learning Mentor for a beginner reading The Qur'an (the Holy Book of Islam). He knew that he would need his wits about him since his young mentee was prone to lapses in concentration and was apt to lark around, distracting himself and others from the tricky task of recitation. After spending much of his life causing violence and chaos, it made Abdurrahman

---

[1] In the Islamic tradition, the names of Prophets are often honoured with the phrase, 'may the peace and blessings of God be upon him'. We use this phrase on this one occasion to acknowledge our respect for this tradition and the person of the Prophet Muhammad. We will not use it hereafter since this book is not a confessional religious text, but a forensic academic account.

[2] In the Islamic tradition, the names of senior Companions (*Sahaba*) of the Prophet Muhammad are often honoured with the phrase 'may God be pleased with him/her'. We use this phrase on this one occasion to acknowledge our respect for this tradition and the senior Companions of the Prophet Muhammad. We will not use it hereafter since this book is not a confessional religious text, but a forensic academic account.

feel calm and grateful that he was bringing his own faith and experience of life to bear to improve someone else's.

Usman

At 1:45pm on 29 November 2019, Usman, a convicted terrorist out on licence and with an electronic tag, sat unobtrusively in a celebration event at Fishmongers' Hall, London Bridge. A group of students, prisoners and academics had gathered to celebrate the success of free citizens, offenders and returning citizens studying together on the 'Learning Together' programme. Like the other attendees, Usman was quietly listening to a storytelling event and giving feedback (Cook and Griffiths, 2019).

In prison, as a convicted terrorist, Usman had participated mandatorily in the UK Government's Desistance and Disengagement Programme, designed to rehabilitate terrorist offenders psychologically and to return them to a state of acceptance both of themselves and their fellow human beings. Usman was regarded as a success story of effective rehabilitation.

At around 1:55pm, Usman left the group almost unnoticed to go to the toilet.

At 1:58pm he emerged bearing two kitchen knives strapped to his wrists and, having ripped off his padded gilet, he appeared in a fake suicide vest. He went on the rampage, fatally stabbing two of the event's organisers, Saskia Jones and Jack Merritt, and wounding three others. He was forced out onto the street by a chef and another prisoner who was out on day licence, restrained by members of the public and then shot dead by police.

Amina

One morning in March 2019, Amina, a 24-year-old Algerian woman, shyly entered the prison chapel. Amina is a recidivist thief, imprisoned for the third time. Her life had been tough: born in war-torn Algeria, with a violent father and a depressed mother, Amina fled Algeria to escape a marriage negotiated for money by her father. As an illegal migrant to Switzerland, Amina lived in shelters for minors, sometimes sleeping in Salvation Army hostels until she was recruited into a criminal racket of prostitution and theft.

Amina is proud to be a Muslim, even when confessing to not being very religious. She is critical of Muslim men who, according to her, do not behave Islamically and try to take advantage of her. Nevertheless, Amina sometimes prays, always fasts, does not wear the *hijab* (because she likes to look pretty) and dances at night alone in her cell for God. Dancing helps her not to fall into depression. Amina sees the contradictions between "fooling around" (stealing), praying and asking God for forgiveness.

Amina interprets her incarceration as God's plan: she needs protection from the criminal network, and God has put her in prison. She receives regular visits from the Christian prison chaplain. She enjoys his visits and trusts him because he really listens to her. Sometimes she also prays with him. On one occasion, she met the visiting Muslim prison chaplain. He gave her hope and had advised her to keep her faith, read The Qur'an and not to forget God. Amina tries to follow his advice and prays for forgiveness, for protection and to keep her away from suicide.

Understanding Islam in prison

These stories, with their startlingly different outcomes, are all tales of the diverse effects of Islam, or what is taken to be Islam, in and around prison. They are stories of significant religious change which can lead to dramatic rehabilitation on the one hand, and on the other to recidivism and even extremist violence.

Apart from the differences in quality of life exhibited by these three stories, another difference between them is that the story of Usman Khan and others like it[3] have been widely reported in the media and analysed in all their macabre horror, not least because of the tragic irony that the two young victims of Khan – Saskia Jones and Jack Merritt – were people who had volunteered to restore the dignity and prospects of people like Khan himself.

The quieter and more hopeful stories of prisoners like Abdurrahman are unreported and are unknown to the public at large, and even to the Prison Service itself.

This is partly because prisons are 'total' enclosed environments (Goffman, 1961) designed to deter, incapacitate and then rehabilitate criminals who remain sealed off from free society. For reasons of security and fear, researchers and journalists are not often let in, and therefore the stories and experiences of prisoners, prison chaplains, prison officers and prison governors are not often let out.

Just as bad news sells copy, bad news also makes policy. Attention to Islam and Muslims in prison by European prison policymakers has tended to be sharply focused on the prevention of extremism rather than the promotion of rehabilitation.

As we saw earlier in the case of Usman Khan, extremist Worldviews (which we document in Chapter 6) *are* held and propagated in prison. Nevertheless, this book intends to bring the calming balance of some proper evidence to bear on the matter.

---

[3] For example, Khalid Masood who was responsible for the attacks on Westminster Bridge in March 2017.

We show that these concerns around the destructive influence of extreme forms of Islamism in prison need to be balanced with the understanding that for many Muslim prisoners, Islam in prison can and does generate productive rehabilitative outcomes such as a reconnection with conscience, discipline, education and work.

The over-representation of Muslims in prison

The sheer numbers of Muslims in prison make it doubly important to present a fair and accurate picture of Islam in prison.

Since the 1940s, mass Muslim migration to Europe (about which we will say more in Chapter 1) has seen increasing numbers of prisoners registered as Muslim in prisons in European jurisdictions. For example, in England and Wales, while Muslims make up circa 5 per cent of the general population, they make up 17 per cent of the prison population (n = circa 13,540) (Sturge, 2019; Statista, 2021).[4] In France – where statistics by religion are illegal – surnames suggest that citizens of Muslim heritage make up circa 10 per cent[5] of the general population but up to 60 per cent of the prison population (World Prison Brief, 2021a). This means that in many European jurisdictions, Muslims, especially Muslim men, are significantly over-represented in prisons.

Of these disproportionately large numbers of Muslims in British and continental European prisons, our research and previous estimates (UK Gov, 2016) suggest that as many as 30 per cent of Muslim prisoners are Converts to Islam, for whom both the productive and the destructive effects of religious belief and practice are particularly pronounced. Yet, despite the urgency of the public need to understand the phenomenon of Islam in prison, including conversion, up until this study there has existed no detailed, specialist, large-scale academic research that focuses on the reasons for and consequences of choosing to follow Islam in prison.

The purposes of this book

Prison policymakers, prison governors, prison officers, prison chaplains and, indeed, prisoners themselves have told us that they need a book to plug this damaging gap in knowledge about Islam in the prisons of Europe. This is why

---

[4] While male Muslim prisoners are significantly over-represented in prison, female Muslim prisoners are only marginally so. Female Muslim prisoners account for 6 per cent of the total female prisoner population: of the 3,213 female prisoners in England and Wales, approximately 250 are Muslim (Ministry of Justice, 2020; HMPPS, 2020).

[5] Due to *Laïcité* (secularism) the French state forbids the collection of statistics according to religion. Estimates of the French Muslim population range from 5 per cent to 10 per cent.

our book aims to be a 'one-stop shop' which will offer its readers a detailed and practical understanding of Islam and Muslims in today's European prisons.

We intend to make this knowledge available in the most accessible way possible designed for busy professionals and general readers who need to know and do more besides gaining a working knowledge of Islam in prison. For readability we intend to filter out as much jargon and academic-speak from the book as possible.

The portrait of Islam in prison that we paint comes out of a fully fledged academic research programme called *Understanding Conversion to Islam in Prison*[6] (UCIP), conducted with the engagement of 279 prisoners and 76 members of prison staff in ten prisons of all security categories in England (five prisons), Switzerland (four prisons) and France (one prison) over three years (see Table I.1 for full details).

The aim of UCIP was to gain a deep and broad understanding of religious change around the practice of Islam in prisons in order to discover how this religious choice might support rehabilitation.

UCIP's interest in religious change around Islam was structured around five Research Questions:

1. Who are Converts to Islam, broadly construed, in socio-demographic and religious terms?
2. Why do many prisoners choose to follow Islam in European prisons?
3. What types of Islam(-ism) are followed in prison?
4. What are the benefits and risks of choosing to follow Islam in prison?
5. How are processes of conversion and religious change managed by prison authorities and the prison chaplaincy?

We discovered that religious change is such a prevalent feature of Islam in prison that this book describes the presence of Islam and Muslims in prison *in general*.

To gain an understanding of the broad patterns of Islamic belief and behaviour we conducted questionnaire surveys, which were analysed statistically. To drill down into the detailed experiences of the practice of Islam in prison, we undertook in-depth interviews and conducted observations, both formally of 32 prison events and informally by being present on the wings.[7] Findings from this research inform the text throughout.

---

[6] UCIP was an independently funded university study undertaken between 2017 and 2021 as a partnership between SOAS, University of London; University of Salford; and University of Fribourg, Switzerland.

[7] See Appendices 1 to 3 for our theory, methodology, ethical framework and sampling and Appendix 4 for full descriptions of our research prisons. See Appendix 5 for an explanation of how we calculated the Worldviews of our sample.

Table I.1 summarises our research engagement from which the evidence base of this book is derived.

The comparative element

Our comparative data from Switzerland and France highlighted fascinating and useful similarities and differences of prisoner Worldviews, chaplaincy practices and national prison culture that constitute a strand of our analysis throughout the book.[8]

As well as this practical understanding of the different types of Islamic Worldviews that are held in European prisons, this book will also give the reader clear guidance on how and why prisoners find their faith, including the different types of conversion and religious change that take place in prison and how conversion affects prisoner rehabilitation.

It will also give an account of Islamist Extremism in prison, its sources and its effects, which, while not our core research focus, emerged through the application of our research tools and by our in-the-field encounters with practices and beliefs in prison that were definitely *not* part of Mainstream Islam.

The structure of this book

Our account of Islam in prison is divided into ten chapters. All the chapters are self-contained and contribute to the 'big picture' by offering a comprehensive portrait of Islam in prison.

Chapter 1: Where does Islam come from and who are Muslim prisoners?

A condensed story of Islam, where Islam comes from, how Islamic civilisation developed, and how and why Islam and Muslims come to be in European prisons today. It includes an account of the characteristics of our sample of 279 Muslim prisoners, who, for reasons that we explain, we regard as characteristic of Muslim prisoners generally.

Chapter 2: What is Islam in prison?

An account of the basic beliefs and practices of Islam and, from prisoners' own voices, how these basic beliefs and practices shape and influence their lives.

---

[8] As Figure I.1 suggests, although our primary focus was on prisons in the jurisdiction of England and Wales our research was actually conducted in five English and no Welsh prisons. So, from now on, we will refer to English rather than English and Welsh prisons.

Table I.1: UCIP research prisons and sample by jurisdiction

Country	Prisons[a]	Security Category of the prison[b]	Questionnaire surveys	Interviews with prisoners	Interviews with chaplains	Interviews with officers	Interviews with governors	Observations: RE classes + Friday Prayers
England	5		191	122	13	25	12	21
	HMP Cherwell	C	57	33	2	8	4	5
	HMP Forth	A	24	19	3	5	2	4
	HMP Parrett	B	52	36	6	8	2	5
	HMP Stour	D	19	12	1	-	3	3
	HMP Severn	B	39	22	1	4	1	4
Switzerland	4		54	25	5	12	1	10
	Mitheilen	A	20	14	1	-	-	2
	Fontgrise	B	15	5	2	11	1	5
	Doriath	A	11	1	1	1	-	2
	La Citadelle	A	8	5	1	-	-	1
France	1		34	11	2	4	2	1
	Hauterive	B	34	11	2	4	2	1
Total	10	4 x A; 4 x B 1x C; 1 x D	279	158	20	41	15	32

Notes: [a] All names of research prisons and participants are pseudonyms; [b] Categories of Swiss and French prisons are approximately based for the sake of consistency on the English categorisation. 'A' corresponds to Maximum Security. 'B' corresponds to High Security.

Figure I.1: Percentages of our sample of Muslim prisoners in each jurisdiction

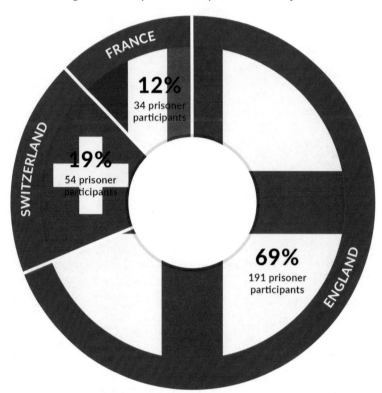

Chapter 3: Finding their faith: why do prisoners choose Islam?

Describes the types of Muslim prisoner, tests, and then challenges the idea that prisoners mainly choose to follow Islam for reasons of 'perks, privileges and protection'.

Chapter 4: What types of Islam do prisoners follow?

Describes the Worldviews of Mainstream Islam, Islamism and Islamist Extremism; details the numbers of prisoners in our characteristic sample that held each type of Worldview and how these Worldviews were connected or not connected to rehabilitation and extremism.

Chapter 5: Mainstream Islam in prison

Describes how Mainstream Islam is brought to life in prison by the majority of Muslim prisoners and how the Worldview of Mainstream Islam shapes their experience of prison life and rehabilitation.

Chapter 6: Islamism and Islamist extremism in prison

Describes, in often graphic and eye-opening terms, how Islamist and Islamist Extremist Worldviews shape the experiences of prison life for a small minority of Muslims.

Chapter 7: The lives of Muslim prisoners: opportunities and risks

Seven different types of Muslim prisoner describe in detail how they experience religious conversion and change in prison, how these changes offer opportunities for rehabilitation, as well as risks.

Chapter 8: Caring for Muslim prisoners: Muslim prison chaplaincy

Describes the critical role of Muslim prison chaplaincy in Muslim prison life through prisoners' experiences of chaplains and the chaplains' experiences of prisoners, with a particular focus on Statutory Duties, Friday Prayer and Islamic Studies classes. This chapter articulates some principles for best practice derived from the views and experiences of Muslim prison chaplains themselves.

Chapter 9: Managing Muslim prisoners: treading a middle path between naïvety and suspicion

In light of the importance of relationships with prison staff in the experience of religion, this chapter articulates some principles for engagement with Muslims on the part of prison officers and prison governors.

Conclusion: The Virtuous Cycle of Rehabilitation and Avoiding the Vicious Cycle of Extremism

A summary of what has been discovered about Islam in prison, how many Muslim prisoners find faith, freedom and fraternity in prison and our plans to assist this process in the future.

Key messages

We offer five key messages about Islam in prison:

1. **Prisons are sites of intense religious change into and within Islam.** Using a broad and original typology of religious conversion and change described in Chapter 3, we discovered that prisons are sites of intense conversion and religious change: Converts who had chosen to follow Islam for the first time in prison, Intensifiers who were born Muslims

who had become significantly more devout in prison and Shifters whose Islamic Worldview had significantly changed represented together 77 per cent of our characteristic sample.

2. **Conversion to and intensification in Islam are significantly associated with positive attitudes to rehabilitation**, in terms of re-engaging with work and education and avoiding criminal behaviour, especially when supported by engagement with prison chaplaincy.

    Conversion to Islam and intensification in Islam also carry some criminogenic risk of prisoners being attracted to the 'Us' versus 'Them' Worldviews of Islamism and Islamist Extremism, especially when they happen on the wings, disengaged from prison chaplaincy.

3. **Muslim prisoners' Worldviews are typically characterised by Mainstream Islam, although pockets of Islamist Extremism do exist in prison**.
    By mapping Muslim prisoners' religious Worldviews in Chapters 4, 5 and 6, we challenge the widespread belief that prisons are wholesale incubators of extremism. On the contrary, Mainstream Islamic values are held by the majority (76 per cent) of prisoners and are likely to support their rehabilitation. In Chapter 6, we also describe how a small proportion of Islamist Extremists can generate an atmosphere of fear and mistrust among staff and other prisoners that belies their relatively small numbers.

4. We identify a **Virtuous Cycle of Rehabilitation** in prison (Figure I.2), consisting of religious Conversion and Intensification, Mainstream Islam, Engagement with Chaplaincy, and Fair Treatment by prison staff, which led to positive attitudes to rehabilitation in the form of work, education and avoiding 'bad behaviour'.

    The more prisoners were moving around or towards this cycle, the less likely they were to be lured towards the **Vicious Cycle of Islamist Extremism**, gangs, suspicious and unfair treatment by prison staff, which leads to further crime.

5. There are **five gaps in prison provision** that should be addressed in order to enhance the rehabilitative potential and reduce the criminogenic risk of Islam in prison:[9]

---

[9] These five gaps in prison provision are being addressed in our follow-up programme, PRIMO (*Prison-based Interventions for Muslim Offenders*).

Figure I.2: The Virtuous Cycle of Rehabilitation

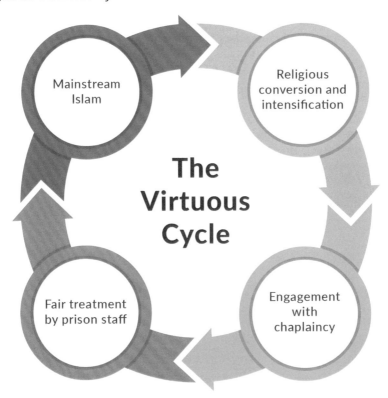

i. to provide an understanding of Islam for prisoners in a way that is relevant to life in prison;

ii. to raise the 'Prisons-Literacy' of Muslim prison chaplains generally;

iii. to raise the 'Prisons-Literacy' of Muslim prison chaplains to the specific needs of female Muslim prisoners;

iv. to raise the 'Religious Literacy' of prison officers;

v. to clarify the management of the process of changing religion in prison through the legal Prison Service Instruction (PSI) in the UK.

For an account of Islam in prison derived from the diverse voices and rich experiences of prisoners and prison staff themselves, we respectfully encourage the reader to read on.

1

Where does Islam come from and who are Muslim prisoners?

Islam is heavily inscribed with the 'presence of the past' (Bhaskar, 2008; Wilkinson, 2019). In other words, forms of Islam that are dominant today have long-standing historical precedents. Also, a wide variety of criminals of different types, both Muslim and non-Muslim, abuse Islam's past to justify their contemporary attitudes and illegitimate activities. Therefore, so that the reader can place Islam and Muslims in prison fairly in historical context, we begin by telling Islam's story in brief, including showing why Muslims come to be found in European prisons today.

Muhammad, son of Abdullah, Prophet of God

The Muslim Declaration of Faith[1] (the *Shahada*) – 'There is no god but God[2] and Muhammad[3] is the Prophet[4] of God' – was first heard in the trading oasis of Mecca in the Arabian Peninsula in 610 CE. It was uttered by one Muhammad, the son of Abdullah, a 40-year-old orphaned minor nobleman from the ruling Meccan tribe of Quraysh. The Arab tribe of Quraysh and Muhammad's own Hashim clan were responsible for the upkeep of the worship that took place in Mecca[5] at an ancient cuboid structure draped in a black cloth, called The Cube (Ka'aba) (see Image 1.1). The Ka'aba was believed to be the site dedicated by the Prophet Abraham to the worship of God (Allah), which had since accrued the worship of myriad religious idols.

The First Revelation

Muhammad was a respected and prosperous merchant known in Mecca as 'The Trustworthy' ('*Al-Amin*'). However, according to Muslim tradition,

---

[1] We give a full account of the basic beliefs of Islam in Chapter 3.
[2] In Arabic, 'Allah', meaning 'The One God'.
[3] Variously spelt in Latin script: Muhammad, Mohammed, Mohammad, Mohamed, Mahmud and Mehmet (Turkish).
[4] In Arabic, 'Rasul Allah' (sometimes translated as 'Messenger of God').
[5] Some Muslims prefer the spelling 'Makkah'.

Image 1.1: Artist's impression of Mecca with the Ka'aba at the time of the Prophet Muhammad

Source: Reproduced courtesy of the Madain Project

Image 1.2: The Cave of Hira where the Prophet Muhammad is believed to have received the first words of The Qur'an

Source: www.islamiclandmarks.com/makkah-other/jabal-al-al-hira

he did not feel satisfied by the affairs of this world and for years had gone on an annual retreat away from the city of Mecca to reflect on life's meaning. The place to which he retreated was a small cave at the back of a mountain overlooking Mecca called Mount Hira (see Images 1.2 and 1.3).

Image 1.3: Mount Hira overlooking Mecca, also known as the Mountain of Light (Jabal al Nur)

Source: Created by Mohamadhaghani, available on wikimedia

One night in Ramadan 610 CE as Muhammad sat in this small cave, Muslims believe that[6] the Archangel Gabriel appeared to him and said,

Read [*Iqra*].

Muhammad was illiterate and formally uneducated and he replied in astonishment,

---

[6] This story of Muhammad is what Muslims believe to be true about Muhammad. The sources of the story of early Islam used in this account are derived from a wide variety of primary and secondary sources, such as Ibn Ishaq's 'Life of Muhammad' written in c. 722 CE and other modern versions. Of course, the reader has every right not to believe this story or the truth of Muhammad's claims. Indeed, there exists a revisionist school of Islamic Studies which casts doubt on the primary sources of Islam. Nevertheless, we do not want to repeatedly write, "Muslims believe that".

> I am not one of those who read!

Twice more the same command to 'Read' was issued. Twice more Muhammad made the same reply until the Archangel Gabriel, holding Muhammad in a fierce embrace, recited:

> Read!
>
> In the name of your Lord who has created humankind from a blood-clot.
>
> Read!
>
> Your Lord is the most Noble who has taught humankind what they did not know before by means of the Pen!
>
> The Qur'an, 96:1–3

These were the first phrases of what became the Book of Islam, The Qur'an,[7] meaning 'The Recitation'.

Muhammad, desperate to flee from this appalling apparition and these terrible words, abandoned the cave, but wherever he turned outside the cave there was the awesome figure of the Archangel Gabriel filling the horizon, repeating the same words (Ishaq, 1955; Lings, 1983).

The message of Islam

After this first revelation, and with the support of his wife Khadija bint Khuwaylid (555–620 CE), Muhammad continued to make the seemingly

---

[7] In transliteration of Arabic, the apostrophe ' stands for the letter 'hamza', which sounds like a glottal stop. With apologies to Islamic Studies purists, throughout the text, we have tried to keep the transliteration of Arabic words as simple and as close to contemporary English as possible. When an Arabic word or name has passed into normal English usage, we do not italicise it, e.g. The Qur'an. We italicise words in Arabic that remain 'foreign' in English.

outrageous claim that the Archangel Gabriel was regularly bringing him words uttered by God Almighty.

At the heart of the message that Muhammad claimed was revealed to him was the idea that God is one Divine Being and that this one Divine Being was the only being worthy of human worship. Muhammad also made the claim that he himself was the last Prophet in a long line of Prophecy stretching back through Jesus, David, Moses and Abraham to Adam, the father of humanity itself. Muhammad's mission was to declare the truth of Divine Unity and to show humanity once again how to worship God and to live in harmony with His Will.

This core belief and the set of practices[8] that Muhammad claimed were revealed by the Archangel Gabriel – such as standing, bowing and prostrating in prayer – were, on the face of it, not threatening. Muhammad did not call for war against his opponents; he did not call for people who followed him to abandon their families as leaders of religious cults often did and do. Moreover, Muhammad did not even claim to bring a new faith. Instead, he claimed that he and his message were merely a continuation of a long line of Prophethood stretching back to Abraham. Nevertheless, it soon became clear that elements of this renewed religion, which its followers called Islam – meaning Submission to God – threatened the Meccan way of life.

Threats to the Meccan way of life

At the time, Mecca was a wealthy trading hub for a region that stretched from Byzantine Damascus in Syria in the north to Yemen in the south (see Figure 1.1). Mecca, as the central trading hub, was sustained by these traders who also gathered to worship the idols of Mecca. By insisting, as the Prophet Abraham had done before him, that only one True God was worthy of worship and that the idols were powerless and meaningless, Muhammad threatened not only a set of ancestral beliefs, but also a significant gravy train.

In addition, the revelations from God to Muhammad through the Archangel Gabriel declared that all humans were created equal by God and that all humans would be judged by God only on the ethical quality of their behaviour and not on their social rank or wealth.

This essential human equality dealt an ideological blow to the strict class structures of Meccan society and to the institutionalised slavery that was enjoyed by the powerful Qurayshi families of the day. Not only did Muhammad's message of basic human equality strike a blow at unjust Meccan class structures, it also struck a blow at the second-class status of women.

The Qur'an (49:13 and 3:195) stipulated that men and women stood as equals before God and it prohibited the abhorrent Meccan practice of

---

[8] For a full account of the basic practices of Islam, see Chapter 3.

Figure 1.1: Trade routes on the Arabian Peninsula at the time of the Prophet Muhammad's birth

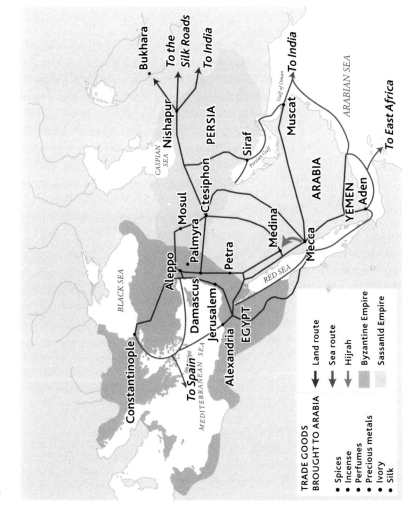

TRADE GOODS
BROUGHT TO ARABIA

- Spices
- Incense
- Perfumes
- Precious metals
- Ivory
- Silk

Land route
Sea route
Hijrah
Byzantine Empire
Sassanid Empire

Source: Image created by Orbital Design; information provided by Ahmed Ben Rezguia; www.eufatwa.com/sharia/concept-for-integrating-sharia/trade-routes-a-d-570/

murdering female infants at birth. This basic equality between men and women meant that women in Islam were afforded a high social status that was unheard of in the early medieval world, when women across the world were usually treated as the dependent possessions of men (Khan et al, 2019).

Muslim women were given the right to choose or reject marriage partners; the right to hold and invest wealth of their own; and the right to work and engage in business independently. Moreover, Islam brought all sexual relations between men and women inside a legally binding marriage in which the rights of children were also protected.

Initially, only Muhammad's immediate family believed that Muhammad's message was a revelation from God: first his wife, Khadija, and next his young cousin, Ali ibn Abi Talib (607–661 CE). Others declared that Muhammad was possessed by a spirit (*Jinn*) or, even though he was illiterate, that he was a poet.

However, gradually the message of Divine Unity, human equality and the poetic beauty of The Qur'an began to attract followers from all levels of Meccan society to embrace Islam. To the horror of Meccan high society, the aristocratic kinsman of Muhammad, Uthman ibn Affan (573/6–656 CE) and the slave, Bilal ibn Rab'ah (580–640 CE), declared each other brothers under God.

The Meccan leadership, after a period of attempting to lure Muhammad away from the new faith and tempting him with offers of tribal prominence and wealth, turned to threats and acts of violence against Muhammad and the growing band of Muslims in Mecca.

The Meccan leadership ostracised Muhammad and his small group of followers from Mecca for a whole year, during which, after a period of terrible hardship, Muhammad's wife, Khadija, died. It became clear to Muhammad that his message and his fledgling community would not survive in Mecca and he started to look around for an alternative place for Muslims to reside and thrive.

The Migration

After a number of false dawns, Muhammad was invited by two warring tribes, the Aws and Khazraj, from an oasis town 200 miles to the north of Mecca called Yathrib, to settle with his community there in order to mediate their feud.

From May to July 622 CE, the Muslims in Mecca started spiriting themselves out of Mecca on a journey called in Arabic *Al-Hijra*, meaning 'The Migration'. Finally, in mid-July[9] 622 CE Muhammad and his close Companion, Abu Bakr al-Siddiq ('The Truthful') (573–634 CE)

---

[9] Either 16 July or 19 July 622 CE.

set out themselves after dark, leaving a decoy in Muhammad's bed. Avoiding trackers and assassins, on 24 September 622 CE Muhammad and Abu Bakr arrived safely in Yathrib. Finally, Muslims felt safe to put down roots and establish a community guided by the principles of The Qur'an.

Muhammad, in his role as a mediator and as guided by The Qur'an,[10] which mandates freedom of religion (The Qur'an, 2:256), was quick to draw up a binding political pact between the resident Arab tribes – including the warring Aws and Khazraj tribes – and the resident Jewish communities and the migrant Meccans.

These groups agreed that they would all defend and protect each other and that they would all be entitled to the same personal rights and the same rights to hold property. This agreement became known as the Constitution of Medina and it was a significant step forward in civil rights, which had previously only been guaranteed through tribal allegiance and protection: the Constitution of Medina gave civil rights a constitutional status (Lecker, 2004).

Yathrib was also renamed by its inhabitants The Town of Enlightened Prophecy (*Medinat Al-Munawarra Al-Nabawiyya*). Seventeen years later, The Migration came to be recognised as such a momentous event in the survival of Islam that 622 CE became the first year of the Islamic calendar.

Permission to fight

With their new-found stability, the Muslim community of Medina resumed their trading businesses from their new home and soon became an emerging power which competed with the traders from Mecca. It was not long before Muhammad's Meccan enemies sought to retaliate against him and bring their errant son to heel.

Those Muslims who had chosen to remain in Mecca or who had been unable to leave Mecca were harassed and persecuted and their property was seized, and their goods were dispatched for sale with trading caravans to Syria and elsewhere.

In this context of the need to defend the lives and property of Muslims, Muhammad, who had previously been pacifist and avoided aggression,

---

[10] The revelations were initially memorised or written down on stone, leather or bark. They were subsequently compiled as a complete text in 650 CE, 30 years after Muhammad's death, initially by the first Caliph Abu Bakr (573–634 CE) and then completed in an authorised edition by the third Caliph 'Uthman (573/576–656 CE).

claimed for the first time that a revelation from God had given him permission to fight to defend Muslim lives and property:[11]

> Those who have been attacked are permitted to take up arms because they have been wronged – God has the power to help them – those who have been driven unjustly from their homes only for saying, 'Our Lord is God.'
>
> The Qur'an, 22:39

The first battles of Islam: the Battle of Badr and the Battle of Uhud

In the context of this permission to fight, the first major showdown between the pagan community of Mecca and the Muslim community of Medina took place on 13 March 624 CE at a place between Mecca and Medina called the Wells of Badr. Here, a Muslim army of around 300 was deployed to intercept a Meccan army and caravan of around 900. After the preliminary single combat between champions, the Meccan army was routed, with 140 dead, including many prominent figures. Among them was Muhammad's most implacable enemy, Amr ibn Hisham al-Makhzumi (570–624 CE), who was known to the Muslim community as Abu Jahl ('The Father of Ignorance') for his intransigence and violence towards them.

After repelling further assaults on Medina, including at the Battle of Uhud (625 CE) and the siege of Medina in 627 CE,[12] Muhammad and his community began to consolidate themselves around the worship of One God in the newly built Mosque of Medina (see Image 1.4). In Medina, the direction of the five Obligatory Daily Prayers was changed from Jerusalem to the *Ka'aba* in Mecca, which symbolised the connection of Islam to the ancient religion of Abraham. This window of opportunity for consolidation

---

[11] For further details about the conditions and regulations of armed combat in Islam, see Chapter 5.

[12] This campaign is notorious for the fact that Muhammad oversaw the execution of the Jewish males of the Banu Qurayza, possibly numbering several hundred, who had violated the Constitution of Medina by entering into alliance with the Meccan pagans to betray the city. Although this event is shocking to modern sensibilities, it should importantly be noted that they were executed for treason in breaking their pact with the community of Medina in times of war and after multiple warnings. They were not executed for being Jewish. The Muslim community retained alliances with a number of Jewish tribes in Arabia after this incident and Jewish communities enjoyed protected legal status throughout centuries of governance by Muslims.

Image 1.4: A model of the Prophet Muhammad's original mosque in Medina based on contemporary accounts

Source: Reproduced courtesy of the Madain Project

was made greater when Muhammad, inspired by a dream, entered into a ten-year non-aggression treaty with the Meccans, called the Treaty of Hudaybiyya (629 CE).

The conquest of Mecca, Muhammad's final sermon and death

After the Meccans violated the terms of the Treaty of Hudaybiyya when one of their allied tribes attacked allies of the Muslim community, in 631 CE a Muslim army of around 10,000 mounted a campaign to capture Mecca and to free the *Ka'aba* from the worship of idols. The Muslim army entered Mecca almost unopposed and, contrary to the norms of warfare of the time, Muhammad spared the lives of his former enemies, the vast majority of whom then accepted Islam, including the leader of Mecca, Abu Sufyan ibn Harb (circa 565–653 CE), and his wife, Hind bint Utbah (circa 584–636 CE).

On 6 March 632 CE, Muhammad preached what is known as his Final Sermon to a gathering of thousands of his community. In this sermon Muhammad reminded his Muslim congregation of the equality of all people of whatever race before God and enjoined them to follow The Qur'an and his own Customary Behaviour (Sunna), which showed them how to put The Qur'an into practice. Muhammad then asked his followers whether he had successfully delivered the message of Islam. His followers replied, 'Indeed, you have.'

On 8 June 632 CE, after a two-week illness, Muhammad died. Medina was in a state of shock. In his grief, one of Muhammad's leading Companions, the irascible Umar ibn Al-Khattab (585–644 CE), threatened to kill anyone who repeated this news until his friend, Abu Bakr, consoled him with the words,

> If anyone amongst you used to worship Muhammad, then Muhammad has passed away, but if anyone of you used to worship God, then God is alive and shall never die.

Through this utterance of monotheistic wisdom, Abu Bakr inadvertently staked his claim to succeed Muhammad as leader of the Muslim community.

Divisions over the Successor (*Caliph*) to Muhammad

Muhammad had been the early Muslim community's unrivalled political and religious leader and his death left a vacuum both of religious authority and of political power. Muhammad had exercised his religious authority differently from his political power: his religious authority, as Prophet, was unquestioned, but his political power, as statesman, was open to question and was challenged (Madelung, 1998).

Prior to his death, Muhammad had not dictated who should be his Successor (*Caliph*) as leader of the Muslim community, nor had he dictated how the Muslim community should govern itself after his death, beyond insisting that Muslims follow The Qur'an and the example of his Customary Prophetic Behaviour (Sunna). Rather, following existing tribal custom, Muhammad had left the Muslim community to choose his Successor and their leader for themselves. While Medina was reeling in grief and disbelief at the death of Muhammad, two factions quickly asserted their rights to lead the community of Medina (Kennedy, 2016).

Sunni Muslims

One group believed the new leader of the Muslim community should be the person with the most appropriate experience for the role. This group believed that Muhammad's close Companion, Abu Bakr as-Siddiq, as the elder statesman of the Muslim community and confidant of Muhammad, was the worthiest candidate to succeed Muhammad. They also inferred that Abu Bakr was also Muhammad's own preference because Muhammad had asked Abu Bakr to lead the collective Obligatory Prayer during his final illness.

These Muslims considered that the Customary Prophetic Behaviour – Sunna – for deciding upon a leader was through a simple, informal tribal consultation process followed by an election (*Shura*). The people who believed in this process of succession became known as the People of the Sunna & Consensus (*Ahl as-Sunna wal Jama*) or, as we now call them, *Sunni* Muslims.

Sunni Islam gradually gained influence and power through the Umayyad dynasty (661–750 CE) and then through the Abbasid dynasty (750–1258 CE and 1261–1571 CE) of ruling Caliphs and conquered territories in the areas of Arabia and North Africa formerly dominated by the Eastern and Western Roman Empires, as well as the rest of the Arabian Peninsula.[13] Through conquest, persuasion and trade, Sunni Islam also spread east to eventually include modern-day Turkey, Afghanistan, Central Asia (now Kazakhstan, Kyrgyzstan, Tajikistan, Turkmenistan and Uzbekistan), India, Pakistan, Indonesia and Malaysia, and West China.

What became known as Sunni Islam also quickly spread west from the Arabian Peninsula so that by 732 CE, within a hundred years of the death of Muhammad, Sunni Islam had spread to Egypt, North Africa, West Africa and Spain. Today, Sunni Muslims comprise roughly 90 per cent of the global Muslim community (*Umma*) (Pew Research Centre, 2017).

Shia Muslims

Another group of Companions of Muhammad – Muhammad's immediate family, known as the People of the Prophetic House (*Ahl al-Bayt*) – had been missing from the process of choosing Muhammad's Successor (*Caliph*) because they had been making the funeral arrangements for the washing of Muhammad's body and for his burial. They were angry that, due to the speed of events following Muhammad's death, they had not been consulted over Muhammad's Successor.

The People of the Prophetic House believed that Ali ibn Abi Talib possessed the most appropriate credentials to become Muhammad's Successor: Ali was the first male convert to Islam after Muhammad himself; as Muhammad's cousin, he was Muhammad's closest living male relative; Ali was Muhammad's son-in-law and the father of Muhammad's grandsons, Hasan ibn Ali and Hussain ibn Ali. He was also notable for his piety, eloquence and bravery.

---

[13] It will be noted that the Prophetic ideal that people should choose their leader for themselves was soon lost and the idea of monarchic dynasties prevailed throughout the early centuries of Islam.

Those early Muslims who believed in the claims to leadership of Ali and his wife, Fatima, and their descendants were later to become formalised as *Shia* Muslims. Shia is short for *Shiat' ul Ali*, which means the 'Party of Ali'. Shia Islam is the second major denomination in Islam after Sunni Islam. Currently, about 10 per cent of the global population of Muslims is Shia (Pew Research Centre, 2017) (see Figure 1.2).

However, immediately after Muhammad's death, those who became Shia Muslims were not in any sense part of a separate community, let alone a different branch of the faith. They were merely a group of Companions who were smarting with the perceived injustice that they had not been consulted about the succession to Muhammad and that Ali's apparently strong claims had been overlooked.

Eventually, after two damaging civil wars between these two different parties during which the grandson of Muhammad, Hussain ibn Ali (626–680 CE), was killed at the Battle of Kerbala (680 CE), the Party of Ali became a separate branch of Islam. Over time, Shia Islam came to develop its own distinctive religious beliefs and practices and became set against the People of Sunna & Consensus, Sunni Muslims.

In time, Shia Islam gained influence in eastern Iraq and Yemen and gave rise to the Cairo-based Fatimid dynasty (909–1171 CE). Shia Islam also gradually took root in Persia (now Iran) through the Safavid dynasty (1501–1736 CE). The Shias came to believe that the true religious and true political authority of the Muslim Community belonged to a series of Imams descended directly from Ali and Fatima. Shia Muslims believe that these Imams are sometimes manifest and known and at other times unknown and hidden, and therefore the spiritual flavour of Shia Islam has often been more spiritualised and esoteric than Sunni Islam.

The differences between Sunni Islam and Shia Islam are therefore not differences of basic religious practice and belief but are differences in belief about by whom and how leadership of the Muslim community can be claimed. But these early violent struggles for power set damaging precedents in the Muslim community, the effects of which have rippled through the Islamic world for centuries.

In this time of upheaval, in 656 CE a third group of Muslims with very different notions of succession also emerged. This group violently rejected the authority of the fourth Caliph Ali outright and then assassinated him. This group claimed that no one could effectively follow Muhammad and that political command belonged to God alone. They were known as Kharijites, meaning 'those who depart from the Caliph's authority', and they set a precedent for politicised violence in Islam which lingers to this day (Timani, 2008).[14]

---

[14] There also exists a body of modern scholarship that casts the Kharijites in a more positive light.

Figure 1.2: The distribution of Sunni and Shia Muslims today in the Muslim-majority world

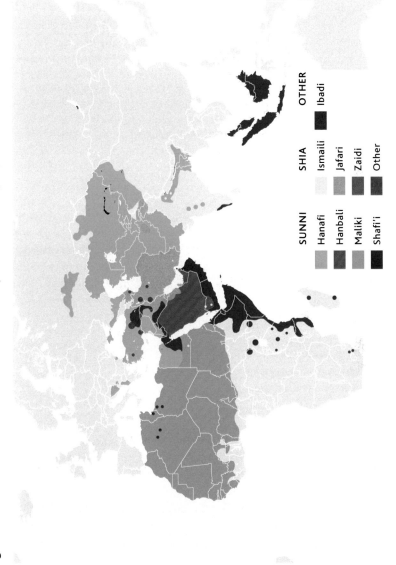

SUNNI
Hanafi
Hanbali
Maliki
Shafi'i

SHIA
Ismaili
Jafari
Zaidi
Other

OTHER
Ibadi

Image by Orbital Design; source of information: www.lib.utexas.edu/maps/ world_maps/muslim_distribution.jpg

The Rightly Guided Successors

In the early years after the death of Muhammad, the Sunni process for electing the Caliph by a simple process of consultation won out because it reflected most closely existing Arab tribal custom.

At the first such election, Muhammad's Companion, Abu Bakr as-Siddiq, was elected the first Successor (*Caliph*) to Muhammad in the leadership of the Muslim community. In fact, the first four Caliphs (Successors to Muhammad) who ruled after the death of the Prophet Muhammad were all elected by a simple vote.

These so-called Rightly Guided Successors (*Khulafa ar-Rashidun*) were:

Abu Bakr as-Siddiq (632–634 CE)
Umar ibn al-Khattab (634–644 CE)
Uthman ibn Affan (644–656 CE)
Ali ibn Abi Talib (656–661 CE)

This period of the Rightly Guided Successors is remembered by Muslims as a 'Golden Age'; a period of the preservation and expansion of Islam when the Four Rightly Guided Successors were seen to practise their faith and to govern fairly according to Qur'anic principles after the pattern of excellence and justice established by the Prophet Muhammad himself.

The great debate: the expansion of Islam

One of the great debates about early Islam is how, in the period of the Rightly Guided Successors and afterwards, did Islam expand so quickly? One hundred years after the death of Muhammad (632 CE), Islam and societies ruled by Muslims stretched from Spain in the west to China in the east (see Figure 1.3).

There are many factors involved in this expansion which add up to the fact that in the 7th century CE the world was ripe for a superpower with a powerful set of new religious ideas. The two superpowers of the day were the Sassanid Empire centred in what is now Iran (224–651 CE) and the Byzantine Empire centred around Constantinople (now Istanbul) (395–1453 CE). Both empires had become corrupt, weakened by war and were unpopular. They had exhausted each other through decades of fighting and both had overtaxed their populaces to fund these military campaigns.

Once the Muslim armies had fought and won 'winner-takes-all' battles with these ailing superpowers against the Byzantines at Yarmuk in Syria (636 CE) and the Persians at Qadisiyya in Iraq (636 CE), defence of Islam turned into occupation and governance of hostile neighbouring territories and there was little to stop the Arab Muslim expansion.

Figure 1.3: The spread of Islam, 622–750 CE

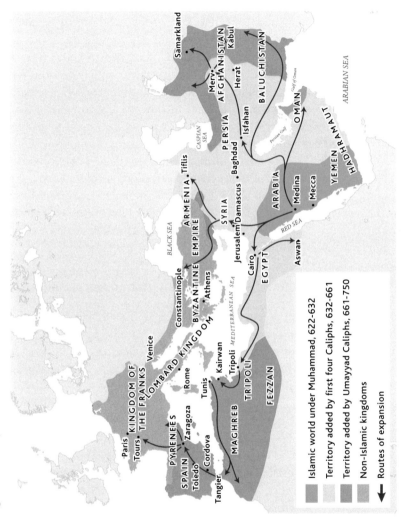

Islamic world under Muhammad, 622-632

Territory added by first four Caliphs, 632-661

Territory added by Umayyad Caliphs, 661-750

Non-Islamic kingdoms

Routes of expansion

Image by Orbital Design; source of information: https://sites.google.com/a/ehschools. org/global-9/unit-2/11-islamic-world/11–2-spread-of-islam

Small Muslim forces dispatched from Medina under generals, such as the accomplished military leader Khalid ibn Al-Walid (died 642 CE), often met with little or no resistance. With only small garrisons, Muslims managed to govern towns and cities such as Jerusalem and Cairo across the Levant, Egypt and North Africa, while letting local populations carry on leading relatively unchanged lives.

For many local Christian and Jewish people, the new relatively light-touch, light-tax Muslim occupation was preferable to the overbearing Byzantine Orthodox Christian rule which they had suffered previously. Moreover, peoples of the Levant and North Africa were also used to being ruled by foreign powers (Hourani, 2005). These local, non-Muslim populations were required to pay a Protection Tax (jizya) to their Muslim occupiers and, to varying degrees, were sometimes subject to other restrictions such as not bearing arms. However, these local, non-Muslim populations were in some respects liberated from religious and burdensome financial oppression.

Moreover, these local, non-Muslim populations were not required to accept Islam. The Qur'an (2:256) mandates religious tolerance: it does not permit forced conversion and it forbids the oppression of non-Muslim faiths. That this Qur'anic mandate of religious tolerance was taken seriously is illustrated by the fact that, after more than 200 years of occupation, Islam was still the minority faith in these lands.[15]

The Muslim Enlightenment leads to Abrahamic Renaissance

This Islamic codification of religious tolerance and of multi-faith coexistence laid the foundations for a society that was led by Muslims and populated by many talented people of a wide variety of faiths. The quest for knowledge, which had originally been made obligatory for Muslims by The Qur'an and Muhammad, now became a cultural passion.

As the Anglo-Saxons, Franks, Normans, Slavs and Vikings fought for control of the kingdoms of Europe in the 9th, 10th and 11th centuries, scholars of all faiths across Europe flocked to Baghdad under the Muslim Caliphs of the Abbasid dynasty (750–1517 CE) (see Image 1.5).[16] They were 'pushed' by conditions of political instability and intellectual persecution in Christendom and 'pulled' by the promise of generous patronage and an open, scholarly environment in the Territory of Islam (Dar al-Islam).[17] For example, a Nestorian

---

[15] Some scholars have also argued that conversion to Islam was actively discouraged since it resulted in a loss of tax revenue from non-Muslims (Abulafia, 2012).

[16] Some of these scholars were fleeing the intellectual persecution of the Orthodox Christian Church, which had shut down centres of philosophical learning such as the Neoplatonic School in Athens, following the edict of the Emperor Justinian in 529 CE, just before the dawn of Islam.

[17] In a process of migration which is the reverse of what we witness happening in our time.

Image 1.5: An artist's impression of the Round City of Baghdad under the Muslim Caliphs of the Abbasid dynasty

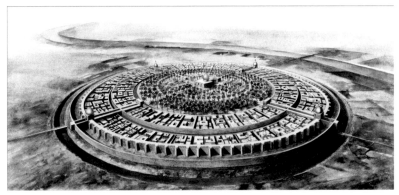

Source: Science Photo Library

Christian called Hunayn ibn Ishaq (809–873 CE) was put in charge of the Grand Library in Baghdad, known as The House of Wisdom (see Image 1.6). Hunayn, under the impassioned sponsorship of the Caliph Al Ma'mun (786–833 CE), initiated a mass movement of scholarly translation of as many of the great texts of the classical European, Hindu and Persian worlds as could be collected (Al-Khalili, 2012).

Inspired by learning derived from many faiths and cultures, from around 750–1300 CE, scholars working in Muslim societies, laid the foundations of many of the branches of scientific and medical knowledge that we take for granted today. For example, Muslim, Jewish and Christian scholars working together in Islamic societies:

- adapted the Hindu number system to create the number systems that we use today – including the use of zero for advanced arithmetic – which facilitated great advances in mathematics, accounting and trade;
- adapted and developed ancient Greek and Persian geometry, trigonometry and algebra for both religious and civic purposes (such as the calculation of inheritance and building irrigation systems);
- made the earliest studies of the circulation of the blood and infection – including by Abu Bakr al-Razi (854–932 CE; see Image 1.7) who established hospitals based upon scientific principles of infection, and who made strides in medical sciences such as ophthalmology (see Image 1.8; Haq and Khatib, 2012);
- reinitiated the study of history and sociology according to systematic principles;

Image 1.6: The public library of the House of Wisdom from a 13th-century CE manuscript

Source: www.1001inventions.com/feature/maqamat/

Image 1.7: Depiction of al-Razi in a 13th-century CE manuscript of a work by Gerard of Cremona

Source: https://en.wikipedia.org

- developed sophisticated models of musical notation and harmony and invented musical instruments such as the lute and the viol, which later became the guitar and the violin (see Table 1.1);[18]
- preserved and developed ancient Greek philosophy, in particular the rediscovery of the Ancient Greek philosopher Aristotle (384–322 BCE). Western Europe was reintroduced to classical scholarship through the

---

[18] There has even existed a long-standing line of argument that the Solfège syllables (do, re, mi, fa, sol, la, ti) that underpin the classical musical scale may be derived from the syllables of the Arabic musical solmisation system Durr-i-Mufassal ('Separated Pearls') (dal, ra, mim, fa, sad, lam) (Smith, 2002). Certainly, the parallels are striking (see Table 1.1).

Table 1.1: Classical music notes compared with Arabic solmisation

Classical music notes	Do	Re	Mi	Fa	Sol	La	Ti
Arabic alphabet solmisation	Dad	Ra	Mim	Fa	Sad	Lam	Sin

Image 1.8: Diagram of the eye with a central lens, from Hunayn ibn Ishaq's *Ten Treatises on the Structure of the Eye* (circa 860 CE)

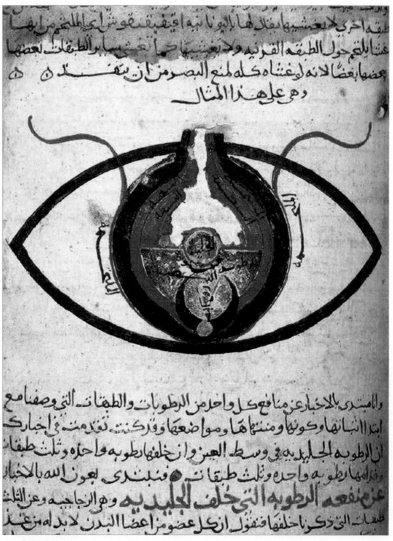

Source: Getty Images

work of Muslim, Christian and Jewish scholars and translators in Muslim Spain, called Al-Andalus. This laid the foundations of Western, empirical scientific method by reintroducing the idea that systematic observation of the patterns and particulars of nature was the means to scientific progress (Al-Khalili, 2012).

Where Muslims settled, scholars gathered to teach different subjects in mosque complexes such as the Qarawiyyin Mosque in Fez, Morocco, which was founded in 859 CE by an enlightened heiress, Fatima al-Fihri (circa 800–880 CE; see Image 1.9).

Soon systems of formalised curricula, quality control and degrees of ability to teach (*ijaza*) were developed, which, in turn, became an inspiration to the processes of education in European universities of Padua, Paris, and then Oxford and Cambridge (Makdisi, 2013).

At the same time, Islamic material culture in the form of glassware, ceramics and musical instruments became the 'must-haves' of late medieval Europe, including the Planispheric astrolabe, which, in the hands of a skilled person, could make astronomical predictions and determine one's exact location and the correct time – day or night (see Image 1.10).

The Abrahamic Renaissance

Although history books do not often explain this, the European Renaissance of the 13th, 14th and 15th centuries drew heavily upon the advances in knowledge made in previous centuries in the Muslim world.

Image 1.9: Reading Room of the Qarawiyyin Mosque

Source: Photograph by Aziza Chaouni

Image 1.10: Planispheric astrolabe, dated 1654–1655 CE

Source: www.metmuseum.org

For example,

- the Polish astronomer Copernicus (1473–1543 CE) developed his heliocentric models of the universe using the astronomical calculations developed by Muslim astronomers from the Maragheh Observatory in Iran founded in 1259 CE (see Image 1.11);

Image 1.11: Astronomers in the Maragheh Observatory, Iran

Source: http://wikimapia.org

- the Italian poet Dante (1265–1321 CE) was inspired to write his great work, *The Divine Comedy*, by the Spanish Muslim mystic poet Ibn Al-Arabi (1165–1240 CE);
- up to the 19th century, all European doctors learnt medicine from *The Canon of Medicine* by Ibn Sina (980–1037 CE) (Al-Khalili, 2012).

It is no exaggeration to say that modern scientific civilisation is heavily indebted to the scholars and patrons of medieval Islam.

What happened to Islamic civilisation?

If in the Middle Ages and Early Modern period, Islam and Muslims were typically associated with science, learning, high culture and medicine, it can fairly be asked: what happened? Why is it that today, Islam and Muslims are more often stereotypically associated with backwardness, religious literalism and terrorist violence?

One of the many causes of the decline of the Islamic civilisation, which are still heatedly debated to this day, was the gradual triumph over centuries of a strong trend of anti-rationalism within Islam itself.

In the context of political turmoil of the Crusades and Mongol invasions (see later), Muslim thinkers such as Al-Ghazali (1058–1111 CE) rejected the existence of secondary natural causes in the world and admitted only the existence of primary causes directly from God. As a result, whereas previously Muslim culture had bred rational scientific inquiry, Islamic religious thinking started to belittle the importance of natural science and reject learning that emanated from outside the Muslim world (Allawi, 2009).

This anti-rational, literalist trend in Islam persists today in elements of the *Wahabi* religious Worldview, together with the historically and theologically false notion that rational, empirical science is 'Western' and therefore must be 'un-Islamic'(Wilkinson, 2015a).

A second cause of the decline of the Islamic civilisation was prejudice. As much for their similarity as for their difference, Muslims posed a threat to Christian Europe. The medieval Catholic Church cast Muslims, along with Jews for their rejection of the divinity of Christ, as the bogeymen of Christendom. The Muslim contribution to learning was minimised and then written off. Muslims were almost universally and inaccurately derided as pagans and infidels, rather than as believers who also accepted Christ as the Messiah and who also worshipped the One God of Abraham.

A third cause of the decline of the Islamic civilisation, and perhaps the most significant, was the Mongols. Between 1200 and 1260 CE, the nomadic tribes of Mongolia united under Genghis Khan (1158–1227 CE) – who called himself 'The Punishment of God' – wreaked havoc across the Muslim world.

In Central Asia, the ancient Muslim cities of Bukhara and Samarkand were sacked and their populations slaughtered or sent into slavery. Genghis Khan's successors, Möngke (1209–1259 CE) and Hulegu (1218–1265 CE), continued their onslaught deeper into the heart of the Muslim Caliphate.

In 1258 CE, after a two-week siege, the Mongols sacked the centre of Muslim power in Baghdad, Iraq: the Mongols slaughtered at least 800,000 people, destroyed all 36 of its public libraries, including the 'House of Wisdom, and destroyed the mosques, the markets and the gardens (see Images 1.12 and 1.13; Graham, 2006). Only those people who sought refuge in the sewers and drains of Baghdad escaped the pillage and the slaughter. Within

Image 1.12: The Mongol Siege of Baghdad in 1258 CE

Source: Bibliothèque nationale de France, Département des Manuscrits, Division orientale,
Supplément persan 1113, fol. 180v-181 licensed by Getty images

Image 1.13: An artist's impression of the Sack of Baghdad in 1258 CE

Source: Image by Sune Reinhardt Fogtmann

a fortnight, the beating heart of centuries of Muslim learning, trade and culture was reduced to a smouldering heap of ruins and piles of rotting skulls.

Although the destruction of the entire Muslim world[19] was averted by the subsequent Muslim victory over the Mongols at the Battle of Ain

---

[19] And probably the Christian West into the bargain.

Jalut[20] in Palestine in 1260 CE by the Egyptian General Saif ad-Din Qutuz (1221–1260 CE), Muslim ascendency and rational scholarship in the Arab world never fully recovered from the destruction of the Mongol raids. Increasingly, power in the Middle East was claimed and held less and less through cultural or spiritual acumen or through a connection to the Prophet Muhammad, and more and more through military power and organisation.

The Crusades leave their mark

Compared to the Mongol invasions, the Crusades (1095–1291 CE) fought by Christian adventurers on the pretext of reclaiming the Holy Land for Christianity were relatively minor calamities. Nevertheless, events such as the Crusader Conquest of Jerusalem in 1099 CE, which resulted in the massacre of at least 30,000 men, women and children and the subsequent occupation of the Crusader states in the Levant, left a lasting legacy of mistrust in the Muslim-majority world of the both the intentions and the methods of Europeans.

In the present day, the Crusades have been referenced by Islamist Extremists – including by the current leader of Al-Qaeda, Ayman Az-Zawahiri (1951 CE–present) – as an example of the supposed eternal hostility of the 'Infidel' (*kafir*) towards Islam.[21]

Muslim civilisation moves east

After the reconquest of Muslim Spain (722–1492 CE) and Sicily (827–902 CE) by Christian powers, authority in the Muslim world shifted eastwards.

In 1280 CE in modern-day Turkey (then Anatolia), a man called Osman Ghazi (1258–1326 CE) of a tribe known as the Othmanis or Ottomans began a process of imperialist expansion of his Muslim Turkic people. After the conquest of Constantinople (renamed Istanbul by his successor Mehmet II (1432–1481 CE) in May 1453 CE), the Ottoman Turks gradually brought the Balkans, modern-day Serbia and the whole of the Middle East under their control, including the Muslim sacred sites of Mecca and Medina.

The Ottomans were astounding military planners and, with Hapsburg Spain, by the 16th century were a superpower of the day with whom

---

[20] The Battle of Ain Jalut was also notable for being the earliest known battle where explosive hand cannons were used in order to frighten the Mongol horses and cavalry and cause disorder in their ranks.

[21] See Chapter 8 for further details.

Western European kings and queens sought prized audiences through their ambassadors at Court for the right to trade in the Middle East.

For the Ottomans, attack was the best form of defence, and they instituted regular aggressive military campaigns styled as religious jihad[22] to expand their sphere of influence into the Balkans and Europe.[23] Nevertheless, in Ottoman-ruled territory, religious tolerance as stipulated by The Qur'an was instituted and regulated. In the 16th and 17th centuries CE, Jews and heterodox Christians sought refuge in Istanbul from the fury of the Inquisition and other religious wars and pogroms that ravaged Western Europe, and some then gained senior positions in the Ottoman civil service and society (see Image 1.14).[24]

Further east, in India, the Mughal tribe under Babur (1483–1530 CE), who was descended from the Mongols, gradually laid claim to the whole Indian subcontinent. Although the population remained largely Hindu, the Mughal dynasty ruled India with forms of Islamic Law for three centuries.

The Mughals developed a material culture of astonishing luxury and beauty that amazed European travellers to India. Buildings such as the Taj Mahal – commissioned in 1632 CE by the Mughal Emperor Shah Jahan (1592–1666 CE) as a mausoleum for his wife Mumtaz Mahal (1593–1631 CE) – expressed the confidence, wealth and technical ability of Mughal civilisation (see Image 1.15).

Colonial incursions

The openness of the Ottomans and the Mughals to outside influences and the wealth brought through trade with Holland, Portugal and England was also their Achilles heel. European trading companies, such as the British East India Company that had acquired trading monopolies with Muslim rulers, started to gain political influence in their own right.

In 18th-century India, small but well-armed forces from these trading companies started to become the power brokers in the dynastic squabbles between local Muslim and Hindu rulers. For example, in Bengal, as the

---

[22] See Chapter 5 for Muslim prisoners' views on religious violence.

[23] The Ottomans have also become infamous for social practices which are certainly offensive to modern sensibilities. For example, a number of Ottoman Sultans engaged in the un-Islamic and immoral practice of fratricide of brothers who they considered potential contenders to the throne and for centuries, captured Christian boys from the Balkans (called devshirme) were forced to convert to Islam before they were inducted into the elite Janissary corps of the Ottoman army or civil service.

[24] Jews who reached high positions in the Ottoman Court and administration include the Finance Minister to Mehmed II (1432–1481 CE), Hekim Yakup Paşa (born circa 1424–1481 CE), the Portuguese physician to Suleiman I (1494–1566 CE), Moses Hamon (1490–1554 CE) and the Master of the Mint in Egypt for Selim I (1470–1520 CE) Abraham de Castro (died 1560 CE).

Image 1.14: A reconstruction of a reception room in Ottoman Damascus 1707 CE

Source: www.metmuseum.org

centralised power of the Mughals in Delhi broke down, the influence of the East India Company rose and, in time, the East India Company came to function as a sovereign power on behalf of the British Crown. These local British rulers and influential merchants – called 'Nabobs' – often took on

Image 1.15: The Taj Mahal

Source: Getty Images

Islamic 'customs' such as polygamous marriage[25] and generally 'went native' in a way that alarmed those back home (Moorhouse, 1984).

After the so-called Indian Mutiny[26] of 1857–1858 CE was put down by troops serving the East India Company, under the provisions of the Government of India Act of 1858 CE the British government liquidated the East India Company and the British government took over its Indian possessions, its administrative powers and machinery, and its armed forces and ruled India directly in the name of the Crown.

The liquidation of the East India Company, which brought much of the Indian subcontinent directly under the control and administration of the British government, produced powerful knock-on effects in the rest of the majority Muslim world. For example, in Egypt the British and the French built the Suez Canal between 1859 and 1869 CE, with the British gradually assuming influence and control of the country so that this vital waterway that connected the Mediterranean Sea with the Red Sea preserved their access to India.

---

[25] It should be noted that today the standard Muslim marriage practice is monogamy between one man and one woman. Although polygamy – the marriage of one man with up to four women – is permitted under certain conditions in Islamic Law, at the time of the revelation of The Qur'an polygamy was both a restriction on the typical marriage practices of the day and also guaranteed women legal rights.

[26] Also named variously the Sepoy Mutiny, the Great Rebellion, the Revolt of 1857, the Indian Insurrection and the First War of Independence.

The First World War and the end of global Muslim power

By the turn of the 20th century, the Ottoman Empire, which had once been the guarantor of Muslim sovereignty and protector of the Sunni Islamic faith,[27] had become an ailing power referred to dismissively by the Great Powers of Britain, France and Russia as 'the sick man of Europe' (see Figure 1.4).

The Ottoman Empire's bureaucratic and systematised central government around the Sultan and his ministers (*Viziers*) was outdone by the mechanisms of emerging constitutional democracy and capital finance operating in Western Europe. Also, while Western Europe had since 1500 CE undergone revolutions in industrial, medical and military science, the Ottomans had, for various reasons, resisted many of the intellectual and technological advances in Europe, including, for example, printing.

After debilitating wars in the Balkans,[28] the Ottomans were desperate for finance, desperate for military hardware and desperate for an ally against Russian influence at their borders. So, upon the outbreak of the First World War[29] in 1914 CE, the Ottoman Empire entered into alliance with the Germany of Kaiser Wilhelm II (1859–1941 CE) (Strachan, 2014). At a blow, the Ottoman Muslim world became the back door to Germany.

Apart from attacking Ottoman Turkey itself with little success, the Allied Powers saw the Ottoman alliance with Kaiser Wilhelm II as an excuse to foment rebellion among Ottoman Arab Muslim subjects, who, as descendants of Muhammad and his tribe of Quraysh, had long resented the rule of Ottoman Turkey.

In order to foment rebellion among the Ottoman Arab Muslims, the Allies made a wartime promise to Arab Muslims in the Ottoman Empire that they would, in return for an Arab military uprising against the Ottomans, recognise a single, unified independent Arab state stretching from Syria to Yemen that would include Palestine. The Allies also offered Palestine as a homeland to the diaspora Jewish community, partly in order to win the participation of the United States in the First World War. After the war, the Allies found it impossible to honour these conflicting promises.

As the end of the First World War came in sight, the Allied Powers carved up the former Ottoman Provinces and began ruling them from London or Paris as international mandates of the League of Nations (Barr, 2012).

---

[27] For nearly 150 years (1514–1639 CE), the Ottoman dynasty fought bitter wars with the Safavid Shia dynasty of Persia for control of Mesopotamia.

[28] … and expensive infrastructure projects such as extending the Orient Express railway from Istanbul to Baghdad.

[29] Also, tens of thousands of Indian Muslims along with Sikhs and Hindus fought alongside the Allied powers on the Western Front and elsewhere.

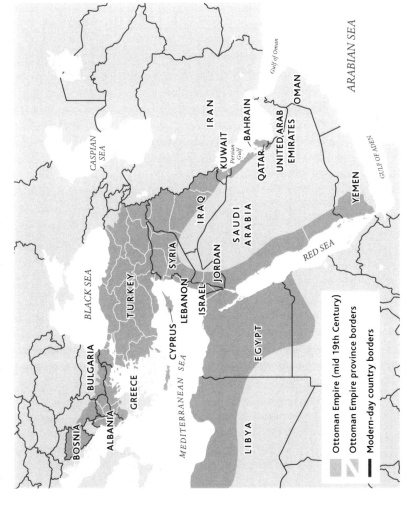

Figure 1.4: Ottoman Empire borders versus modern-day borders of states in the Near and Middle East

Image by Orbital Design; information provided by Ahmed Ben Rezguia.

Legend:
- Ottoman Empire (mid 19th Century)
- Ottoman Empire province borders
- Modern-day country borders

Britain took control of Iraq, Jordan and Palestine; France took control of Syria and Lebanon.

As the Allies forced Ottoman Turkey into a surrender, with the loss of its territories, a group of revolutionaries called the Young Turks rose up and abolished the Ottoman Sultanate (1922 CE) and the Caliphate (1924 CE). The Turkish Republic was internationally recognised in the Treaty of Lausanne on 29 October 1923 CE, with Ankara as the country's new capital.

A 1,300-year history of centralised Muslim power, governance, Islamic Law and Islam-centred education came abruptly and bloodily to an end: the new Turkish Republic abolished the Sultan, the religiously trained jurists (*Ulema*) were removed from office, and Islamic courts and Islamic schools were closed.

By the 1930s CE, the Muslim-majority world was almost entirely ruled by non-Muslim powers. Within 200 years, Muslim civilisation had shifted from being a mover-and-shaper of global civilisation to being entirely shaped by political, technological and educational processes that had their source in the non-Muslim West.

The Muslim crisis of faith and responses to modernity

This loss of global leadership, power and influence generated a crisis of faith within Muslim intellectual circles and in their leaders in India, Egypt and elsewhere. Muslims asked themselves: if God had guaranteed Islam and Muslims success in This World and The Next World when they had followed Islam (The Qur'an, 23), did their failures in This World mean that the Muslim world had not been following Islam properly? Or did these failures mean that God's favour had passed out of Islam to the successful Christian West (Shepard, 2004)?

Responses to this crisis of faith and confidence came from a group of intellectuals who collectively came to be known as the Muslim Reformers (Taji-Farouki and Nafi, 2004). They were described as 'Reformers' because they sought to define a reformed relationship of Islam and Muslims with the modern, post-Caliphate world of nation states, global finance and high technology.

Broadly speaking, the Muslim Reformers fell and fall into three groups: Secularists, Modernists and Islamists.

The Secularists

The Secularists might be grouped under the banner 'Islam is the problem'.

The Secularists believed – and still believe – that Islam with its religious jurists (*ulema*) and compendious religious law had prevented the Muslim-majority world from harnessing the benefits of modern empirical science, of technological progress and of access to investment through banking and the capital markets for the development of the economy.

Mustapha Kamal Atatürk (1881–1938 CE) was a well-known political exponent of the Secularist position. As the founding President of the Turkish Republic, Atatürk set about stripping Turkey of its Ottoman Islamic heritage and legal infrastructure so that Turkish citizens could access the technological and cultural achievements of Europe.

Another, though very different, Secularist political leader was General Gamal Abdul Nasser (1918–1970 CE). Nasser seized power in Egypt in 1956 and envisioned an Egypt that sat at the heart of a nationalist, pan-Arab and pan-African revival. Nasser's opposition to British control of the Suez Canal made him a hero of the Arab Muslim-majority world. Saddam Hussein (1937–2006 CE) in Iraq was also an exponent of the Secularist position, which was often coupled with forms of Arab nationalism and brutal one-party dictatorships.

For Secularists, Islam was to be reduced either to a strictly private, individual faith or to be simply part of a national cultural heritage but without any role in law, education or governance (Shepard, 2004).

The Secularists, their intellectuals and their regimes generated a great influence over wide swathes of Muslim society as thousands of Muslim citizens of Turkey, India, Iraq, Egypt and other countries abandoned the daily practice of Islam. As a result of the influence of Secularist intellectuals, today Islam for millions of Muslims is no longer connected with regular religious practice and belief and persists mainly in cultural habits and manners, for example in the importance of family and of welcoming hospitality.

The Modernists

The second group of Reformers, the Modernists, might be grouped crudely under the banner 'Islam has problems, and Islam contains solutions'.

The Modernists pointed to problems within Islam, such as centuries of outdated religious law, which had prevented Islam and Muslims from adapting to the challenges of modernity. For example, the influential Modernist Egyptian theologian and jurist Muhammad Abduh (1849–1905 CE) believed that by stripping Islam back to the basics of the faith of the earliest community of Muslims (called the *Salaf*), Muslims could and should realign themselves with the values of scientific reason and flexible law making. Muhammad Abduh argued that Muslim society should both learn from the scientific and technological achievements of the West and be critical of the values of Western materialism (Kerr, 1966).

The Modernists were and remain influential throughout the Muslim world in thinking about the relationship between Islam and the West. They have consistently argued that Islam and Muslims can and do fit in with the modern world.

The Islamists

The third group of Reformers – the Islamists – might be grouped crudely under the banner 'Islam is the solution'.

The Islamists believed and still believe that, in order for Islam and Muslims to return to their days of power and influence, Islam needs to be purified of non-Muslim influences and they brooked no accommodation with either 'Western' values or liberal democracy.

Islamists stress what they see as the complete difference between Islam and Unbelief (*kufr*) and the complete difference between the ideas of Muslims and non-Muslims. Islamists believe that Muslims can only be fully and properly Muslim if they are governed purely by Islamic Law.

Islamists' belief that Islam was in need of radical purification from alien beliefs and practices had been presaged in the 18th century by Muhammad ibn Abdal Wahab (1703–1792 CE), who was the founder of the eponymous *Wahabi* religious ideology and whose pact with a tribal leader of the Hijaz called Muhammad ibn Saud (1687–1765 CE) laid the foundations of the Kingdom of Saudi Arabia.

With the breakdown of colonial influence in the 20th century, the Worldview of Islamism was given renewed life and vigour by ideologues in India/Pakistan such as Abul Ala Maududi (1903–1979 CE) and in Egypt by Hassan Al-Banna (1906–1949 CE). Both Maududi and Al-Banna drew inspiration from the totalitarian ideologies of Communism and Fascism to argue that Islam was a comprehensive system of living that needed to hold sway over every aspect of a person's public and private life (Al-Banna, 1975; Maududi, 1980; Rahnema, 1994).

Maududi argued that this comprehensive Islamic way of life was only possible in the context of a modern Islamic state governed by Sharia Law and purified of Western influences.

Al-Banna argued that without this Islamic state, which must be constitutionally based on The Qur'an, all Muslims were sinful and sunk in western materialism. In order to carry out their Islamist agendas to return Islam to political greatness and governance by Islamic Law, Al-Banna founded the Society of the Muslim Brothers in 1928 CE in Egypt (often known as the Muslim Brotherhood), and Maududi was a founding figure of the Jamaat e-Islami political party of India/Pakistan in 1941 CE.

In the 1950s and 1960s, in a titanic struggle with Secularists in Egypt and elsewhere for the post-colonial control of government, the

Islamists ultimately failed to provide the post-colonial blueprint for the Muslim world.[30]

The Islamist Extremists

As a result of this Islamist failure to provide the post-colonial blueprint for the Muslim world, and often in conditions of political oppression, disaffected splinter groups from the Muslim Brotherhood in Egypt began to advocate the more extreme idea that Muslim-led regimes in the Muslim-majority world were actually not Muslim at all because they dealt with non-Muslim powers and did not fully implement Islamic law. These extreme splinter groups believed that 'true' Muslims should violently oppose these 'fake' Muslim regimes by resurrecting the practice of armed struggle (jihad) directed against them (Faraj, 1979).

These extreme splinter groups were inspired by the highly influential Egyptian ideologue Sayyid Qutb (1906–1966 CE), whose theological manifesto 'Milestones' (1964 CE) (*Ma'alim fi al-Tariq*) was instrumental in laying the foundations of the Islamist Extremist Worldview of absolute difference between 'Us'/Muslims versus 'Them'/Non-Muslims and 'wrong Muslims' (Qutb, 1964).

By the end of the 20th century, this extremist Worldview underscored the thinking of Violent Islamist Extremist groups such as Egyptian Islamic Jihad, the Islamic Group and later, Al-Qaeda.

For Islamist Extremists, non-Muslims and 'wrong Muslims' who did not fight for Islam were the eternal enemies of 'true' Islam, and only armed struggle (which they called jihad) would rid the world from the influence of Infidelity (*kufr*) and pre-Islamic Ignorance (*jahiliyya*). For example, it was one of these Islamist Extremists, Khalid Al-Islambouli (1958–1982 CE) of the Egyptian Islamic Jihad group who in 1981 CE assassinated President Anwar Sadat of Egypt with the Islamist cry, 'We have killed Pharaoh'; in other words, Al-Islambouli believed that he had killed a leader of pre-Islamic Ignorance (*jahiliyya*) in the name of Islam (see Image 1.16).

At the end of the 20th century and in the first decades of the 21st century, vicious conflicts across the Muslim-majority world, including the Soviet–Afghan War (1979–1989 CE), the Palestine–Israel conflict (1948 CE–present; see Image 1.17), the Gulf War (1991 CE), the Bosnian War (1992–1995 CE; see Image 1.18), the War in Afghanistan (2001–2021 CE)

---

[30] This failure was partly due to the political persecution of Islamists by Secularists, and partly because Islamists lacked enough popular Muslim support for what often appeared austere and backward-looking religious and political agendas.

Image 1.16: The 1981 CE assassination of President Anwar Sadat of Egypt

Source: Getty Images

Image 1.17: Palestinians being expelled from their homes in Haifa in 1948 CE, weeks before Israel declared independence

Source: Getty Images

Image 1.18: Muslim Croatian and Muslim Bosnian prisoners at a Serbian concentration camp on Mount Manjača during the Bosnian War 1992 CE

Source: Photograph by Sovfoto

and, as part of the War on Terror (2001–2021 CE), the US-led Invasion of Iraq (2003 CE), all added fuel to the core Islamist Extremist myth that the non-Muslim West was the eternal enemy of Islam and bent on its destruction.

During this time in the Middle East, rampant male unemployment caused by a population explosion and weak economies across the region provided willing recruits to groups such as Al-Qaeda ('The Base'), which were formed from foreign fighters of the Soviet–Afghan War (1979–1989 CE) (Burke, 2003). Al-Qaeda spawned offshoots and affiliates, including in Somalia, *Al-Shabaab* ('The Youth') and in Nigeria, *Boko Haram* ('Western Education is Forbidden').

In Iraq and Syria, the chaos of the Syrian Civil War (2012 CE–present) provided an opportunity for a rogue outgrowth of Al-Qaeda in Iraq, the so-called Islamic State group, to declare a Caliphate and 'govern' a territory in Iraq and Syria the size of Wales in accordance with a brutal literalistic version of Islamic Law (McCants, 2015).

The young men who join these groups often enjoy few prospects in life and are beguiled by the offers of a salary, religious certainty, sex through the provision of a wife, and, if martyred in the cause, sainthood. The soft power of these Islamist Extremist groups has extended into the migrant Muslim populations in Europe and America, where some young Muslim males, including traumatised migrants from war zones, find themselves unemployed and unwelcome by non-Muslim populations, which confirms them in the Islamist Extremist Worldview that all non-Muslims are evil.

Three key Islamist Extremist events

In the last 45 years, three particular Islamist Extremist events have presented to the world a politicised and extreme form of Islam. These three Islamist Extremist events have for many people come to represent Islam as a whole and, as such, have tarnished the global Muslim 'brand'.

The first Islamist Extremist event occurred in December 1978 CE with the overthrow of the Shah of Iran (1919–1980 CE) and the Iranian Revolution of early 1979 CE that installed Ayatollah Ruhollah Khomeini (1902–1989 CE) as an Islamist President of Iran (see Image 1.21). Three years earlier in 1975 CE, Amnesty International's assessment of Iran stated:

> The Shah of Iran retains his benevolent [world] image despite the highest rate of death penalties in the world, no valid system of civilian courts and a history of torture which is beyond belief, the total number of political prisoners has been reported at times throughout the year [1975] to be anything from 25,000 to 100,000. (See Images 1.19 and 1.20)

The subsequent Iranian Revolution's acts of bloody purging and the virulent anti-Westernism that this regime change generated convinced many Muslims

Image 1.19: Shah Mohammad Reza Pahlavi with his wife Empress Farah and their son Crown Prince Reza at their coronation, 26 October 1967 CE

Source: Photograph by Jack Garofalo

Image 1.20: An exhibition in a former Tehran prison run by the pre-Revolution intelligence service, Savak, now a museum, where wax mannequins of interrogators and prisoners are displayed

Source: Photograph by Future Publishing

Image 1.21: 1 February 1979, Ayatollah Ruhollah Khomeini returns to Iran after 14 years in exile

Source: Photograph by Alain Dejean

Image 1.22: Tehran, 12 February 1979 CE. A woman dressed in a black chador

Source: Photograph by Kaveh Kazemi

– both Sunni and Shia – that it was not democracy but Islamism that was the most effective means for Muslims to regain ascendency in the world over their brutal Western-backed governments (see Image 1.22).

For many Muslims, the Iranian Revolution also cemented the idea of the United States of America as the Great Satan, and the idea that the West and Islam were necessarily opposed (Wilkinson, 2019).

Image 1.23: The Al-Qaeda attacks on the World Trade Center, New York, 11 September 2001

Source: Photograph by Spencer Platt

The second Islamist Extremist event that this anti-Western, anti-American feeling dramatically enacted was the attacks by Al-Qaeda on the Twin Towers of the World Trade Center in New York on 11 September 2001 CE, so-called 9/11 (see Image 1.23). The images beamed continuously around the world for weeks afterwards of two passenger jets being forced by Al-Qaeda terrorists to crash into the Twin Towers and into the Pentagon on 11 September 2001 CE stunned the world and traumatised many Americans, since they expressed the suicidal hatred of some Islamist Extremist Muslims for the United States and the West.

The third Islamist Extremist event was the capture of Iraq's second city, Mosul, and the 'Declaration of Caliphate' in June 2014 CE by the so-called Islamic State (see Images 1.24 and 1.25). This event suggested that Islamist

Image 1.24: The 2014 invasion of Iraq by the so-called Islamic State group

Source: Uncredited/Militant website

Image 1.25: The 2014 occupation of Mosul, Iraq by the so-called Islamic State group

Source: Uncredited/Militant website

Extremism posed a real political threat to the established global order of nation states beholden to international law.

Together, these three events – the 1979 Iranian Revolution, the 2001 Al-Qaeda attacks on the United States, and the 2014 'Declaration of Caliphate' by the so-called Islamic State group – accompanied by a myriad of smaller but vicious acts of terrorism in the Muslim-majority and Muslim-minority worlds, have meant that Islam and Muslims have been firmly installed as the new folk devils (Shain, 2011) of the West. These acts of Islamist Extremists have confirmed for many commentators and members of the public that the West and Islam are indeed locked in a 'Clash of Civilisations' (Huntingdon, 1996).

Notwithstanding the fact that the 20th and 21st centuries have been periods of turmoil for much of the Muslim world, in 2015 there were 1.8 billion Muslims in the world, making Muslims a quarter (24 per cent) of the global human population and an influential component of the contemporary geo-political world (Lipka, 2017).[31]

Muslims in prison

Prisons and imprisonment have formed an important part of this story of Islam and Muslims with both constructive and destructive outcomes in the world.

Some of the most esteemed founding figures of early Islam fell foul of the authorities of their day for their religious views, including the jurists Malik ibn Anas (711–795 CE) and Ahmad ibn Hanbal (780–855 CE) who developed some of their most enduring legal ideas in prison as 'prisoners of conscience'.

In the 1960s CE in the United States, prisoner Converts to the religious and political movement the Nation of Islam – including the activist Malcolm X (1925–1965 CE) – are credited with de-escalating tensions between prison authorities and prisoners during critical points in the civil rights movement and with encouraging an ethos of self-discipline and self-improvement and a commitment to study (Hamm, 2013).

Destructively, in the 20th century, prisons in the Middle East were vicious and inhumane mechanisms of radicalisation into Islamist Extremism. For example, the 1964 CE 'urtext' of Islamist Extremism 'Milestones' (*Ma'alim*

---

[31] Globally, Muslims represent a diversity of nationalities and ethnicities:
- 62 per cent of Muslims live in the Asia Pacific region.
- 20 per cent of Muslims live in the Middle East and North Africa.
- 16 per cent of Muslims live in Sub-Saharan Africa.
- 3 per cent of Muslims (circa 48,600,000) live in Europe, including Turkey, and they make up about 6 per cent of the total European population.
- 0.2 per cent of Muslims live in North America.
- 0.1 per cent of Muslims live in Latin America or the Caribbean (Desilver and Masci, 2017).

fi al-Tariq) was written by the ideologue Sayyid Qutb in incarceration under allegations of attempting to assassinate President Gamal Abdal Nasser (1918–1970 CE) of Egypt.

In the 21st century, the late head of Al-Qaeda in Iraq, Abu Musab Az-Zarqawi (1966–2006 CE), and the former leader of the so-called Islamic State group, Abu Bakr al-Baghdadi (1971–2019 CE), both identified prison as a key mechanism that led to their embrace of Violent Islamist Extremism (McCants, 2015).[32]

Muslims in European prisons

Since the 1960s, Muslims have begun to present in increasing numbers in European prisons. This is because from the mid-20th into the early 21st centuries, there have existed strong 'push' and 'pull' factors bringing successive waves of Muslims as migrants to Europe (see Figure 1.5).

'Push' factors have included such seismic events such as the Partition of India (1947 CE) and devastating conflicts across the Muslim-majority world such as those discussed earlier. 'Pull' factors have included labour shortages in Europe after the Second World War, which brought millions of Muslims to migrate to Europe and become permanent residents for the first time. There are now about 45 million Muslim residents of Europe, excluding Turkey, who represent about 6 per cent of the European population and about 3 per cent of the global Muslim population (Pew Research Centre, 2017).

Over-representation of Muslims in European prisons: disadvantage, youth and discrimination

This mass Muslim migration – which has accelerated since 2015 with turmoil in Iraq, Syria and Afghanistan – has resulted in increasing numbers of prisoners registered as Muslim in prisons in European jurisdictions. For example, in England and Wales, Muslims make up circa 5 per cent of the general population but make up 17 per cent of the male prison population.[33]

Moreover, between 2007 and 2019 CE in England and Wales there was a 47 per cent increase in the Muslim prisoner population: from 8,864 in 2007 CE to 13,563 in 2021 CE (Sturge, 2019; Statista, 2021). This means that Muslims, especially Muslim men, are significantly over-represented in European prisons.

---

[32] Moreover, a number of leaders of Islamist militias in the Syrian Civil War became better 'trained' while incarcerated in the American-run Camp Bucca in Iraq (McCants, 2015).

[33] While male Muslim prisoners are significantly over-represented in prison, female Muslim prisoners are only marginally so. See p 4, note 4.

Figure 1.5: The major Muslim populations of Western Europe

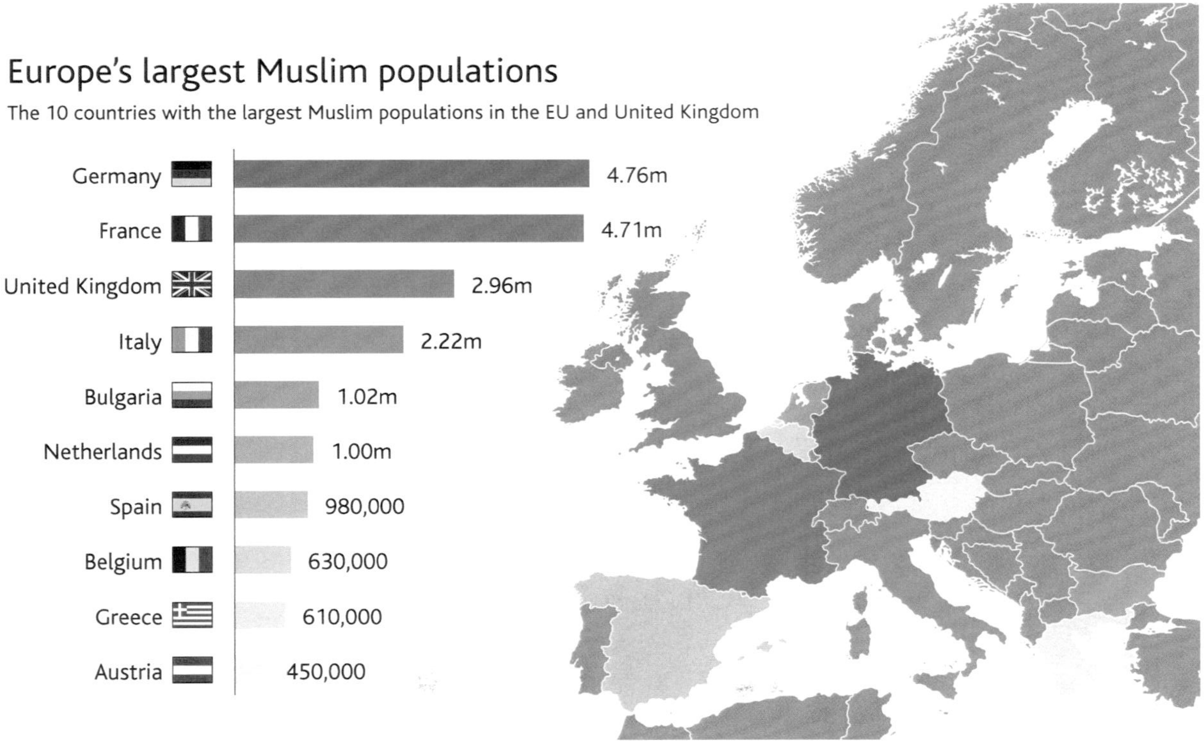

Europe's largest Muslim populations

The 10 countries with the largest Muslim populations in the EU and United Kingdom

Germany	4.76m
France	4.71m
United Kingdom	2.96m
Italy	2.22m
Bulgaria	1.02m
Netherlands	1.00m
Spain	980,000
Belgium	630,000
Greece	610,000
Austria	450,000

Image by Orbital Design; source of information: Statista, 2015.

Perhaps the most significant reason for this over-representation of Muslims in prison is that in Britain, France, Switzerland and other European jurisdictions Muslims tend to come from poor communities and tend to be disadvantaged by low educational achievement, poor housing and high levels of unemployment (Hussain, 2008).

The knock-on effects of Muslim disadvantage in terms of crime have been aggravated in the last 30 years by the collapse of industrial manufacturing in places of traditional Muslim migration such as the north of England (Quraishi, 2005). This collapse of the type of heavy labour that young Muslims have often been educated to expect (Archer, 2001) makes dealing in drugs and sex, for example, seem to some Muslims the only viable and reliable money-making alternative to manual labour (Webster and Qasim, 2018).

Some research suggests that Black, Asian and Minority Ethnic (BAME) populations are disproportionately represented in all stages of the British criminal justice system (Phillips and Bowling, 2017; Irwin-Rogers, 2018; Fatsis, 2021). This, in turn, suggests that BAME populations, including many Muslims, are victims of racial and faith-based discrimination. Little concrete evidence has been established, however, about discrimination in sentencing decisions, particularly with regard to Muslim defendants. A recent British study sampled 8,437 offenders and concluded that those with traditional Muslim names on average received sentences 9.8 per cent longer than the rest of the sample, which is consistent with our sample (Pina-Sánchez et al, 2019). However, once the authors controlled for types of offence and other characteristics, such as public protection factors, they found no evidence of discrimination even in cases of terrorism.[34]

Moreover, it has been noted that Muslims in European countries constitute a young community (aged 16–30), and young people are invariably over-represented in prison populations (Lammy, 2017).

Thus, in a global context of post-colonial conflict and migration, the collapse of employment in heavy industry and the experience of different types of discrimination, Muslims, especially young Muslim men, have come to be a significant presence in prisons in Europe.

Our characteristic sample of Muslim prisoners

In this context, the socio-demographic, criminal and religious backgrounds of our Muslim sample of 279 prisoners were characteristic of what is already known about the Muslim prison populations in England, Switzerland and France in terms of:

---

[34] Independent researchers do not routinely have formal access to detailed sentencing decisions and defendant records kept by the Ministry of Justice to enable more refined statistical analysis despite recent calls to undertake more research in this area (Lammy, 2017).

- **ethnicity**, which was typical of the ethnic constituents of Muslim prisoners in England, France and Switzerland (see Infographic 1.1a for further details);
- **age**, which was similar to the average and median ages of prisoners in France and Switzerland and slightly younger in England where the Muslim population has a youth bulge (see Infographic 1.1a for further details);
- **gender**, which was overwhelmingly male as per the general prison population;
- **mental health**, which was typical of the general prison population;[35]
- **migration profile/nationality**, with 85 per cent of the English sample being British nationals, 71 per cent of the French sample being French citizens, and 91 per cent of the Swiss sample being foreign, non-Swiss nationals;
- **religiosity**, which by denomination and Worldview was typical of what we already know about the denominational affiliations and religious Worldviews of Muslims in England, Switzerland and France.[36]

---

[35] In England, 21 per cent of our data sample declared that they had mental health conditions. We have no reason to believe that our data sample differs significantly from the general Muslim prison population, and 21 per cent is similar to what is known about the general prison population of England.

In Switzerland, 33 per cent of our data sample declared that they had mental health conditions. This is similar to what is known about the general prison population in Switzerland at 32 per cent.

In France, only 6 per cent of our data sample declared that they had mental health conditions. Six per cent is much lower than the general prison population in France at 25 per cent.

[36] There are no official percentages of the different sectarian affiliations of Muslims in European countries. However, 75 per cent of Muslims in Europe tend to associate themselves with one of the four main Sunni Schools of Law (*madhahib*): Hanafi School of Law, Maliki School of Law, Shafi School of Law and Hanbali School of Law. See Chapter 3 for further details.

Recently, there has been an increase in the number of Muslims who consider themselves Salafi Muslims, which is estimated now to be around 12 per cent. Salafi Muslims tend not to subscribe to any of these four traditional Schools of Law. Salafi Muslims refer only to The Qur'an and the sayings (*ahadith*) of the Prophet Muhammad for their religious teachings. Salafi Muslims are often second- or third-generation European-born Muslims who want to return to what they regard as a purer, less compromised faith than that of their parents (Bowen, 2013). Second- and third-generation European-born Muslims can also identify as 'just Muslim', that is, they have no particular sectarian affiliation.

Even though the majority of Muslims in Europe are Sunni, there are smaller pockets of Twelver Shia (10 per cent) communities across Europe (Buijs and Rath, 2002). In Britain, there are also small communities of Ismaili Shia (2 per cent) and some Zaydi Shia. In Switzerland, France and Britain, there are small minorities of Ibadi Shias as well as members of the Ahmadiyya denomination.

Our sample of Muslim prisoners also displayed:

- **higher levels of education**; and
- **higher levels of pre-prison employment** than the general prison population.

This suggests that Muslim prisoners tend to come from 'higher' socio-economic backgrounds than non-Muslim prisoners and/or that more educated and employable Muslims tended to volunteer for our study.

Our Muslim prisoner participants were also serving

- **significantly longer prison sentences**; and
- **were more prone to reoffending/reconviction**

than the general prison population, which is characteristic of Muslim prisoners in Europe generally (Pina-Sánchez et al, 2019).

Given the close correspondence of the characteristics of our own research sample of Muslims with what has already been discovered about Muslim prisoners in Europe, we believe that we are justified to claim that our sample was broadly 'characteristic' of Muslim prisoners in our jurisdictions more generally.

Infographics 1.1a and 1.1b plot these characteristics in full.

Infographic 1.1a: The socio-demographic features of Muslim prisoners

		FRANCE	SWITZERLAND	ENGLAND
ETHNICITY	North African	76	39	•
	Turk	80	4	•
	White (French/Swiss/British)	9	6	17
	Black African	1	29	4
	Balkan	9	22	•
	South Asian	3	1	45
	Black (British/Caribbean)	0	0	68
	Mixed Heritage	0	0	22
	Other	0	0	6
Legend: Muslims in prison; Muslims outside prison[1]				
Observations		Overwhelming North African prison population reflects French Muslim community	Predominantly migrant, non-Swiss national prison population	Higher levels of 'white', 'black' and 'mixed' Muslim prisoners due to high rate of conversion
AGE	Under 26	14	8	23
	26 - 35	47	46	44
	36 - 45	21	31	21
	46 - 55	18	13	9
	Over 55	0	0	3
Legend: Muslim prison population				
Observations		Average age = 34, median age = 32 which is similar to General Prison Population (GPP)	Average age = 37, median age = 34 which is similar to General Prison Population (GPP)	Average age = 33, median age = 32 which is younger than General Prison Population (GPP)
EDUCATION	No qualifications	19 / 49	19	20 / 52
	Compulsory	0	2	36 / 33
	Further	26 / 5	7	11 / 4
	Higher	6 / 14	21	20 / 4
	Vocational	3 / 62 / 17	51	14 / 4
Legend: Muslim prison population; General prison population (GPP)				
Observations		Muslim prison population more educated than GPP. Higher levels of vocational training than GPP	Low levels of compulsory education reflects largely non-Swiss migrant population	Muslim prison population more educated than GPP. Higher levels of vocational training than GPP
PRE-PRISON EMPLOYMENT	YES	77 / 80	66 / 80	60 / 76
	NO	23 / 9	34 / 5	40 / 4
Legend: Muslim prison population; National average				
Observations		Unemployment 250% higher than the French national average[2]	Unemployment 700% higher than the Swiss national average[3]	Unemployment 1000% higher than the UK national average[4]
PERCENTAGES		10 20 30 40 50 60 70 80 90 100	10 20 30 40 50 60 70 80 90 100	10 20 30 40 50 60 70 80 90 100

Sources: [1] 2011 Census, UK. [2] World Book 2018 for French national average. [3] World Book 2018 for Swiss national average. [4] Office of National Statistics, UK, 2020 for UK national average. • Data not available

Infographic 1.1b: Crime-related and religious characteristics of Muslim prisoners

		FRANCE	SWITZERLAND	ENGLAND
NUMBER OF CONVICTIONS	1	40	55	49
	2	15	26	15
	3	18	4	18
	4	15	4	4
	5 OR MORE	12	11	14
Observations	Muslim prisoners are more prone to re-offending	60% of Muslim prisoners had served more than one sentence compared with 46% of GPP.	45% of Muslim prisoners had served more than one sentence compared with 38% of GPP.	51% of Muslim prisoners had served more than one sentence compared with 48% of GPP.
LENGTH OF SENTENCE	Less than 1 year	38	7	3 / 7
	1 - 5	19	26	15
	5 - 10	31	55	30
	10 - 20	46	20	19
	More than 20 years	21	27	21
	IPP[1]	14	9	47
	LIFE	10 / 5	12 / 4	11 / 6 / 6 / 2 / 14 / 9 / 10
	Muslim prisoners / *General population*			
Observations	Sentencing is different in France, Switzerland and England	Muslim prisoners serving similar sentences to General Prison Population in France	Muslim prisoners serving longer sentences the General Prison Population in Switzerland	Muslim prisoners serving longer sentences than General Prison Population in England
RELIGIOUS DENOMINATIONS	No particular group	42	57	39
	SUNNI	39	38	43
	SALAFI	13	4	14
	SHIA	0	0	1
	AHMADI	0	0	1
	OTHER	6	2	2
Observations		Similar to Muslim religious denominations outside prison in France	Similar to Muslim religious denominations outside prison in Switzerland	Similar to Muslim religious denominations outside prison in England
RELIGIOUS WORLDVIEWS[2]	MAINSTREAM TRADITIONAL	44	51	48
	MAINSTREAM ACTIVIST	32	35	28
	ISLAMIST	18	11	22
	NON-VIOLENT ISLAMIST EXTREMIST	6	2	1
	VIOLENT ISLAMIST EXTREMIST	0	0	0.5
Observations		Similar to what is known about Muslim religious Worldviews outside prison?	Similar to what is known about Muslim religious Worldviews outside prison	Greater number of Islamist prisoners converted with high conversion rate in England
PERCENTAGES		10 20 30 40 50 60 70 80 90 100	10 20 30 40 50 60 70 80 90 100	10 20 30 40 50 60 70 80 90 100

Notes: [1] Indeterminate Sentence for Public Protection. [2] Please see chapters 4, 5 & 6 for further details. [3] Please see chapters 4, 5 & 6 for further details.

62

2

What is Islam in prison?

We have seen in Chapter 1 where Islam comes from and how Muslims came to be in European prisons, and we have offered the reader a brief socio-demographic portrait of Muslims in prisons in England, Switzerland and France.

In this chapter, we will describe the basic sources, beliefs and practices of Islam to inform the prison professional and the general reader.[1] We will explain how these basic elements of practice and belief inform and shape the lives of Muslim prisoners and also describe the experiences of those prisoners who are apathetic or non-committal about their faith.

The primary sources of Islam

There are two primary sources from which all Mainstream Islamic belief and practice are derived, both of which feature strongly in prison life:

1. The Qur'an (literally 'The Recitation');
2. The Sunna (the Customary or Everyday Behaviour of the Prophet Muhammad).

The Qur'an in prison

The Qur'an is believed by Muslims to be the inimitable word of God. Muslims believe that it was brought from God by the Angel Gabriel, in stages, to be delivered upon the tongue of the Prophet Muhammad over a period of 23 years from 610 CE to 632 CE.

Our Muslim prisoners understood that The Qur'an is a core primary source of their religion. The Qur'an formed a central feature in the religious Worldviews of the participants, as evidenced by the fact that The Qur'an was referenced by 86 of our 158 interviewees. We found that The Qur'an was seminal to the individual and institutional life of Muslims in prison, and participants engaged with The Qur'an for a variety of spiritual purposes.

---

[1]   These are common to both the Sunni and Shia Schools of Law.

THE QUR'AN (2:3) DESCRIBES ITSELF AS
'guidance for those who are mindful of God'.

- The Qur'an is made up of 114 chapters (*surahs*) and 6,236 verses (*ayats*).

- Eighty-five chapters were mainly revealed while the Prophet Muhammad and the early Muslim community lived in Mecca from 610 to 622 CE.

- Twenty-nine chapters were mainly revealed after the emigration (*Hijra*) of the Prophet Muhammad and the early Muslim community to Medina in 622–632 CE.

- The verses (*ayats*) that were revealed in Mecca tend to deal with big cosmic themes such as: Divine Unity; the need for worship and social responsibility; the Day of Resurrection and the Afterlife and Stories of the Prophets.

- The verses (*ayats*) that were revealed in Medina deal more with basic practical principles of life and law governing matters such as marriage, inheritance, business.

- Therefore, The Qur'an reflects the context into which it was revealed since it was only in Medina that the Prophet Muhammad came to govern the legal and political life of an entire community of over 10,000 souls, that included Muslims, Jews, Christians and Pagan 'non-believers'.

For example, Abdu[2] (male, 24, British Black African, Born-Muslim, HMP Cherwell, Category C Prison) read The Qur'an in Arabic as a way of finding inner peace.

> In the Seg[regation Unit] ... I used to get into a lot of fights because, like I said, I was a bit hot-headed and ... I would just end up reading. I would read The Qur'an ... It would bring peace to my heart ..., it would bring me happiness, although I'm in a bad situation.

---

[2] All names of individuals and prisons are pseudonyms that bear no resemblance to their original names.

Abbas (male, 50, British Asian Pakistani, Born-Muslim, HMP Stour, Category D Prison) read The Qur'an in English translation specifically to derive spiritual guidance from it.

> Yeah I keep reading it, but I'm not reading it in Arabic, I'm reading it in English. Because ... The Qur'an is a book of guidance.

As well as individual prisoners' experiences of The Qur'an, in prison The Qur'an also acted as a focal point of religious education and chaplaincy provision.

At HMP Cherwell (Category C Prison), once a week Imam Abdullah gave a two-hour recitation class of The Qur'an in which he had instituted a mentoring system with more accomplished prisoner reciters bringing on the beginners. This meant that learning to recite The Qur'an could continue on the wings after the chaplaincy class, and the mentoring also created a bond and feeling of brotherhood and responsibility between prisoners. By contrast, such encouragement was prohibited in Switzerland and in France as 'proselytising'.

In HMP Severn (Category B Prison), once a week Imam Abdul Ghani conducted a one-hour Qur'an class in which we observed the intense focus of 12 prisoners who did not break their concentration for the whole hour. Among these prisoners, study of The Qur'an generated a 'sense of the sacred' (Otto, 1958) that was in stark contrast to the often noisy and raucous atmosphere on the wings, in the workshops and during association.

The Sunna in prison

The second source of Islam – the Customary or Everyday Behaviour (Sunna) of the Prophet Muhammad – is absolutely central to Islam. Quite simply, without the Sunna of Muhammad there would be no Islam. As one early Muslim scholar put it (Brown, 2009), 'The Qur'an ordains it; the Sunna explains it' **(see Information Box on p 66)**.

Hadith

The Sunna is itself derived from a vast corpus of recorded sayings and actions of the Prophet Muhammad as he interacted with his family and Companions. These recorded sayings and actions are called *hadith*. These *hadith* were recorded by reliable and trusted chains of narrators (*isnad*) which started during the life of the Prophet Muhammad, but gathered momentum

AN ILLUSTRATION OF THE RELATIONSHIP BETWEEN THE QUR'AN AND THE SUNNA IS THE OBLIGATORY PRAYER (*AS-SALAH*):

- The Qur'an (4:103) declares that the Obligatory Daily Prayers must be conducted at prescribed times during each day.

- The Sunna illustrates what these times are, how these times are calculated across the year and the actions and words that must be performed to complete the Obligatory Five Daily Prayers.

- The Qur'an describes the Prophet Muhammad as an 'Excellent Example' (The Qur'an, 33:21) and the Sunna of the Prophet Muhammad as 'Wisdom' (The Qur'an, 62:2).

straight after his death. *Hadiths* have traditionally been ranked according to their quality and the number of their narrators.[3]

The Sunna was important to prisoners

Twenty-seven of our research participants in our interviews cited the Sunna as a significant component of their Islamic Worldviews.

For example, Karim (male, 34, British Mixed Heritage, Born-Muslim, HMP Cherwell, Category C Prison) cited the Sunna of the Prophet Muhammad as a key element in his coping with the challenges of prison life:

> The Prophet, peace be upon him, said if you're standing in your anger, sit down. If you're sitting, lay down. If you're angry, go and do Wudu [ablution] because the water extinguishes the fire, pray two Rakats, seek assistance from Allah for whatever you are going through. So, for me, the deen [religion] has helped me with my emotional side, with the direction that I'm moving in with my life.

---

[3] Although often used synonymously, the *hadith* and the Sunna are not the same:
- the *hadith* are the records of the sayings and actions of the Prophet Muhammad;
- the Sunna is the religious and sometime legal practice derived from the *hadith* (Kamali, 2003).

And because Karim was an inmate of a working prison, he referenced the Sunna as an inspiration to develop a strong work ethic.

> I'm motivated to work because the Prophet always promoted a positive work ethic. When you're paid to do something, you do that job. ... So, my work ethic is part of my deen [religion] ... and I work hard and I'm efficient and I get it all done.

The Sharia, its schools and its purposes

Religious and legal stipulations derived from The Qur'an and the Sunna comprise the Islamic Sharia. Sharia means 'the legal straight path'. Sharia is an Arabic word of pre-Qur'anic origin that means 'a pathway to a spring of pure water'. Therefore, the Sharia is understood by Muslims as a religious pathway from birth to death which is to be travelled in obedience to God (Wilkinson, 2015b).[4]

The Schools of Law (madhahib)

The majority of legal judgements of the Sharia which are derived from The Qur'an and Sunna are therefore human legal interpretations of divine and prophetic principles (Kamali, 2017). In other words, the majority of legal judgements of the Sharia are fallible and changeable because they are legal interpretations made by humans and dependent on context.

Over centuries, these judgements of Sharia clustered into five different Schools of Law.

The four Sunni Muslim Schools of Law are named after their founders:

- Hanafi School of Law[5]
- Maliki School of Law[6]

---

[4] To many non-Muslims, and indeed Muslims, the Sharia has come to be associated with the severe and literalist penal code (hudud) adopted by some Muslim-majority states, such as Saudi Arabia. However, these have often violated the merciful spirit of The Qur'an and Sunna. Moreover, the hudud require such a high evidence threshold that they are very seldom prosecuted and rather represent symbolically the fact that sins such as adultery greatly displease God and greatly damage society.

[5] Named after its founder Imam Abu Hanifa (699–767 CE).

[6] Named after its founder Imam Malik bin Anas al-Asbahi (713–795 CE).

- Shafi School of Law[7]
- Hanbali School of Law[8]

The one Shia Muslim School of Law is called the Jafari[9] School of Law.

All Islamic Schools of Law are different legal expressions of Mainstream Islam as expressed in The Qur'an and the Sunna.

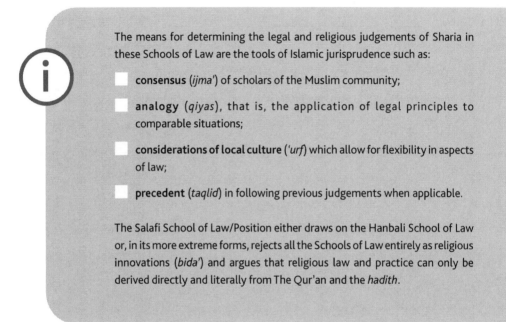

The means for determining the legal and religious judgements of Sharia in these Schools of Law are the tools of Islamic jurisprudence such as:

consensus (*ijma'*) of scholars of the Muslim community;

analogy (*qiyas*), that is, the application of legal principles to comparable situations;

considerations of local culture (*'urf*) which allow for flexibility in aspects of law;

precedent (*taqlid*) in following previous judgements when applicable.

The Salafi School of Law/Position either draws on the Hanbali School of Law or, in its more extreme forms, rejects all the Schools of Law entirely as religious innovations (*bida'*) and argues that religious law and practice can only be derived directly and literally from The Qur'an and the *hadith*.

The purposes (maqasid) of the Sharia

Critically, in the early centuries of Islam, scholars reviewed The Qur'an and the Sunna to identify the core divine purposes (*maqasid*) behind the Sharia. These, with some variants and derivatives in different times and places, were determined to be:

- Protection of Life
- Preservation of Faith

---

[7] Named after its founder Imam Muhammad Idris al-Shafi (767–820 CE).
[8] Named after its founder Imam Ahmad bin Muhammad bin Hanbal (780–855 CE).
[9] Named after its founder Imam Ja'far ibn Muhammad al-Sadiq (702–765 CE).

- Preservation of Lineage
- Protection of Property
- Protection of Intellect

Importantly, the purposes of Sharia indicate that the religious law of Islam is not arbitrary, but that there are reasonable and consistent principles behind it. The purposes behind the Sharia have become an important element of religious and legal decision making in Islam, in particular in the modern, technological era when relevant analogy or legal precedent may be difficult to identify.

The articles of faith in Islam

THE ARTICLES OF FAITH IN ISLAM

According to the Sharia, all Muslims are required to believe in the following Articles of Faith (Hussain, 2012):

1. GOD (ALLAH)

The One who is uniquely God without partners (in Arabic, Allah): Creator, Sustainer and Lord of the entire created Universe and other Worlds that we do not know about. Islam, like Judaism, is an uncompromisingly monotheistic faith.

2. THE ANGELS

Invisible beings that carry out the Divine Command (*Amr*). The Archangels are believed by Muslims to be:

Gabriel (Jibra'il) – responsible for human–divine communication, for revealing The Qur'an to Muhammad verse by verse, and for announcing the miraculous birth of Jesus to Mary;

Raphael (Israfil) – will usher in The End of Time;

Michael (Mika'il) – charged with the distribution of material provision and natural resources;

Azrael (Azrail) also known as Malak al-Maut, the Angel of Death – responsible for removing the Spirit (*ruh*) from the body upon death (The Qur'an, 79:1–2).

3. GOD'S BOOKS

The Books of Revelation given to Abraham, Moses, David, Jesus and Muhammad. These books are the Torah, the Psalms, the Gospels and The Qur'an. Muslims tend to believe that only The Qur'an is still known to us in its pristine revealed form.

4. GOD'S MESSENGERS

The Qur'an refers to 25 known Prophets. The Prophets who were given Books of Revelation are Abraham, Moses, David, Jesus and Muhammad.

As well as the Prophet Muhammad, other renowned Prophets of Islam include Adam, Noah, Aaron, Lot, Ismael, Isaac, Jacob, Joseph, Solomon and John the Baptist.

Other lesser-known Prophets include Enoch, Shiloh, Eber, Job, Zachariah, Jethro, Ezekiel, Elijah, Elisha and Jonah.

The Qur'an requires believers to make no distinction between the Prophets in that they all deliver the message of Divine Unity without partners and the need to worship and obey Him (The Qur'an, 2:285).

5. THE DAY OF RESURRECTION AND JUDGEMENT

The Day of Resurrection and Judgement when every human being will stand before God to account for their life. It is fundamental to Islam that every human being is individually accountable before God Almighty for their actions and their intentions without intermediary or the need for a priesthood.

6. THE DECREE

God Almighty has determined and has power over the good and the bad of everything that happens.[10,11]

---

[10] All four Schools of Sunni Law – Maliki School of Law, Hanafi School of Law, Hanbali School of Law and Shafi' School of Law – and the one Shia Muslim School of Law – Jafari School of Law – and the Traditions of Islam are agreed on these core elements of Islamic belief (*Aqeedah*). In addition to these Six Articles of Faith, the Shia Muslim Articles of Faith include the principle of Divine Justice (*Adala*) and the Principle that God has designated specific religious leaders to follow the Prophets in the guidance of mankind (*Imama*).

[11] Tensions between Article 5 and Article 6 have been debated throughout the centuries of Islam.

What the Articles of Faith meant to Muslim prisoners

These Articles of Faith were important to many Muslim prisoners, not merely as abstract doctrine but as realities that impacted on the meaning that they give to prison life. For example, the idea of The Decree – that God has preordained all of existence, including their prison sentence – acted as a powerful coping mechanism for many Muslim prisoners.

On many occasions, prisoners articulated the feeling or belief that their conviction and sentence were part of a Divine Destiny which had spared them from a worse fate, such as death, and had given them the opportunity to find Islam.

Bashir (male, 33, Asian, Born-Muslim, HMP Cherwell, Category C Prison) was unequivocal:

> I think I'm just being saved, God's put me through the hardship, but only because he loves me, that's what I believe? … Allah is saving me, so maybe there was something bad going to happen around the corner or the next years, maybe it was on a plane journey or this or that. So, just have patience, because look where God's put you. This is what you need to understand about life. Don't take prison as a punishment.

Seeing imprisonment as part of God's plan helped participants move on from fixating on the circumstances of their conviction, including in many cases feelings of anger, resentment and injustice, and to reframe their lives in prison as an opportunity from God to bring about positive personal change.

Muslim prisoners also regularly expressed how their belief in standing before God in Judgement and the prospect of the afterlife (*Akhira*) of Heaven or Hell acted as a powerful 'carrot and stick' for them to reflect upon their former life of crime and to make an intention to abandon it.

For example, Troy (male, 28, British Black, Muslim Convert, HMP Stour, Category D Prison) feared meeting God with unatoned crime on his hands:

> Yeah, 100 per cent because I know it's [crime] wrong. I know I'll be judged but I will be accountable for my actions. … So I'd rather just live in one of these paths where I abstain from crime, abstain from things, because I know it's not the judge that's in the courts

or the police that's going to hurt me the most, it's when I'm in front of Allah Subhana Watala and He says, "What have you done? I gave you this, what have you done with it?" It's one of them things where I don't want to be walking round with victims and their judgement and saying, "Look, he's done this to me, take him [to Hell]."

99

Troy's belief that he would have to answer for his actions to God and his victims on the Day of Judgement acted as a powerful incentive to aspire to avoid further crime.

Figure 2.1: The Pillars of Islam

The Pillars of Islam

As well as mandating certain religious beliefs, Islam also mandates five types of obligatory religious action (see Figure 2.1).

As the Prophet Muhammad said:

> Islam has been built upon five things: testifying that there is no god but God and that Muhammad is the Messenger of God, establishing the Obligatory Prayer, paying the Poor Tax, making pilgrimage to the House of Allah, and fasting the month of Ramadan. (Narrated by Al-Bukhari (died 870 CE) and Muslim (died 874/5 CE))

Following on from this *hadith*, the scholars of Islam over many centuries (Hussain, 2012) have stated that Islam has Five Pillars of basic religious obligation – which are often referred to as the Five Pillars of Islam – that every individual Muslim must perform (*Fard 'Ayn*):[12]

THE PILLARS OF ISLAM ARE …

1. THE WITNESSING (*SHAHADAH*)

This is the Declaration of Faith,

that there is no god but God (Allah) and that Muhammad is the Messenger of God (Allah).

Upon declaring this in front of two witnesses, a person enters Islam.

This Declaration of Faith means that he or she agrees to perform the following four practices:

---

[12] Twelver Shia Muslims add the following six obligatory actions to these basic Five Obligations:
1. Payment of the Fifth (*Khums* = 20% capital gains tax paid in charity)
2. Struggle to obey God (*Jihad*)
3. Enjoining good (*Amr bil M'aruf*)
4. Forbidding evil (*Nahil 'anil Munkar*)
5. Drawing near God and to righteous people (*Tawalia*)
6. Turning away from Evil and from wrong-doers (*Tabarra*).

2. THE OBLIGATORY DAILY PRAYER (*SALAH*)

Five daily prayers that are performed at prescribed times of day that move according to the position of the sun:

i.   *Salat al-fajr*: at dawn, before sunrise;
ii. *Salat al-dhuhr*: midday, after the sun passes its zenith;
iii. *Salat al-'asr*: the late part of the afternoon after the mid-point between noon and sunset;
iv. *Salat al-maghrib*: just after sunset;
v.   *Salat al-'isha*: between sunset and midnight.

The Prayer is comprised of rotations of standing, bowing and prostrating before God, called *Rak'ahs*, together with the recitation of certain phrases and verses of The Qur'an.

The Obligatory Daily Prayer is the means by which the believer connects with and accounts for himself or herself before God five times a day. See Figures 2.2 and 2.3.

3. THE FAST OF RAMADAN (*SAWM*)

This is to abstain from all food, drink and sexual relations from dawn to sunset during the month of Ramadan.

The purpose of The Fast is to teach self-restraint and moderation of the appetites, gratitude to God for His provision and empathy with the poor (The Qur'an, 2:183–185). The Prophet Muhammad said,

God will not accept the Fast from food and drink of someone who does not fast from lying and acting ignorantly.

(Sahih al-Bukhari (73/83))

4. THE POOR TAX (*ZAKAH*)

This is a tax on 2.5 per cent of a Muslim believer's unused savings which is paid to a religious authority for the maintenance of the poor and a variety of other categories of needy people. It is paid once someone's unused annual savings have reached a threshold (*nisab*) of c. £400.

5. THE PILGRIMAGE (*HAJJ*)

Once in a lifetime if s/he is able to afford it while still fulfilling their duties to provide for their family, the believer agrees to make pilgrimage to perform the rites of *Hajj* at the first place dedicated to the worship of God: the Ka'aba in Mecca and surrounding areas.

THESE FIVE PILLARS MAKE THE COMPLETE MUSLIM

These are the only obligatory acts of worship in Islam that combine to make the Muslim the complete believer and fulfil the believer's covenant with God. This is illustrated, Muslims believe, by the *hadith* of the Prophet Muhammad:

A man asked the Messenger of God (may blessings and peace be upon him):

Do you think that if I perform the obligatory prayers, fast in Ramadan, treat as lawful that which is lawful and treat as forbidden that which is forbidden, and do nothing further, I shall enter Paradise? He (Muhammad) said: Yes.

(Narrated by Muslim (d. 874/75 CE))

Figure 2.2: Positions of the Muslim Prayer, First *Rak'ah*

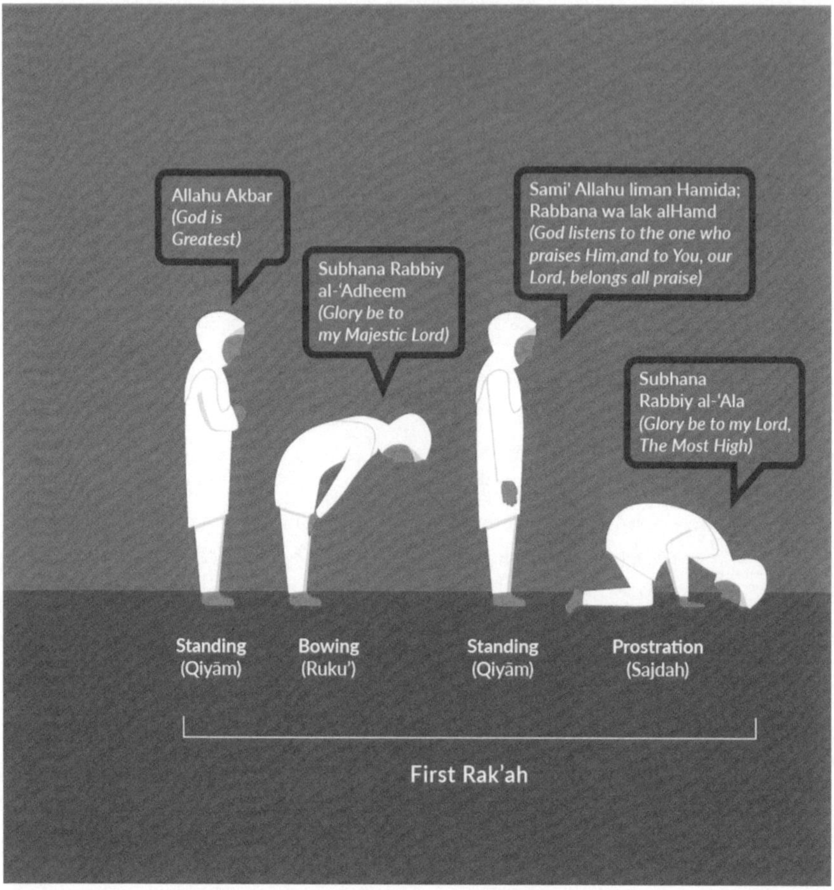

Note: These diagrams do not depict the complete words and actions of the Obligatory Prayer.

For many of our Muslim participants, the ability to perform the Five Obligatory Practices was often of paramount importance to their identity as Muslims. The Obligatory Daily Prayers, in particular, structured their day and their week, and many prisoners were grateful for the opportunities that they had received in prison to relearn and return to Obligatory Daily Prayer, often with rehabilitative outcomes.

For example, for Omar (male, 35, Asian Bangladeshi, Born–Muslim, HMP Severn, Category B Prison) the act of seeking repentance for his crime was specifically connected to his return to performing the Prayer in prison:

Figure 2.3: Positions of the Muslim Prayer, Second *Rak'ah*

Allahu Akbar (God is Greatest)

Subhana Rabbiy al-'Adheem (Glory be to my Majestic Lord)

Sami' Allahu liman Hamida; Rabbana wa lak alHamd (God listens to the one who praises Him, and to You, our Lord, belongs all praise)

Subhana Rabbiy al-'Ala (Glory be to my Lord, The Most High)

The Tashahhud (The Witnessing of Faith)

Standing (Qiyām)   Bowing (Ruku')   Standing (Qiyām)   Prostration (Sajdah)   Sitting (Jilsah)

Second Rak'ah

> Interviewer:
>
> Has your practice of Islam made you think about that [your crime]? ... make tawba [repentance]?
>
> Omar:
>
> I did tawba every day and even though, I don't know why it's happening, I never ever prayed five times a day [outside prison]. ... But since I've been in prison, if I miss one salat [Obligatory Prayer] or get late, I'm getting crazy.

These regular acts of repentance through the Obligatory Prayers helped prisoners construct and then sustain a positive identity in which they could move past their crimes towards a more positive new life (Maruna et al, 2006; Williams, 2018).

The connection with the Obligatory Daily Prayers was strongly connected with prisoners regaining balance, calm and inner peace. This type of connection was cited 121 times at interview.[13] For example, according to Fahd (male, 34, British Asian Pakistani, Born-Muslim, HMP Parrett, Category B Prison):

> It [the Prayer] gives you like peace and that. ... It makes you feel better after you've done a prayer because when I'm outside, I don't pray. I don't pray, to tell you the truth, and when I'm in prison, I do pray. I come to Jumu'ah and that. It's very rare I pray outside or read The Qur'an ... it makes me feel better and that, it makes me feel cleaner and that, if you know what I mean?

Fahd's account was typical of several prisoners who contrasted the ease of practising the Obligatory Prayer in prison with the difficulties and distractions that they faced outside prison.

It was common to both men and women in our English, Swiss and French cohort that they were often unable to sustain the spiritual practices and gains that they had achieved in prison when re-exposed to the outside world. Therefore, for some repeat offenders, prison acted as a regular religious retreat from crime (cf. Webster and Qasim, 2018).

Ablution for prayer

In order to perform the Obligatory Prayers, Muslims are required to perform a ritual washing or ablution (*wudu*), which involves wiping their hands, face, hair, arms, ears and feet with fresh water (see Figure 2.4). Before the Friday Prayer and after sexual emissions, Muslims are expected to perform a major ablution (*ghusul*), which is a form of full-body wash or shower in fresh water.

---

[13] 'Balance' was cited 11 times; 'Calm' was cited 54 times; 'Inner peace' was cited 47 times.

Figure 2.4: Ablution in Islam

When conditions for washing on the wings were insanitary, Muslim prisoners felt uncomfortable about doing their ablution, and this could affect their state of mind and their satisfaction more generally with prison life. Farhad (male, 30, British Asian, Born-Muslim, HMP Cherwell, Category C Prison) felt strongly that facilities at HMP Cherwell were inadequate for major ablution before the Friday Prayer because the prison authorities did not understand its significance.

> There's only about five showers on the wing and that's on the ground floor. ... Somebody said to them, "Give them half an hour access" because they get up from work from 11.45, go to break, grab our lunch and then come back at 12 o'clock and then we're back over here in the masjid at five past 12, quarter past 12. Which doesn't give us no time, five minutes, to have a bath [*Ghusl*] and get dressed is so quick, it's too quick, especially when you've got 30 inmates on one wing. They said, "No." But it's, you can't blame the Imam for this because the Imam is one man, as much he can do, he can do. Brothers have fought for it, and it just didn't work out because they don't know how it's important to us. They do not know what deen [religion] is for us, inside jail. But could you blame them?

The lack of understanding by some prison staff about the obligations on Muslims to perform ablution before the Obligatory Prayers and that, after using the toilet, Muslims are required to wash their private parts in order to be 'clean' for the Obligatory Prayer caused unnecessary contention between prisoners and staff. For example, Jamil (male, 30, Black British, Born-Muslim, HMP Cherwell, Category C Prison) complained that he was repeatedly stopped and challenged by prison officers for carrying a small plastic water bottle across the wing for cleaning himself after using the toilet.

Charity

The vast majority of our participant prisoners were poor and did not meet the threshold to pay the obligatory Poor Tax (*Zakah*) of 2.5 per cent of savings. Nevertheless, many prisoners engaged in other voluntary acts of charity (*Sadaqa*), which they often regarded as a means of atonement for the damage that they had caused to victims and to society. For example, Rick (male, 40, White British, Convert, HMP Cherwell, Category C Prison) set aside some of his monthly earnings to send to charity:

> I give money every month to different charities. … I've got a bit of money behind me, and this job's good for wages, you know what I'm saying? I'm on £25 a week and plus I get a bit of cash sent in. … So, it's not a lot money, I send but it's a few quid, you know what I'm saying? But that few quid helps every month, you know what I'm saying?

Other prisoners spoke about sharing the best bits of their canteen, such as chocolate biscuits and good shampoo, with other prisoners – both Muslim and non-Muslim – which were acts of kindness and solidarity that made them feel better about prison life.

The Fast of Ramadan

Fasting the month of Ramadan is a core practice for many Muslim prisoners. The Fast of Ramadan is facilitated in all English prisons according to protocols drawn up by Her Majesty's Prison & Probation Service (HMPPS) Muslim Advisors. To the credit of the English prison authorities, Ramadan thermos boxes were provided to all registered Muslim prisoners. These boxes included food to break the fast (*iftar*) at sunset and for the pre-dawn breakfast (*suhur*).

Like other core Islamic practices, prison had afforded some prisoners the occasion to observe the Fast of Ramadan properly for the first time. Osman (male, 45, British Asian, Born-Muslim, HMP Parrett, Category B Prison) was typical in this respect:

> Before prison I didn't really used to fast. I used to cheat. When I came in prison, I thought okay I can do it and so I tried fasting and managed all of them.

Yusuf (male, 22, Mixed Heritage, Convert, HMP Parrett, Category B Prison) relished the solidarity and brotherhood with other Muslims that fasting Ramadan brought him:

> I've done it before on the outside, but where I've been in jail, I've tried and you know what it is as well? When I'm on the wing with so many brothers ... I've done two Ramadans in jail, I've done one in this jail and one in another jail and the other jail I was in ... there were so many brothers on the wing, it was just tight. We was [*sic*] all doing it together, we're not going to break our fast ... we all encourage each other and I think, on the outside I haven't got all of that. I've got loads of my friends that are Muslims, but there's not going to be so many.

On a visit to the kitchens at HMP Stour, we witnessed some prison staff taking special care with the preparation of the Ramadan boxes. When this happened, it was particularly welcomed by Muslim prisoners. This care shown by the prison staff at HMP Stour had a knock-on effect of generating greater trust between Muslim prisoners and prison staff more generally.

For example, we observed that the head chef at HMP Stour, Mike (male, circa 40, British White, non-Muslim), was particularly sensitive to the needs of Muslim prisoners. Mike explained how every "Muslim brother" received the special Ramadan box during Ramadan:

> even if one day they are seen eating during the day, since ... doing the fast in prison and out of prison are not the same; in prison they may have had a bad telephone call or something has not gone right. So, if they say at lunch, "I want some chips," I give it to them. Then they go back to the Fast the next day. ... Ramadan in prison is like running two separate regimes: it's difficult.

Nevertheless, despite the difficulties, Mike was adept at liaising with key trusted Muslim prisoners to see that Ramadan was observed to everyone's satisfaction. Mike's approach generated appreciable trust and good feeling between prisoners and staff.

Mike's sensitivity to the challenges of observing Ramadan in prison aptly exemplifies a model of good prison practice and an example of how respect for this religious observance managed to bring people of different types together.

By contrast, we also heard from two prisoners of occasions when prison officers were not respectful towards the fasting prisoners by, for example, withholding or appearing to withhold the Ramadan boxes from them.

The Permitted (halal) and The Forbidden (*haram*) in prison

As well as the basic elements of Islamic belief and practice, all of the Islamic Schools of Law – including the Shia Jafari School of Law and the Salafi School – concur on the major behaviours that are permitted (halal) and forbidden (*haram*) by God and His Prophet in Islam.[14]

Theologically, if a Muslim performs an action that is permitted (halal), it is believed to count as a Good Deed in the Balance (*mizan*) of their Account (*hisab*) with God. If a Muslim performs an action that is forbidden (*haram*), it is believed to count as a sin in the Balance (*mizan*) of their Account (*hisab*) with God.

Since considerations of what counts as permitted (halal) and what counts as forbidden (*haram*) are a significant part of the Worldviews and experiences of Muslim prisoners, it is worth listing here the basic elements of the halal and *haram*. Observing The Permitted and The Forbidden are believed by Muslims in general, and by our characteristic sample of Muslim prisoners in particular, to represent a holistic account of the human being's Covenant with God.

---

[14] There are also other legal categories such as *makruh* (disliked by God, such as divorce) and *mubah* (religiously neutral, such as eating).

THE PERMITTED (HALAL) INCLUDES:

■ worship of God that is not idolatrous;

■ just government;[15]

■ knowledge and learning of all types that we would term both secular and sacred;[16]

■ trade;[17]

■ productive work of all types that does not involve the manufacture or sale of things that are forbidden;[18]

■ consumption of all foods that are both good and not forbidden (see later);[19]

■ fully expressed sexual relations within the legal parameters of a contractually binding marriage;[20]

■ friendly relationships and affection between groups of all types;[21]

■ artistic expression, so long as is it does not celebrate or encourage what is forbidden;[22]

■ under very strict conditions, regulated warfare, because it is a part of the Natural Way (*fitra*) by which human beings must occasionally protect themselves from greater harm and by which worship of God is sometimes necessarily protected.[23]

---

[15] The Qur'an 5:8; 42:38; 3:159.

[16] The Qur'an 20:114; 39:9; 35:28.

[17] The Qur'an 2:275.

[18] Imam Ja'far as-Sadiq reports the Prophet Muhammad as saying, 'It is necessary for the believer to work hard even if he feels the scorching heat of the sun.' Taking charity unnecessarily or begging if one can work are disliked in Islam. The performance of good deeds (*amal salih*) – which includes earning a living – is an idea repeated 360 times in The Qur'an.

[19] The Qur'an 2:168; 5:4.

[20] The Qur'an 2:223.

[21] The Qur'an 60:8–9.

[22] The Qur'an 7:32. Also *The Psalms of David*, in which Muslims are required to believe, mandates singing to God.

[23] The Qur'an 22:39–40.

THE FORBIDDEN (*HARAM*) INCLUDES

(IN APPROXIMATE ORDER OF RELIGIOUS-LEGAL SEVERITY):

- ▪ idol-worship of other-than-God (*shirk*);[24]

- ▪ gratuitous violence, terrorism (*hiraba*) and unregulated and unjust war;[25]

- ▪ political oppression, rebellion, injustice and anarchy (*fitnah*);[26]

- ▪ murder;[27]

- ▪ suicide;[28]

- ▪ theft;[29]

- ▪ sexual acts outside a legally binding heterosexual marriage;[30]

- ▪ breaking of contracts;[31]

- ▪ usury/charging interest (*riba*) and other forms of financial malpractice;[32]

- ▪ slander;[33]

- ▪ lying;[34]

- ▪ gambling;[35]

- ▪ intoxicants, including alcohol and drugs;[36]

- ▪ the meat and all products from pigs and carrion and food that has been consecrated to other-than-God.[37]

---

[24] The Qur'an 4:48; 5:72; 31:13.

[25] The Qur'an 2:190; 5:33–34.

[26] The Qur'an 2:191.

[27] The Qur'an 4:93; 5:32.

[28] Qur'an 4:29–30 and numerous authentic *hadith*.

[29] The Qur'an 5:38–39 and numerous authentic *hadith*, and the fact that Muslims accept Mosaic Law, which forbids theft.

[30] The Qur'an 17:32; 24:2 and numerous authentic *hadith*. These forbidden acts include fornication, adultery and homosexuality.

[31] The Qur'an 16:91.

[32] The Qur'an 2:275.

[33] The Qur'an 49:12.

[34] The Qur'an 24:8.

[35] The Qur'an 5:3, 5:90–92.

[36] The Qur'an 5:90–92.

[37] The Qur'an 5:3; 5:90–92. What does and does not constitute *halal* meat is a debate in Islam which is beyond the remit of this book to rehearse.

These are Forbidden (*haram*) because they are believed by Muslims to disrupt or destroy the conditions under which the basic purposes of Islam can be pursued: the worship of God together with human flourishing (Wilkinson, 2015a).[38]

In these prohibitions, Islam reflects the Abrahamic heritage of the Torah, the Psalms and the Gospels, as well as The Qur'an, and the reader will notice a considerable overlap of The Forbidden (*haram*) with behaviours that are regarded either as criminal or as unethical in Western religious and legal traditions.

FORBIDDING THE PERMITTED IS ITSELF FORBIDDEN

Crucially, The Qur'an also expressly forbids people to prohibit things that are not prohibited in The Qur'an:

'Oh you who believe!

Do not forbid [make haram] the good things which God has permitted [made halal] for you, and do not go to excess; indeed, God does not love those who go to excess.

And eat of what God has provided for you, lawful and good, and be mindful of God, in whom you believe.'

(The Qur'an, 5: 87–88)

In Islam, it is as wrong for Muslims to prohibit things that are permitted as it is to permit things that are forbidden.

There are also many types of action about which The Qur'an and the Sunna have remained silent, and therefore Muslim believers must examine their own conscience and make up their own moral minds.

The halal and *haram* for our sample of prisoners

For our Muslim prisoners, the aspiration to fulfil The Permitted (halal) and to avoid The Forbidden (*haram*) was often a core element of their

---

[38] Actions that support The Permitted are often termed 'Recommended' (*Mustahab*). Actions which run a risk of someone falling into The Forbidden are often termed 'Disliked' (*Makruh*).

understanding of what it means to be a Muslim and could also inspire and reinforce a desire to avoid future crime.

This framing of certain activities as not simply illegal or wrong but forbidden by God often added a protective layer against reoffending. This was especially the case when it was done in the company of other trusted and respected Muslim prisoners. For example, Imran (male, 24, British Turkish, Muslim-Born, HMP Cherwell, Category C Prison) explained:

> Yes, so I see big changes from selling drugs, not caring about many things, to not doing anything [*haram*] and believing in Islam ... so I was getting more into Islam, hanging around with the brothers more. Then they showed me guidance ... they were showing me that selling drugs is no go. ... So, the brothers have showed me what's right, what's wrong, what's haram.

Imran framed 'right' and 'wrong' in terms of avoiding the *haram* as a core part of his identity as a Muslim.

Halal food

In prison, while there is ample scope for prisoners to engage in activity that is Islamically either halal or *haram*, issues of halal and *haram* tend to focus around two prevalent features of prison life: food and music.

For meat to be halal, the animal must be treated with compassion during its rearing, handling and transport, as well as being slaughtered in compliance with Islamic law, as The Qur'an (2:168) commands believers to eat 'what is permitted and good' (The Qur'an, 2:168).

The need to fulfil The Permitted (halal) inspired in Muslim prisoners a desire to eat halal food and to be confident that their food was not 'contaminated' by the *haram*. Suspicions that prison food, although labelled as halal was, in fact, contaminated with *haram* food, such as pork fat, fed off and into existing prisoner suspicions that prison authorities, and prison officers in particular, were trying to deceive them (Liebling & Arnold, 2012). Therefore, as well as being inspired by a genuine desire to follow the Sharia, food also became a means by which Muslim prisoners could assert their Muslim identity and difference from other non-Muslim prisoners and prison staff.

Wade (male, 20, British Mixed Race, Convert, HMP Parrett, Category B prison), for example, was typical in his view that halal food was often 'contaminated' in prison kitchens by *haram* food:

> So, basically a cross-contamination goes on all over the place, so basically, the first thing I done was worked in the kitchen, when I got here. ... There was a lot of cross-contamination going on.

Jameel (male, 31, British Mixed Heritage, Convert, HMP Forth, Category A prison) felt that Muslim prisoners were sometimes tricked into eating *haram* food, such as pork, and the idea that their food was being purposely 'contaminated' by prison authorities played on the minds of several Muslim prisoners:

> Well, the first night I arrived in the segregation from HMP Thames I got placed into a cell. ... Oh, no, on the bus they said, we've got the famous Toad-in-the-Hole, York Toad-in-the-Hole, so I went into my cell, opened the box, looked at it, and asked the Prison Officer, "Is this Halal?" and he said, "Oh, it should be, what's made you suspicious?" Then I cut open the sausages, looked at it and it was pink and, like I said, "To my knowledge, Toad-in-the-Hole is normally always cooked with pork sausages." So, I didn't eat it, but the other prisoner that I arrived with from Thames actually ate it, and he didn't know that it wasn't halal, and when I told him after he was outraged.

In France, prisoners raised concerns about the lack of halal red meat and were troubled by the idea that in making a request for halal food, a prisoner became an object of suspicion to the authorities. For example, Nabil (male, 47, French National, Algerian, Born-Muslim, Hauterive, Category B Prison) said:

> That's the problem, we only eat halal. And that's also a problem here, well it's all over France, they have a problem with halal, as soon as they hear halal, boom, it's blocked see. People like us are gone for years, see it's still hard not to eat red meat, it's only chicken, after all depends on the prisons.

In Switzerland, some prisoners explained that because out of prison they had not always eaten meat that was slaughtered in a halal way (with the exception of pork), they continued to eat whatever meat was served to them in prison. To some Muslim scholars, this is an acceptable position because The Qur'an permits Muslims to eat meat that is slaughtered by Jews and Christians (The Qur'an, 5:6).

On the whole, Muslim prisoners felt that the respect or lack of it that the prison authorities showed for their need for halal food reflected more generally their respect or lack of respect for Islam and Muslims.

Music

Music of diverse types is a ubiquitous feature of prison life in individuals' cells, on the wings and in workspaces. Another point of contention for Muslim prisoners focused around whether or not music was halal.

There exist a wide variety of religious opinions about the status of music in Islam, on which The Qur'an is silent. Many Muslims, especially Salafi and some Deobandi Muslims, opine that the Prophet Muhammad forbade almost all music except the unaccompanied voice and a type of drum.

Other Muslims, following the rulings of classical scholars such as Al-Ghazali (1058–1100 CE), believe that music is permitted (halal) except if music explicitly celebrates aspects of life which are themselves forbidden (*haram*), for example adultery (Al-Ghazali, circa 1080/2009).

As we noted in Chapter 1, classical Muslim scholars such as Al-Kindi (circa 800–870 CE) made pioneering contributions to music theory, which led to *solfège* annotation (*do-re-me*) and the possibility of sophisticated harmonies and melodies, and to the development of musical instruments including the guitar and the violin.

Muslim prisoners reflected this wide diversity of opinion over music. Some prisoners, often at the direct instruction of prison chaplains, most of whom are the graduates of Deobandi seminary schools, were strongly of the opinion that all music is forbidden in Islam.

Liam (male, 33, White British, Convert, HMP Parrett, Category B Prison) was one of those:

> I followed the opinion that it's [music's] haram. ... Because I've listened to some talks and also read other things about it saying that it's one of the instruments of the shaytān [Satan]. ... It can corrupt your actions, it can control you as well, it's a very, very powerful tool. So, I follow the opinion that it's haram.

Other prisoners thought that music contained spiritual benefits such as Suleiman (male, 26, British Black, Born-Muslim, HMP Parrett, Category B Prison):

> there's meditation from just praying salat [Obligatory Prayer] but you can get meditation even ... from music.

Because it was widely known that Muslim prisoners tended to avoid music, sometimes prison staff and non-Muslim prisoners appeared to weaponise loud rock music to annoy Muslim prisoners. For example, in the segregation wing of HMP Forth, Jameel (male, 31, British Mixed Race, Convert, HMP Forth, Category A Prison) explained,

> The prison officers, the seg[regation] officers. They were playing heavy metal music, Rock FM all the time, very loud, I could hear it in my cell. So, I asked them to turn it down because I found it at an unacceptable level, while I was praying, while I was reading.

On the three occasions that we visited this segregation unit, there was indeed loud rock music being played by prison staff. Here, music had become a point of 'Us'/Muslim prisoners versus 'Them'/non-Muslim staff contention partly because, as the Christian Prison chaplain at HMP Cherwell put it:

> They're at it [in prison] 24/7 and they can't get away.

Muslim prison chaplains tended to teach that music is forbidden (haram) in Islam

While there was diversity of opinion among prisoners about music and, practically speaking, a high degree of tolerance and flexibility, the Muslim prison chaplains strongly and almost uniformly propagated the idea that music is forbidden in Islam.

Prison chaplain Imam Abdullah (male, circa 35, Bangladeshi, Born-Muslim, HMP Cherwell, Category C Prison) was typical in this respect:

> the thing is, music is haram of course, that's ... what the scholars have said.

This teaching that all music is forbidden had been absorbed by prisoners and it sometimes confused them, especially Converts (see Chapter 7, 'The Converts'), who had grown up in cultures in which listening to music was the norm.

For example, Troy (male, 28, British Black, Convert, HMP Stour, Category D Prison) felt considerable guilt about his inability to stop listening to music:

> Troy:
>
> I listen to music. My thing is music. I don't know how to get rid of it. It's something that I can't [get rid of]
>
> Interviewer:
>
> Why should you "get rid of" it?
>
> Troy:
>
> Because as a Muslim that's what I've been told. Of course, my understanding of it as well, of course, why music is forbidden within Islamic culture, Islam in itself because, of course, after the Ka'aba was built, they used to put the idols in the Ka'aba and they used to sing and dance around it, playing instruments. That's my understanding of it and I get it.

Intellectually, Troy had accepted the opinion that music was forbidden because in his mind it was connected to the worship of idols, but culturally and emotionally he could not 'kick the habit'.

On the whole, though, Muslim prisoners were realistic: even if they believed that music was forbidden, they accepted that music was not going to disappear from prison. Typically, Muslim prisoners merely wanted music to be played in workspaces and on the wings at a civilised volume, and turned down or off at the specific times when they were trying to pray.

Non-observant Muslim prisoners

Almost all our Muslim participants seemed to know what the Obligations of Islam require. Moreover, typically, 70 per cent of registered Muslims turned up for the Friday Congregational Prayer. Nevertheless, we do not want to give the impression that our characteristic sample of Muslim prisoners was uniformly observant of the Five Pillars or consistent in their beliefs.

We encountered many Muslim prisoners – 10 per cent of our sample (n = 27) – who did not always or ever perform the Obligatory Prayers, especially in Switzerland and France. They either performed the Obligatory Prayers 'sometimes' or else they had abandoned it or had never done it at all.

Cemtar (male, 37, Kosovon, Born-Muslim, Mitheilen, Category A Prison) expressed the non-committal attitude to Islam that was typical of prisoners from the Balkans in Switzerland:

> Before, I didn't go to the mosque very often before. It was not the most important thing for me. In Kosovo, for example, religion doesn't play such a big role. We also have holidays for New Year, Bairam or something. And when I came here, it wasn't that important either.

As we will see in Chapter 7, for the majority of prisoners both their faith and their commitment to practise Islam fluctuated, sometimes greatly, depending on their mood, the news from outside and, in particular, the quality of the company of other prisoners.

For Badr (male, 25, British Bangladeshi, Born-Muslim, HMP Severn, Category B Prison) the only consistent factor in his faith was its inconsistency:

> for me, it's been on and off so I'd have periods where I was for six months fully on the deen [religion] so I'd be praying, observing everything, not doing anything bad at all but then I have my off moments where I go completely off the rails. That's consistent for me.
>
> That's been since, I'd say 2007 is when I fully, that was the first time I fully started practising and it's been like that on and off. So, I'd go six months fully on it and six months off.

Our female prisoner participants, in particular, expressed the view that prison was dirty and an inappropriate place in which to pray (Schneuwly Purdie et al, 2021). For example, Noma (female, 19, British Pakistani, Born-Muslim, HMP Parrett, Category B Prison) said:

> I don't really get the time to pray. Since I've been here, I've wanted to pray, but I haven't got time to. It's like when we clean the cells, I don't know what happens, but within seconds there is

> dust all over the floor and I don't want to pray on a dirty floor ...
> and you haven't got anything to [do wudu] with, so I had to keep
> an empty bottle to wash me.

In France and Switzerland, there was a prevailing feeling among many Muslim prisoners that, in one prisoner's words:

> You don't come to prison to do religion.

In this way, Muslim prisoners often reflected both the religious cultures of their jurisdictions and the differing levels of religious commitment of Muslims outside prison with even greater degrees of volatility and fluctuation. They also reflected the wide range of reasons that Muslims – like those of other faiths – often give for not observing what they know to be the basic practices and values of their faith (Wilkinson et al, 2021).

Conclusion: Beliefs are living realities in prison

This chapter has outlined the essential elements of belief and practice of Islam. It has shown how the Articles of Faith, the Five Pillars of Islam and The Permitted and The Forbidden are not merely beliefs in prison but living realities. They brought structure, meaning, purpose and identity to the lives of a majority of Muslim prisoners who drew upon them and encouraged them to reflect upon their crimes, to feel remorse for them and to find charitable ways to repent and atone.

We have also seen how The Qur'an acts as a focal point for Islamic instruction in prison and also how many prisoners often turned to the example of the Prophet Muhammad to cope with the pains, privations and provocations of prison life.

By contrast, a significant minority of our characteristic sample of Muslim prisoners neglected or chose not to follow the basic tenets of their faith.

Also, the commitment of Muslim prisoners to their faith tended to fluctuate greatly, as we illustrate with our case studies in Chapter 7.

Finding their faith:
why do prisoners choose Islam?

In the previous chapter we have described the basic 'spiritual architecture' of Islam in prison and how this affects prisoners' lives. This chapter explores the types of Muslim prisoner and what motivates prisoners to choose Islam.

Conversion to Islam in prison

Religious conversion in contemporary contexts[1] has primarily been understood as the act of leaving one faith – or no faith – to join another faith, that is, between-faiths conversion.

The process of between-faiths conversion involves adopting the beliefs, values and religious practices of the new faith, as well as typically joining a new faith community and taking on its identity (Rambo and Farhadian, 2014). In other words, it involves adopting a new Worldview (Wilkinson, 2018) together with a new associated in-group (Tajfel, 1981).

Importantly, religious conversion in prison often involves the construction of a new pious, non-criminal identity (van Nieuwkerk, 2014). Because Converts often reinterpret their own autobiography based on their new religious Worldview, the construction of this new pious self can allow prisoners to move away from crime and from former criminal associates (Maruna et al, 2006; Spalek, El-Hassan, 2007; Williams, 2018).

Conversion to Islam

Research on conversion to Islam *outside* prison shows that it is not necessarily a sudden change; rather it often involves a long process of reflection and search for meaning, whereby a person may initially reject a previous belief and then, after several years, take up an Islamic Worldview (van Nieuwkerk, 2006; Hermansen, 2014).

---

[1] Historically, religious conversion usually meant a denominational change within a religion, for example a conversion from Protestant to Roman Catholic Christianity.

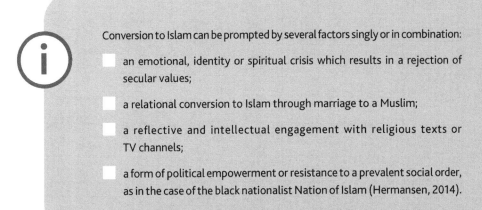

Conversion to Islam can be prompted by several factors singly or in combination:

- an emotional, identity or spiritual crisis which results in a rejection of secular values;

- a relational conversion to Islam through marriage to a Muslim;

- a reflective and intellectual engagement with religious texts or TV channels;

- a form of political empowerment or resistance to a prevalent social order, as in the case of the black nationalist Nation of Islam (Hermansen, 2014).

The appeal of religious ritual often plays a significant role in conversion to Islam: Converts may initially be attracted to Islam by observing Muslim rituals such as prayers, fasting or religious remembrance such as the ritual recitation of the 99 Names of God (*dikhr*).

The appeal of religious ritual is particularly relevant in the prison environment where prisoners live in close proximity to one another and where Islamic beliefs are regularly articulated on the wings, and Islamic rituals and objects are often on display. Prison life naturally provides the opportunity for prisoners to try out different religious identities, beliefs and behaviours.

Within-faith conversion

While it is more common for religious conversion to be understood as a change from one faith or from no faith to another faith, within-faith conversion refers to significant changes of interpretation and/or of religious commitment and practice that can occur to someone within their existing faith (van Nieuwkerk, 2006).

A prisoner's practice and understanding of religion can vary significantly over different parts of their sentence or during different convictions (Sarg and Lamine, 2011). This points to the changing and shifting nature of religious belief in prison as a site in which many prisoners regularly re-evaluate their core life values, which we exemplify with the case study of Ethan in Chapter 7 (Hermansen, 2014).

As with between-faiths conversion, within-faith conversion may also be connected to a prisoner's desire to leave behind a criminal identity and criminal behaviour (Maruna et al, 2006). For example, as we report in Chapter 6, the crimes of some serious offenders such as terrorist and sex offenders will often have been accompanied or justified by a skewed or misunderstood version of religion. Therefore, a change of their religious Worldview within their existing faith is vital for their chances of leaving crime.

Types of Muslim prisoner

Using our understanding of various forms of Islam/Islamism as Worldviews[2] and the idea of both between-faiths and within-faith conversion, for our study we construed religious conversion broadly as:

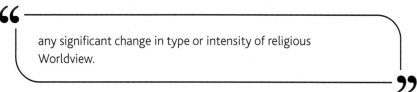

any significant change in type or intensity of religious Worldview.

This definition, which emerged from our theory in conversation with our data, allowed us to identify the following five types of Muslim prisoner:[3]

---

[2] Worldviews are integrated ways of being-in, behaving-in and understanding the world. See Chapter 5 for a detailed explanation.

[3] Although some prisoners' lives exhibited more than one type of significant religious change, we categorised their predominant change. We captured a snapshot of the types of prisoner conversion though our Attitudinal Questionnaires and we explored the factors and deep motives for them in one-to-one interview and through observations of Islamic Studies classes and Friday Prayer.

1. CONVERTS

were those who chose Islam for the first time from another faith or from no faith, that is, a between-faiths conversion.[4]

2. INTENSIFIERS

were those who became significantly more devout in prison in terms of finding their faith 'more important' and 'praying more' in prison, that is, a form of within-faith conversion.

3. SHIFTERS

were those who experienced significant changes of Islamic Worldview in prison according to the framework outlined in Chapter 5, that is, a form of within-faith conversion.[5]

4. REDUCERS (INCLUDING LEAVING ISLAM ENTIRELY)

were those who became significantly less devout in prison in terms of 'praying less' and finding the faith 'less important'.

5. REMAINERS

were those who experienced an unchanged Islamic Worldview and an unchanged commitment to worship in prison.

Significant levels of religious conversion in prison

Our characteristic sample of Muslim prisoners was distinguished by a high degree of significant religious change: **Converts to Islam** and **Intensifiers in Islam** predominated in our data sample.

---

[4] Muslims sometimes refer to Converts as 'Reverts' which evokes a Prophetic saying that everyone is born Muslim, i.e. in a state of natural submission to God, and becoming Muslim is a reversion to this natural state.

[5] This was identified through our interviews with prisoners and is discussed in Chapter 7.

- **Converts** who had chosen to follow Islam for the first time from another faith or from no faith in prison represented **21 per cent** of the sample.[6]
- **Intensifiers** who had become *significantly more devout* in terms of performing the Obligatory Daily Prayers more regularly and finding their religion 'more important' than before they went to prison represented **48 per cent** of the data sample.
- By contrast, **Remainers**, whose understanding and commitment to their faith remained *broadly the same* in prison as before prison, represented **23 per cent** of the data sample (n = 62).
- **Reducers**, whose commitment to their faith had decreased, represented **8 per cent** of the data sample.

Conversion to and intensification in Islam was most likely in England

We found that prisoners in English prisons were significantly more likely to convert to Islam or intensify in Islam than their Swiss or French counterparts.

Converts (28 per cent) and Intensifiers (56 per cent) predominated in our five English prisons; whereas Remainers and Reducers characterised prisons in Switzerland and France (see Infographic 3.1).[7]

This difference was, in turn, generated by differences in the provision of Muslim Chaplaincy in England, Switzerland and France and differences in prison culture around religion, which we will discuss in Chapter 8. Also, it was relevant that Muslim prisoners in England started from a significantly lower baseline religious commitment to Islam than in Switzerland or France.[8]

The faith of men tended to intensify; the faith of women tended to reduce

The experience of prison also had tended to generate an **Intensification** in **Muslim men's** religiosity; by contrast, the experience of prison was more likely to generate a **Reduction** in **Muslim women's** religiosity.

---

[6] Decimals are rounded up if ≥ 0.5 or down if < 0.5.

[7] We discovered statistically significant differences in median 'Intensification' scores between:
- England (4.5) and Switzerland (3.5) (p = 0.008) and
- England (4.5) and France (3.0) (p < 0.0005)
  but not between:
- France (3.0) and Switzerland (3.5).
  This confirmed that religious Intensification, as well as conversion, was significantly higher in England than in Switzerland and France.

[8] In response to the variable statement 'Before I came to prison, my religion was very important to me':
- in England 30 per cent of our Muslim prisoners agreed with this statement;
- in Switzerland 56 per cent of our Muslim prisoners agreed with this statement;
- in France 44 per cent of our Muslim prisoners agreed with this statement.

Infographic 3.1: Types of Muslim prisoner

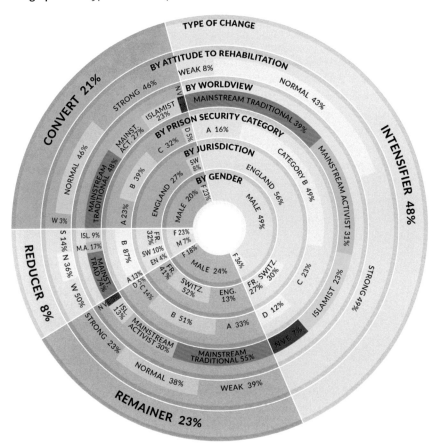

Note: NVE = Non-violent Islamist Extremism

As Infographic 3.1 shows:

- **49 per cent** of **men intensified** their religiosity;
- **36 per cent** of **women intensified** their religiosity.

By contrast,

- **7 per cent** of the **men reduced** their religiosity;
- **23 per cent** of the **women reduced** their religiosity.

The differences between male and female Converts and Remainers were less marked.

Our interview data allowed us to explain the differences in the types of conversion by gender, which we report fully elsewhere (Schneuwly Purdie et al, 2021). In short:

- Chaplaincy provision was much more developed and consistent in the male prison estate than in the female estate.
- In the male prison estate, the identifiers of Islam, such as wearing a beard and using Islamic terms in conversation, were high status; in the female prison estate, the identifiers of Islam such as the Islamic headscarf (*hijab*) were low status.
- Also, importantly, Muslim women prisoners were much more likely than the men to see themselves as the *victims* rather than the perpetrators of crime, which meant that women prisoners felt the need to draw on the inner resources of faith – such as repentance (*tawba*) – less than the men.

Prisoners' faith intensified as their sentences progressed

Our questionnaires also showed that **Intensification in Islam** was **significantly and inversely related** to **Prison Security Category**[8] (see Infographic 3.1). In other words, using prison category as a proxy for period of sentence, prisoners were likely to become more committed to their faith as their sentences progressed. This statistical finding ran contrary to some perceptions of prisoners captured in our qualitative data that as their release date approached the religious commitment of prisoners tended to weaken. However, our interviews also indicated that if prisoners retained their faith during a long sentence, they were more likely to have intensified their faith by the end of their sentence, even if they practised it in a less obvious way than at the start.

Once we had identified the types of religious change and their effects typically experienced by Muslim prisoners, we were keen to discover what motivated prisoners to choose Islam.

Conversion to Islam in prison: the cynical view

In public discourse and research, choosing to follow Islam in prison has often been seen as a strategic or as an insincere choice. Conversion to Islam

---

[8] • Intensifiers were 79 per cent (n = 15) of the Category D prison estate.
- Intensifiers were 53 per cent (n = 30) of the Category C prison estate.
- Intensifiers were 46 per cent (n = 64) of the Category B prison estate.
- Intensifiers were 36 per cent (n = 21) of the Category A prison estate.

in prison is often regarded as a means to gain protection and the safety of belonging to a group (similar to gang affiliation), or to obtain other perks and privileges such as better food, power on the wings, a means to intimidate staff or time out of the cell for the Friday Prayer (Spalek and El-Hassan, 2007; Hamm, 2009; Liebling et al, 2011; Phillips, 2012). Islam has also been seen as the new 'fast fame' religion adopted by Converts to 'look cool' without any sincere understanding or commitment to the faith (Phillips, 2012).

The views of prison officers and prison governors

Some of the prison officers and prison governors whom we interviewed echoed these popular ideas that conversion to Islam in prison is likely to be a strategic choice to gain perks, or to become part of the gang culture of the prison. This was born out of their genuine experiences on the wings and from the fact that, by the frank admission of the governor of HMP Parrett, prison staff's view of prisoners is often skewed by having to deal with the disciplinary consequences of their bad behaviour, which can obscure their acts of goodness.

Most prison officers were more aware of the risks associated with following Islam in prison than they were of any benefits. The accounts of prison officers tended to portray choosing Islam by a prisoner as an opportunistic, gang-related or superficial choice. For example, a prison officer (female, white, HMP Parrett, Category B Male and Female Prison) said:

> The only time I see people sort of turning to religion is for their own personal gain. So, if it's a time when they're fasting and they get their Ramadan packs or if they don't really have any friends and they then decide, "Actually, I will be …" because it puts them in like a friendship group like a protection group.

Other accounts from prison officers construed conversion to Islam as a facet of gang culture, characterised by coercion and seeking protection. For example, a prison officer at HMP Parrett (male, white, Category B Male and Female Prison) said:

> I generally feel that a vast majority of these conversions are gang related. What tends to happen on some of the wings is, a prisoner

> will come in and he will get a visit, and then he might be a Muslim the next day or say he's a Muslim. Yes, and they might do it for protection.

Despite a prevailing sceptical attitude and genuine concerns around risks associated with prisoners choosing Islam, other prison officers also recognised the advantages of having a faith in prison and that prisoners exhibited mixed motivations for choosing their faith. For example, according to a prison officer (male, white, HMP Severn, Category B Male Prison):

> I would say, in my experience, the white Converts fall into three very specific categories: you get those that kind of have got the dreams of jihad; we've got those that do it because they're bullied into it or for their own protection or to feel part of something; you've got those who use it as an actual source of faith. I mean, I could introduce you to two white prisoners on this wing, one is a very, very pious man who converted to Islam, and the other one did it because he was pressurised into it and wants out of it as soon as possible.

Some prison officers and prison governors also witnessed the importance of having faith for the emotional well-being of prisoners in their care. For example, a prison governor (male, white, HMP Cherwell, Category C Male Prison) said:

> I think it [faith] plays a huge part I really do ... I see from attending the church services. I see from attending particular festivals that it means an awful lot to the individual with regards to what either keeps them on an even keel. It might be what gives them hope again. It might be what provides some balance and some priority and something to focus on in their life.

A few prison officers spoke about the importance to a prisoner of feeling a sense of belonging and companionship, which joining a faith group provided.

Muslim prison officers also acknowledged that they had a bridging role to play in mitigating the 'Us', prisoners versus 'Them', prisoner officer culture that typifies most prisons, which we explore in depth elsewhere (Quraishi and Wilkinson, 2022 forthcoming).

According to a prison officer (male, white, HMP Parrett, Category B Male and Female Prison):

> It's very, very different. On the male side, from what I've seen, if you're a Muslim you, get looked after in the sense that there's unity between them. If you want to go pray [the dawn prayer] together so there's that sort of … that's automatic.

The views of prisoners

Against this background of competing understandings about why prisoners choose to follow Islam,[9] and in a prevailing professional culture that tended to be sceptical about the sincerity of religious conversion, we asked Muslim prisoners in our questionnaire to tell us why they chose to follow Islam.

Our Survey Question 31 asked:

'I CHOOSE to follow Islam in prison because …'.

Respondents could tick as many options as they felt were applicable. The questionnaire also included an open option: 'None of these, I follow my religion because … (please write here)'.

See Infographic 3.2 for the results.

Even allowing for some social desirability bias,[10, 11] our data from canvassing Muslim prisoners themselves presents a challenge to the cynical idea that prisoners tend to choose Islam primarily for 'perks, privileges and protection'. Of the reasons that our Muslim prisoners gave for choosing to follow Islam, 93 per cent were related to reasons of:

- **Faith** (42 per cent);
- **Emotional coping** (34 per cent);
- **Company** (17 per cent).

---

[9] See, for example, 'Lags Go Muslim for Better Food', *The Sun* (2010).

[10] 'Social-desirability bias' is a type of bias in questionnaire responses that refers to the tendency of respondents to answer questions in a manner that will be viewed favourably by others.

[11] Also the fact that 'strategic' Converts might have participated less than sincere Muslims in our research.

Infographic 3.2: The reasons prisoners choose Islam

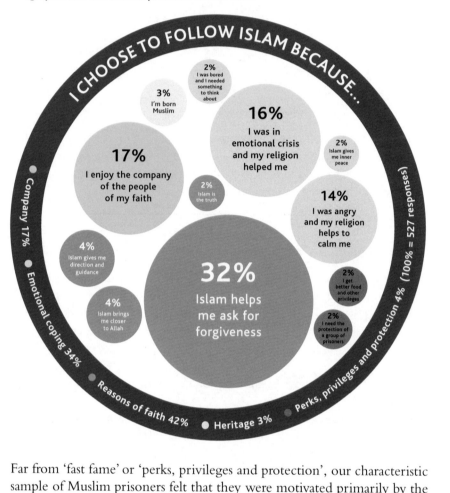

Far from 'fast fame' or 'perks, privileges and protection', our characteristic sample of Muslim prisoners felt that they were motivated primarily by the search for the inner resources of spiritual and psychological support in order to survive and make the most of their prison sentence. We explore these motivations more deeply in our seven case studies in Chapter 7.

The connection between conversion to Islam and strong Attitude to Rehabilitation

This finding that prisoners were primarily motivated to choose Islam for sincere reasons of faith, emotional coping and good company was corroborated by the fact that statistical analysis[12] showed that **Converts**

---

[12] Using Attitude towards Rehabilitation as our independent variable, we ran a Multiple Linear Regression Model to test the factors which influenced attitudes towards rehabilitation in our data sample.

to Islam and **Intensifiers** in Islam were significantly more likely[13] than **Remainers** and **Reducers** to have strong, positive **Attitude to Rehabilitation**.[14]

Moreover, the factors Religious Intensification[15] and Engagement with Chaplaincy[16] together explained 30 per cent of the variance in Attitude towards Rehabilitation.[17, 18] Relatedly, **Remainers** and **Reducers** were prone to significantly weaker **Attitude to Rehabilitation** than **Converts** and **Intensifiers** (see Infographic 3.2).

We explore this rehabilitative force of converting to or intensifying in Islam in the case studies of Chris and Nadim in Chapter 7.

The Islamist risk in conversion to Islam

The values encouraged by conversion to and intensification in Islam were not, however, uniquely conducive to prisoners aspiring towards a renewed commitment to rehabilitation and engagement with prison chaplaincy.

---

[13] P<0.001.

[14] To test this, our questionnaire was designed to measure prisoners' attitudes towards rehabilitation. The underlying factor 'Attitude to Rehabilitation' was calculated by adding and calculating mean scores on response to the following three statistically related variables:

1. Question 20 'Because of my Islam, I have taken up a class, a training course or some private study in prison'.
2. Question 21 'Because of my Islam, I am motivated to work hard in prison'.
3. Question 10 'I give up bad behaviour for my religion'.

[15] A factor underlying the variables "I pray more", "I find religion more important" and "I understand religion more in prison".

[16] A factor underlying the variables "I learn about Islam from Muslim prison chaplains" and "I turn to Muslim prison chaplains for advice about Islam".

[17] R^2 for the overall model was 31.5 per cent with an adjusted R2 of 30.9 per cent, a moderate size effect. The regression model was statistically significant F (2269) = 61.72 p < 0.0005).

[18] There were statistically significant differences in Attitude to Rehabilitation scores in England compared with France and Switzerland and Religious Intensification scores in England compared with France and Switzerland. Muslim prisoners in England were more likely to intensify their faith inside prison and they were more likely to have higher scores on the factor Attitude towards Rehabilitation than in Switzerland or France. These differences added weight to our finding that intensifying in Islam was a significant driver of positive attitudes to rehabilitation in the form of a commitment to work, education and the avoidance of crime.

The differences in Religious Intensification and Attitude towards Rehabilitation between England, Switzerland and France were also linked to the differences in Muslim chaplaincy provision in the three countries. Differences in the Muslim chaplaincy provision in England, Switzerland and France are discussed in more detail in Chapter 8.

There was also a significant[19] over-representation of Converts and Intensifiers in the exaggeratedly separate 'Us' versus 'Them' Worldview of Islamism, and in the absolutely divided and antagonistic 'Us' versus 'Them' Worldview of Islamist Extremism.

Together, Converts and Intensifiers constituted 69 per cent of our whole data sample. However,

- **Converts** and **Intensifiers** together constituted 81 per cent (n = 43) of those in the category of Islamism with an exaggerated 'Us' versus 'Them' Worldview.

Moreover,

- **Converts** and **Intensifiers** together constituted 83 per cent (n = 9) of those in the category of Islamist Extremism with an absolutely divided 'Us' versus 'Them' Worldview.

This showed up some risk connected with conversion to and intensification in Islam in terms of adopting an 'Us' versus 'Them' Worldview and suggested that conversion to Islam can play into the existing 'Us'/The prisoners versus 'Them'/ prison officers of the prison environment, especially when conversion happened in an unmanaged way on the wings.

The hazards of unmanaged conversion were harrowingly brought home to us by one prisoner who told us that he had been 'converted' by another prisoner on the wing without the awareness of the prison chaplains and had been persuaded to self-circumcise in his cell, which resulted in his hospitalisation.

We explore this Islamist risk connected with conversion to and intensification in Islam and its implications for prison practice more deeply in Chapter 6 and through the detailed case study of Ethan in Chapter 7.

Conclusion: Prisons are sites of intense religious change

Prisons in Europe, especially in the male estate in England and Wales, are places of significant conversion activity into and intensification in Islam. Muslim prisoners cluster into five basic types:

1. **Converts** who choose Islam for the first time from another faith or from no faith;
2. **Intensifiers** who become significantly more devout in prison in terms of participants finding their faith 'more important' and 'praying more' in prison;

---

[19] P = 0.021.

3. **Shifters** who experience significant changes of Islamic Worldview in prison according to the framework outlined in Chapter 4, that is, a form of within-faith conversion;
4. **Reducers** (including leaving Islam entirely) who become significantly less devout in prison in terms of 'praying less' and finding the faith 'less important';
5. **Remainers** who experience an unchanged Islamic Worldview and an unchanged commitment to levels of worship in prison.

Although opportunistic and gang-related conversion to Islam does occur, as observed by prison staff, prisoners are more likely to choose their faith primarily for reasons of faith, emotional coping and good company than for 'perks, privileges and protection'.

Conversion to or intensification in Islam in prison are significantly connected with positive Attitude to Rehabilitation in terms of engagement with work, education and the avoidance of criminal behaviour; whereas remaining the same or experiencing a reduction in faith are significantly connected with less positive Attitude to Rehabilitation.

Conversion to or intensification in Islam in prison also carry some risk of prisoners shifting towards an 'Us' versus 'Them' Islamist Worldview.

We exemplify these opportunities and risks through detailed case studies of individual prisoners in Chapter 7.

What types of Islam do prisoners follow?

The Worldviews of Muslim prisoners: Islam, Islamism and Islamist Extremism

In the previous chapters, we have described the history of Islam and of Muslims in prison, the 'spiritual architecture' of Islam in prison, the basic types of Muslim prisoner and the reasons why prisoners choose Islam. In this chapter, we offer the reader an overview of the types of Islamic Worldview that Muslim prisoners hold and how these types of Worldviews affect their lives in prison.

A 'Worldview' approach

From here on, we will describe different forms of Islam as different 'Worldviews'. 'Worldviews' have been defined as 'unified ways-of-being in the world, together with ways-of-knowing the world in which knowledge and action are knit-up together and organized into a single view of life' (Orr, 2001: 6). In other words, by Worldview we mean 'walking-the-talk' and 'talking-the-walk', which we all do to varying degrees of consistency in order to form a coherent idea of who we are in relation to the rest of the world.[1]

As well as this idea of individual Worldviews as an integrated way of understanding and acting consistently in the world, a second key aspect of Worldviews is that they are often shared both consciously and unconsciously by collectives, such as families and nations (McCarthy, 1978), and also by deviant and criminal 'in-groups', such as criminal gangs, and terrorist organisations and states.

The idea of a Worldview is also useful to us in this context because it corresponds with the Islamic idea of religion as a *deen*, which means an integrated combination of belief in God together with related actions and outcomes in the world.

---

[1] Thus, for example, the majority of citizens recognise and obey the law not as a result of an analytical decision about the law's innate justice but because the majority of citizens are enculturated into a law-abiding Worldview, together with an awareness of the penalties involved in breaking the law.

Islam, Islamism and Islamist Extremism as Worldviews

This idea of the Worldview provides our framework for understanding the differences between different religious forms in prison, which, on the surface, all look and sound Islamic and yet, in reality, are very different (Wilkinson, 2019; see also Figure 4.1).

Figure 4.1: Islamic Worldviews

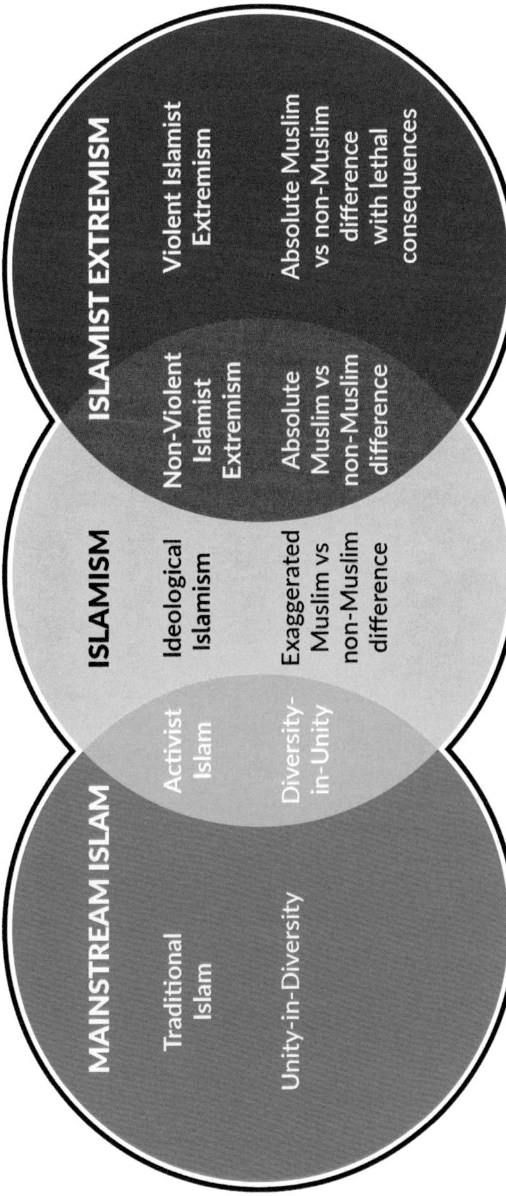

Note: The different Islam-related Worldviews described refer to the qualities and characteristics of Mainstream Islam, Islamism and Islamist Extremism and not the numbers of people that hold to them. Attitudinal research of Muslim populations suggests that globally Muslims are overwhelmingly 'Mainstream' in their Worldview (Wilkinson, 2019).

Source: Wilkinson, 2019

IN THIS BOOK, WE REFER TO THESE DIFFERENT ISLAMIC WORLDVIEWS AS:

MAINSTREAM TRADITIONAL ISLAM

This is the Worldview of those who believe in the fundamental equality of all human beings as God's creatures, regardless of secondary differences in religion, race, gender or any other characteristic. We describe this quality as 'Unity-in-Diversity'.

Mainstream Traditional Muslims accept and follow, to varying extents,[2] the basic injunctions of The Qur'an and the Customary Behaviour of the Prophet Muhammad (Sunna) in a way that is appropriate to their circumstances without foregrounding personal or social change.

MAINSTREAM ACTIVIST ISLAM

This is Mainstream Islam characterised by Diversity-in-Unity and an ethos of change when Islam is practised to bring about either personal change and/or legal, transformative change in the public space according to Islamic principles.

ISLAMISM

Islamism is an 'Us'/Muslim versus 'Them'/Infidel (*kafir*) Worldview characterised by an exaggerated difference between Muslim and non-Muslim peoples, cultures and political ideals. This is also the Worldview of Islam as revolutionary political ideology directed at overthrowing – rather than transforming – existing political structures and replacing them with an Islamic state governed by an Islamist interpretation of Islamic Law.[3]

NON-VIOLENT ISLAMIST EXTREMISM

This is the Islamist Worldview as it sharpens antagonistically into an absolutely divided 'Us'/ Muslim versus 'Them'/Infidel (*kafir*) Worldview that stresses the absolute difference between the 'true' Muslims who want to live separately in an

---

[2] And notwithstanding the limitless ability of human beings throughout history to make moral and intellectual mistakes and to fall well short of our aspirations and ideals.

[3] Islamism is sometimes called Political Islam.

Islamic state versus the 'non-Muslims' and 'wrong Muslims' who are afforded a less human or sub-human status, as if damned by God.[4]

VIOLENT ISLAMIST EXTREMISM

This is the absolutely divided 'Us'/Muslim versus 'Them'/Infidel (*kafir*) Worldview which understands the cosmos as a manifestation of the eternal struggle between Islam and Unbelief (*kufr*) and in which the 'non-Muslim' and 'wrong Muslim' (those who do not struggle violently to establish a global Islamic state) are construed as eternal enemies of 'true' Islam and are therefore considered fit to be exterminated.[5]

Mapping the Worldviews of Muslim prisoners

The Worldviews of prisoners in numbers

Using variables and methods detailed in Appendix 5 across the whole sample, we identified that those prisoners whose Worldview was characterised as **'Mainstream'** were significantly in the majority at **76 per cent**, with those categorised as **'Islamist Extremist'** representing only **4 per cent** of our characteristic sample. The breakdown was as follows:

- **48 per cent**[6] (n = 133) were characterised as **Mainstream, Traditional**;
- **28 per cent** (n = 79) were characterised as **Mainstream, Activist**;
- **19 per cent** (n = 54) were characterised as **Islamist**;
- **4 per cent** (n = 11) were characterised as **Islamist Extremist, Non-violent**;
- **0.4 per cent** (n = 1) was characterised as **Islamist Extremist, Violent**.

We conducted a statistical test[7] to determine if there were differences in Worldviews according to prisoners' ethnic groups, gender, sentence lengths, jurisdictions, Attitude to Rehabilitation and prison security categories

---

[4] Non-violent Islamist Extremism is sometimes referred to after its principal protagonist Sayyid Qutb (1906–1966 CE) as 'Qutbism'.

[5] Violent Islamist Extremism is also known popularly as Jihadism. This runs the risk of conflating what Islamist terrorists do with the noble doctrines of struggling to please God (*Jihad fiy sabil-illah*).

[6] Figures are rounded up or down, which accounts for the fact that these percentages total 99.4 per cent.

[7] Kruskal–Wallis Test.

Infographic 4.1: The characteristics of the Worldviews of Muslim prisoners

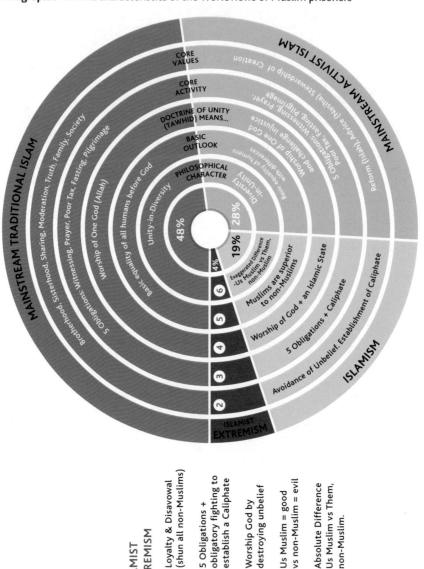

ISLAMIST
EXTREMISM

2. Loyalty & Disavowal (shun all non-Muslims)

3. 5 Obligations + obligatory fighting to establish a Caliphate

4. Worship God by destroying unbelief

5. Us Muslim = good vs non-Muslim = evil

6. Absolute Difference Us Muslim vs Them, non-Muslim.

Infographic 4.2: Differences in the Worldviews of Muslim prisoners

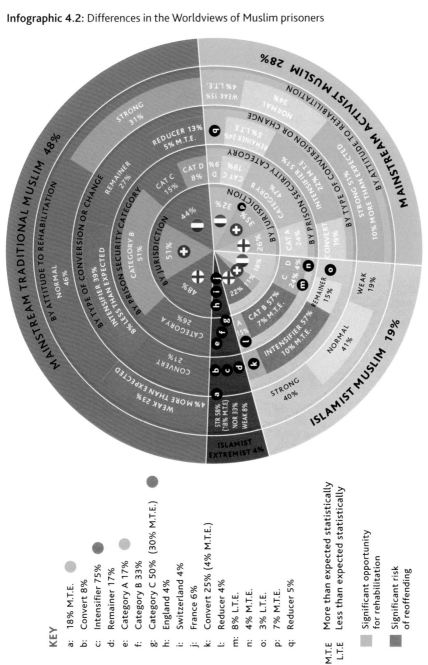

KEY

a: 18% M.T.E.
b: Convert 8%
c: Intensifier 75%
d: Remainer 17%
e: Category A 17%
f: Category B 33%
g: Category C 50% (30% M.T.E.)
h: England 4%
i: Switzerland 4%
j: France 6%
k: Convert 25% (4% M.T.E.)
l: Reducer 4%
m: 8% L.T.E.
n: 4% M.T.E.
o: 3% L.T.E.
p: 7% M.T.E.
q: Reducer 5%

M.T.E   More than expected statistically
L.T.E   Less than expected statistically

Significant opportunity for rehabilitation

Significant risk of reoffending

(see Infographics 4.1 and 4.2 for a detailed overview of the characteristics and differences in the Worldviews of our sample of Muslim prisoners). The test showed up differences in Worldview by:

- **type of prisoner** (see Chapter 3);
- **prison security category;**
- **attitude to rehabilitation;**
- **jurisdiction.**

Converts and Intensifiers were more Islamist than Remainers and Reducers

- As discussed in Chapter 3, there was an over-representation of Converts to Islam and Intensifiers in Islam in the 'Us' versus 'Them' Worldview of Islamism and in the Absolutely Divided 'Us' versus 'Them' Worldview of Islamist Extremism.[8]

English prisoners were more Islamist than Swiss ones

- The most obvious variation between jurisdictions was the different levels of Islamists in England (22 per cent) and Switzerland (11 per cent).[9]
- This difference was related to the significantly higher levels of Conversion to and Intensification in Islam in our English prisons than in our Swiss prisons.

Category D prisoners were the most Mainstream

Prisoners in our Category C Medium Security Prison, HMP Cherwell, were less Mainstream and more Islamist than prisoners in either our Category A Maximum Security Prisons or our Category D Open Prison.[10]

---

[8] In our characteristic sample, 'Converts' and 'Intensifiers' formed 69 per cent (n = 185) of our total data sample. 'Converts' and 'Intensifiers' constituted 81 per cent (n=43) of those holding the Worldview of Islamism and 83 per cent (n = 9) of those holding the Worldview of Islamist Extremism. The only recorded Violent Islamist Extremist (100 per cent, n = 1) was a 'Convert' from HMP Cherwell, England, Category C Prison.

[9] Post hoc analysis revealed statistically significant differences in median 'Worldview' scores between England (3.4) and Switzerland (3.5) (p = .008), but not England and France (3.6) or any other pairing. Most obvious of these were the differences in the levels of Islamism in England (22 per cent) and Switzerland (11 per cent).

[10] Analysis revealed statistically significant differences in Worldview scores between the 'C-Medium Security training prison' (108.08) and 'A-Maximum Security' (160.52)

Prisoners in our Category D Open Prison, HMP Stour, were significantly the most Mainstream of all our participant prisoners. Considering that these prisoners were closest to release of all our participants,[11] this finding allows us to make the suggestion that prison sentences had tended to produce a moderating effect on prisoners' religious Worldviews in terms of helping them to develop an outlook of Unity-in-Diversity and a commitment to lawfulness.

Mainstream Activist Muslims display the strongest Attitude to Rehabilitation

There was a significant ($\tau b = .0.215$, $p = .001$), positive association between **Attitude to Rehabilitation**[12] and the question used to check for Mainstream Activist Islam:

'It is part of Islam to challenge things that are unfair in society.'

- **51 per cent** of those Muslims prisoners categorised as **Mainstream Activist Muslims** exhibited a **'Strong' Attitude to Rehabilitation**, compared with
- **31 per cent** of Mainstream Traditional Muslims and
- **41 per cent** of Islamist Muslims.

This suggests that the Worldview of Mainstream Activist Islam, which we shall illustrate more fully in the next chapter using prisoners' own accounts, and the ethos of religious change that underscored it, was strongly conducive to prisoners' making efforts to reform their personal behaviour and to re-engage with education and work.

(p=0.002) and between 'C-Medium Security training prison' and 'D-Open prison' (170.42) (p=0.019), but not between the 'B-High Security prison' (136.19) or any other group combination.

[11] And using Security Category as a proxy for prison length.

[12] Prisoner attitudes towards rehabilitation were measured by three related variables that loaded onto a single underlying factor:
1. "I give up bad behaviour because of my religion."
2. "I have taken up some course, training or private study due to my religion."
3. "I am motivated to work hard because of my religion." We called this underlying factor **Attitude to Rehabilitation**.

Conclusion: Mainstream Islam predominates in prison

In this chapter, we have presented a strong challenge to the widespread belief that the Islam of Muslim prisoners is characterised primarily by the Worldview of **Islamist Extremism**.

We found that:

- **76 per cent** of our characteristic sample of 279 Muslim prisoners held the Worldview of **Mainstream Islam**, which is characterised by an ethos of the basic equality of all humans before God and the need for universal justice and respect;

  - **48 per cent** held a Worldview of **Mainstream *Traditional* Islam**, which is characterised by an ethos of the basic equality of all humans before God and the need for universal justice and respect, *but which did not particularly stand for change*;

  - **28 per cent** held a Worldview of **Mainstream *Activist* Islam**, which is characterised by an ethos of the basic equality of all humans before God and the need for universal justice and respect, *and also drew upon a targeted ethos of personal and social change*;

- **Mainstream *Activist* Islam** was strongly and significantly associated with strong **Attitude to Rehabilitation**, which was a factor underlying the *Avoidance of Bad Behaviour* and *Commitment to Work* and *Commitment to Education*;

- **Mainstream *Activist* Islam** was the Worldview associated, in particular, with **Intensifiers** in Islam. See Infographic 4.2.

- **19 per cent** of our characteristic sample of 279 Muslim prisoners held the **Islamist** Worldview of exaggerated difference between 'Us', Muslim versus 'Them', non-Muslim, in particular **Converts** and **Intensifiers**.

- **4 per cent** (n = 12) held a Worldview **of Non-Violent Islamist Extremism**, in particular **Converts** and **Intensifiers**.

- **0.4 per cent** (n = 1) held a Worldview that was unequivocally committed to **Violent Islamist Extremism**. This one prisoner was a **Convert**.

It should be noted, however, that even this small cohort (4.4 per cent; n = 13) of **Islamist Extremists** displayed a **strong Attitude to Rehabilitation**. This suggests that even Islamist Extremist prisoners, including those convicted of terrorist offences, are likely to be open to reform and rehabilitative change, which is a notion that we explore fully in the case study of Nadim in Chapter 7.

Mainstream Islam in prison

In the previous chapter, we gave basic definitions and painted a statistical picture of Muslim prisoners' Worldviews, which showed that the Worldview of **Mainstream Islam** was the most *significant* feature of Muslim prison life.

In this chapter, we flesh out our description of the Worldview of Mainstream Islam and illustrate how this Worldview of **Mainstream Islam** was brought to life by Muslim prisoners.

THE FUNDAMENTAL CHARACTER OF MAINSTREAM ISLAM: UNITY-IN-DIVERSITY

Mainstream Islam is the Worldview of Unity-in-Diversity generated by the religious practice of those who accept and follow, to the best of their ability,[1] the basic injunctions of the Book of Islam – The Qur'an – and the Customary Everyday Behaviour – the Sunna[2] – of the Prophet Muhammad in a way that is appropriate to their circumstances.

Because Muslims believe that The Qur'an was sent to call all humankind to right action and to worship Him, Mainstream Muslims regard the primordial unity of humankind as a fundamental premise of The Qur'an (Haleem, 2010). Many passages of The Qur'an are directed at humankind in general without any distinction being made between Muslim and non-Muslim (for example The Qur'an 56:57–74 and The Qur'an,10:45–47). Take the following passage, for example:

> It was We who created you: will you not believe? Consider [the semen] you eject – do you create it yourselves or are We the Creator? We ordained death to be among you. Nothing could stop Us if We intended to change you and recreate you in a way unknown to you. You have learned how you were first created: will you not reflect? Consider

---

[1] And notwithstanding the limitless ability of human beings throughout history to make moral and intellectual mistakes and to fall well short of our aspirations and ideals.

[2] See Chapter 2 for an account of The Qur'an and the Sunna.

the seeds you sow in the ground – is it you who make them grow or We?

(The Qur'an 56:57–65[3])

Furthermore, the **essential spiritual covenant** that all human beings share with God is specifically alluded to as existing even before the existence of created matter:

> [Prophet], when your Lord took out the offspring from the loins of the Children of Adam and made them bear witness about themselves, He said, 'Am I not your Lord?' and they replied, 'Yes, we bear witness.'
>
> (The Qur'an, 7:172)

Within this essential unity, The Qur'an also recognises natural diversity:

> People! We created you from a single man and a single woman, and have made you races and tribes so that you should get to know one another. In God's sight, the most honoured of you are the ones most mindful of Him: God is all knowing, all aware.
>
> (The Qur'an, 49:13)

Thus, the essential unity and equality of humanity before God is also characterised in Islam by real, second-order differences: men and women are different; nations, countries and tribes are different; there exists a plurality of different religions, that is, not everyone is born to be a Muslim. Nevertheless, as this verse describes, these secondary differences are intended by God to be the source of greater cultural enrichment and mutual understanding, and not of conflict.

---

[3] Translations taken from Haleem (2016).

The Mainstream Islamic values of our prisoners

As a product of their varied commitment to believe and practise Islam as outlined in Chapter 2, Muslim prisoners understood and enacted Mainstream Islamic values in a wide range of ways.

Unity-in-Diversity

For Riyad (male, 28, British Indian, Born-Muslim, HMP Stour, Category D Prison), the equality of humanity before God was a core element of his Islamic belief:

> we're all God's creation. … Nobody is above nobody and we all come from one place. We all come from Adam. If you're a believer, you believe we come from Adam, so [we are] all the same.

Asif (male, 45, British Asian, Born-Muslim, HMP Cherwell, Category C Prison) had been struck by the importance of diversity in belief and practice within Islam when he had performed *The Lesser Pilgrimage to Mecca (Umrah):*

> I went to Umrah, which is a small Hajj, and that kind of opened my eyes up as to the diversity of Islam, you know, the peace and tranquillity it gives when you worship Allah.

Respect for humanity regardless of faith or none

Mainstream Muslim prisoners also emphasised the importance of translating this idea of equality and diversity into practice by treating both Muslims and non-Muslims fairly and as equals.

Adnan (male, 27, British Black Caribbean, Muslim Convert, HMP Cherwell, Category C Prison) explained the value that he placed on the Islamic ethos of fairness:

> Even when we're talking about Sharia Law or judgements …, Allah says, 'deal with people just' and as a Muslim, if I want to deal with a person, whether they're a Muslim, non-Muslim, whether they're

pink, gold, purple, all the colours of the rainbow, Allah says deal with people fairly. And if you're not going to deal with that person fairly, it's called ['Allah's Justice'], you need to fear Him.

99

MERCY AND COMPASSION

As well as basic human equality and Unity-in-Diversity, the theme of **Mercy and Compassion** is central to The Qur'an and the Sunna. For example, every chapter of The Qur'an, except Surah 9, 'Repentance', starts with the phrase 'In the name of God, the Compassionate, the Merciful' (*Bismillahi Ar-Rahman, ir-Raheem*).

Eighty-four times in The Qur'an, God describes Himself as the 'Oft-Forgiving, most Merciful' (*al-Ghafur, ar-Raheem*). This makes Mercy by far the most referenced attribute of God in The Qur'an (Sherif, 1995).

Our **Mainstream Muslim** prisoners recognised (18 citations) the centrality in Islam of forgiveness and showing compassion towards others despite their negative behaviours.

For Suleiman (male, 26, British Black Caribbean, Born-Muslim, HMP Parrett, Category B Prison) the Prophet Muhammad himself provided the best exemplar of Islamic mercy:

It's like taking note from the Prophet Muhammed, sallallahu alayhi wa sallam [peace and blessings be upon him] … he went through a lot of struggle and he would still help people. Because I remember there's a beautiful story about a woman that would always throw stones at him every time he was walking. And then, I remember, there was a day when she didn't throw no stones at him, she was very ill, he was the only one that come to check up on her and then from that day, she reverted to Islam.

99

Sharing and caring for other Muslim brothers and sisters

As part of a Worldview foregrounded by Mercy, **Mainstream Muslim** prisoners were strongly characterised by looking out and caring for other Muslims. For many Muslim prisoners an important way of giving positive meaning to life in prison could be found in sharing resources, participating in rituals together, and guiding and helping other Muslims.

For example, Imran (male, 24, British Turkish, Born-Muslim, HMP Cherwell, Category C Prison) described how he became more serious about practising Islam because of the generosity of Muslim prisoners who had made him feel that he was not alone but part of their community:

> It feels more brotherhood type of ... it's like everyone's there for each other. That's what it feels like. It feels like I'm not riding out [seeing out] this sentence alone, you know.

Neighbourliness and good manners

The Islamic ethos of caring and sharing for others spilled out onto the wings and was not restricted to the kind treatment of fellow Muslims. For example, Sajid (male, 37, British Asian Pakistani, Born-Muslim, HMP Severn, Category B Prison) stressed the importance of an ethic of proactive neighbourliness and good manners in the prison environment, regardless of "colour" or religion:

> I mean my neighbours in my cell now, one on the left and the right, they're both white people and I really respect them a lot. The reason why, because Islam teaches us to respect your neighbours regardless of their colour, regardless of their religion. ... Islam teaches you a lot of things like how you approach people, you should be the first one to approach them, you should be the first one to show love and respect. If you want that love and respect back, you know, it's you, you're the first one to approach that person regardless of his age, regardless of his gender, regardless of his religion.

This Islamic ethos of caring and sharing as brothers and sisters acted for many prisoners as an essential coping mechanism for the pains of imprisonment and generated considerable hope for them that they were destined for a better, non-criminal life after release from prison.

MODERATION

Since the War on Terror (11 September 2001–present), there have been many appeals for Muslims to adopt a 'moderate' Islam and the idea of inculcating 'moderation' has been at the core, for example, of several deradicalisation programmes in Saudi Arabia.

It has almost gone unremarked that the ethic of moderation (*wasatiyyah*) has always been at the core of Mainstream Islam and is a divinely mandated religious principle (Kamali, 2015) (The Qur'an, 2:143; 4: 171; 5: 77).

Similarly, the Prophet Muhammad said,

> Beware of going to extremes in religion, for those before you were only destroyed by becoming extreme. (Sunan An-Nasai, 3057, Sunnah.com, 2022a)

Moderation among Muslim prisoners

Despite the hardships and isolation associated with imprisonment, a strong theme to emerge in the interviews was the need to maintain a sense of balance and moderation in prison. For example, Peter (male, 52, White British, Muslim Convert, HMP Forth, Category A Prison) spoke about how the ethos of moderation inculcated in him by a prison chaplain now guided him to avoid extremes:

> I hear so many times, like, over the ten years I was a Muslim, [the prison] Imam used to say to me, "Peter," he'd say, "make sure that you maintain the Middle Path" you know, "Do not go left to right" you know, "extremities meet. ..." So, I was ever conscious of that, like, these people guided me.

For Zaki (male, 40, British Asian Pakistani, Born-Muslim, HMP Cherwell, Category C Prison) the values of moderation engendered by his faith extended to respect for items that might have been considered specifically anti-Islam such as the novel *The Satanic Verses*:[4]

> I've read 'Satanic Verses' on the 30th anniversary of 'Satanic Verses'. A prisoner saw it in my cell and said, "Brother, I want to burn it." ... Now, this is where my deen [religion] helped me. Even though that is something sacrilegious in my religion, I know that I still have the sense of duty that I have an amana [religious trust] from the library that I have to give [the book] back to the library and I'm not going to burn it. Sticks and stones.

This account was typical of the fact that, for many of the prisoners that we interviewed, their religious faith was more likely to moderate their behaviour than it was to make it extreme.

It was also typical that prisoners with a sincere commitment to **Mainstream Islam** tended to play an important role in moderating the extreme views of others and to be a calming influence on the wings.

---

[4]   *The Satanic Verses* is a novel by British-Indian writer Salman Rushdie. It was first published in 1988 and is a fantasy inspired in part by the life of the Prophet Muhammad. It was regarded as insulting and blasphemous by sections of the Muslim community in the UK and overseas and sparked riots and violence across the Muslim-majority and Muslim-minority worlds. It resulted in a legal judgement (*fatwa*) being issued by the Supreme Leader of Iran Ayatollah Khomeini (1902–1989 CE) in 1989 calling for the assassination of Rushdie. This fatwa is regarded as invalid by the majority of Muslim jurists and leaders on the grounds that:

- the book did not meet the legal threshold for blasphemy or apostasy which must also involve a seditious political act against the Muslim community;
- Rushdie had not been given the opportunity to repent or submit a defence as part of a legal process;
- extra-judicial execution is forbidden in Islam.

FAMILY AND SOCIETY IN ISLAM

At the heart of the Mainstream Islam Worldview of Unity-in-Diversity is the centrality of the family and the extended family of kith and kin.

Respect for parents, kith and kin, and society in general is specifically connected in The Qur'an to worship of God:

> Worship God; join nothing with Him.
>
> Be good to your parents, to relatives, to orphans, to the needy, to neighbours near and far, to travellers in need, and to those under your authority.
>
> (The Qur'an, 4:36)

Civic cohesion was also central to the message of the Prophet Muhammad, who himself maintained his family ties throughout the period of his mission, even with those who did not believe in his Prophetic calling (Lings, 1983).

In linking belief to sound actions, prisoners with a **Mainstream Islamic Worldview** said that they attached a lot of importance to maintaining good interpersonal relationships both with kith and kin, and also sometimes with prison staff in lieu of kith and kin.

For example, Karim (male, 34, British Mixed-Race, Born-Muslim, HMP Cherwell, Category C Prison) was typical in this respect:

> The other day, I was at work and I work for an older woman and she's like, "Why are you always so helpful?" 'Cause she's got a bad back as well. ... 'Cause a lot of the brothers that go down there and they're very rude to her they have this misogynistic behaviour. But she's like but, "Why are you always so helpful?" I said to her "'Cause my mum's got a bad back. Me helping you, I then in return hope that Allah will bless me with someone that will look after my mum when she goes to work the same way." And that's happened. And she goes, "I've never thought about it like that." ... So, I try to

be pious so that Allah will then protect those closest to me, those who mean a lot to me and I feel they're doing alright.

99

In prison where participants were separated from their role as carers of their own families, care for others was seen by some Muslims as a way of attracting divine blessings towards their family members on the outside.

Finding respect for the law

As part of the **Mainstream Islamic** ethic of responsibility towards family and society, a respect for the law of the country was an important part of ethical behaviour for Mainstream Muslims, for **Intensifiers** and **Converts** who had returned or turned to Islam for the first time in prison as well as for **Remainers** and **Reducers**. Figures 5.1 and 5.2 summarise our sample's responses to two questions (respect for the law and the sacred nature of human life) which helped us interpret their Islamic worldview (see also Chapter 7).

Figure 5.1: Islam teaches that I must follow the law of this country

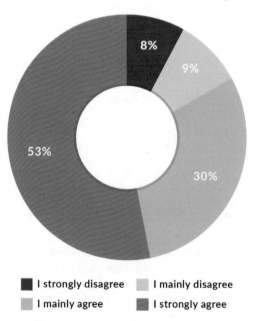

8%

9%

53%

30%

■ I strongly disagree   I mainly disagree
I mainly agree   ■ I strongly agree

For example, Nadim (male, 49, British Pakistani, Born-Muslim, HMP Forth, Category A Prison) explained how turning to religion was an important part of his rehabilitation in terms of his new determination to respect the law of the land, which he regarded as an Islamic value and which he wanted to draw upon to avoid crime after release:

> Interviewer: Tell me more about that, how will it [religion] help you avoid crime when you leave prison, "definitely"?
>
> Nadim: To respect the law of the land where you're living. And, if I disagree or find that some parts of the law are not compatible with me, then it's only right that I move from here and go somewhere where the law is suitable for me. But I don't think, really, that's going to be a situation. So, if I choose to live here then, Islamically, there is no way that I can, you know, justify breaking the law or going against the law.

Through the auspices of the HMPPS Muslim Chaplaincy, Nadim had tapped into the Mainstream ruling (Al-Oadah, 2014) that if a Muslim feels that secular laws and society are in contradiction to Islamic law and teachings then the correct course of action would either be to lobby peacefully for a legal change through, for example, an MP or by joining a campaign group, or to move to a country where this contradiction was not present.

THE SANCTITY OF LIFE IN ISLAM

The Sanctity of Life, and especially human life, is a fundamental value in Mainstream Islam:

> On account of [his deed], We decreed to the Children of Israel that if anyone kills a person – unless in punishment for murder or spreading corruption in the land – it is as if he kills all mankind, while if any saves a life it is as if he saves the lives of all mankind. (The Qur'an, 5:32)

What needs to be noted in the Qur'anic verses quoted earlier is that the sanctity of each individual human life is comparable to the sanctity of an entire community. This principle of the sanctity of life is given full expression during the rites of *Hajj* when a Pilgrim may kill no living creature, not even a mosquito.

In respect of the sanctity of life, **83 per cent** of our characteristic sample of Muslims prisoners 'strongly agreed' that 'Islam teaches me that human life is sacred'. In other words, there was a high degree of consensus among Muslim prisoners over this core Islamic value.

Figure 5.2: Islam teaches that human life is sacred

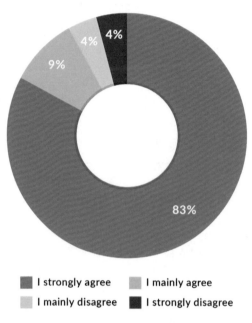

I strongly agree   I mainly agree
I mainly disagree   I strongly disagree

For example, Hussain (male, 41, British Pakistani, Born-Muslim, HMP Cherwell, Category C Prison) drew on the Qur'anic teaching of the **Sanctity of Life** to support his rejection of religious extremism:

> I said, "Yeah, bro, let me remind you of the hadith of Rasul Sallallahu Alaihi wasallam [the Messenger of God, peace and blessings be upon him] said, 'Oh, son of Adam, Allah says, verily if you kill one innocent person, regardless of his religion, race, colour or creed, you will gain the sin as if you've killed the whole of mankind.
>
> Verily, oh, son of Adam, if you save one innocent person, regardless of his religion, race, colour or creed, you shall gain the reward as if you've saved the whole humanity.' Where does this leave extremism?"

Within this understanding of the **Sanctity of Life** as a core religious and legal principle of **Mainstream Islam**, we need to consider what jihad means and how our prisoners understood it.

Struggle (jihad) in Islam

STRUGGLE (JIHAD) IN ISLAM

The Arabic word jihad simply means 'struggling'. By extension, it means 'struggling in the way of God'. In The Qur'an, words derived from the root *j-h-d* (to struggle) appear 41 times, and only ten of these are unambiguous references to fighting in an armed jihad (Bonner, 2006).

Following Qur'anic usage, for the early Muslim community jihad came to mean the struggle to establish or preserve the religion of Islam. Occasionally, if there was no other way open, it meant struggling to defend Islam by force of arms.

TYPES OF JIHAD

In the Prophet's lifetime, there existed no formal Doctrines of Struggle (jihad). Doctrines of jihad derived from The Qur'an and the Sunna were developed by Muslim thinkers in the centuries following the Prophet Muhammad's death.

Following the lead of The Qur'an and the Sunna, classical jurists – such as the Andalusian jurist Ibn Rushd (Averroes) (died 1198 CE) – classified jihad into four main categories:

- Struggle of the heart (*jihad bil qalb/nafs*). This struggle is concerned with combating the evil insinuations of the ego and the devil. This type of jihad was regarded classically as the greater jihad (*al-jihad al-akbar*) as it concerns the daily business of training the rebellious ego to obey God's injunctions.

- Struggle by the tongue (*jihad bil lisan*). This struggle is concerned with speaking the truth and spreading the word of Islam.

- Struggle by the hand (*jihad bil yad*). This struggle refers to choosing to do what is right and combating injustice with action. We might call this 'activism'.

- Struggle by the sword (*jihad bis saif*). This struggle refers to armed fighting in the way of God (*Qital fi sabilillah*), the final resort, if all other types of jihad have failed and the integrity of the Islamic religion and safety of the Muslim community is threatened.

THE STRICT LEGAL CONDITIONS OF ARMED JIHAD (*QITAL*)

All **armed jihad** in Islam has always been subject to strict ethical procedures. During his life, the Prophet Muhammad gave various injunctions to his forces and adopted practices toward the conduct of war. The most important of these were summarised by the Prophet Muhammad's Companion and first Caliph, Abu Bakr (died 634 CE) in the form of *Rules for the Muslim Army*:

People! I charge you with these rules; learn them well!

1. Do not betray or misappropriate any part of the booty.

2. Do not practice treachery or mutilation.

3. Do not kill a young child, an old man, or a woman.

4. Do not uproot or burn palms or cut down fruitful trees.

5. Do not slaughter a sheep or a cow or a camel, except for food.

6. You will meet people who have set themselves apart in hermitages; leave them to accomplish the purpose for which they have done this.

7. You will come upon people who will bring you dishes with various kinds of foods. If you partake of them, pronounce God's name over what you eat.

8. You will meet people who have shaved the crown of their heads, leaving a band of hair around it [monks]. Leave them in God's name, and may God protect you from sword and pestilence. (Al-Tabari (died 923 CE))

Therefore, the conditions for armed combat in The Qur'an and Sunna which are applied by Muslim jurists up to the present day are clear (Kamali, 2013):

1. Armed combat (*Qital*) must be conducted in defence of life and property.

2. Armed combat (*Qital*) can only be considered when overtures for peace have failed.

3. Armed combat (*Qital*) can only be against an armed aggressor and not against civilians.

4. Armed combat (*Qital*) can only be for a just cause.

5. Armed combat (*Qital*) can only be conducted under authorised and legal leadership.

6. Armed combat (*Qital*) can only be conducted with a view to suing for peace as soon as possible.

The prisoners' views on religious violence

The idea of religious Struggle (jihad) did not form a notable part of Muslim prisoners' everyday experience. Jihad of any sort, armed or otherwise, was only mentioned at interview by seven of our 158 Muslim prisoners. Nevertheless, there existed a consensus amongst **Mainstream Muslim prisoners** that the taking of innocent life was both illegal and against The Qur'an and the Sunna. For example, Abbas (male, 50 years, British Asian Pakistani, Born-Muslim, HMP Stour, Category D Prison) said,

> I totally disagree with all these bombings and all that, killing innocent people, because it doesn't teach you, nowhere in The Qur'an to kill innocent people.

Many of our cohort of Mainstream Muslim prisoners were repelled and ashamed by the use of such violence in the name of Islam. For example, Ethan (male, 43 years, White British, Muslim Convert, HMP Forth, Category A Prison) said,

> Every time you see a news clip where someone is killing someone or hurting someone and saying, "Allahu Akbar" that is shameful, it is completely sinful. ... He should not be saying, "God is Great" for killing one of His creatures.

Mainstream Activist Islam in prison

As well as forbidding illegitimate violence, The Qur'an advocates transformative change, rather than revolutionary change, in a way that explicitly gives primacy to personal change over institutional change in the cause of changing the status quo:

> God does not change the state of a people until they change what is in themselves.
>
> (The Quran, 13:11)

Moreover, the Prophet Muhammad advocated challenging and changing wrong-doing in the famous *hadith*,

> Whosoever of you sees an evil, let him change it with his hand;
> and if he is not able to do so, then [let him change it] with his tongue;
> and if he is not able to do so, then with his heart – and that is the weakest of faith.
>
> (An-Nawawi, Hadith 34, Reported by Muslim, Sunnah.com, 2022b)

We also found from our questionnaires and our interviews that a commitment to personal and structural change formed a key component of those prisoners with the Worldview of **Mainstream Activist Islam**, who formed 28 per cent of our characteristic sample.

We have seen in the previous chapter how this Worldview of **Mainstream Activist Islam** was significantly associated with strong **Attitudes to Rehabilitation**, and this came across strongly at interview.

Those prisoners who held a Worldview of **Mainstream Activist Islam** attached importance to actions that created conditions for more harmonious and fairer prison life and actions that promoted the care of God's creation.

We found examples of Muslim prisoners joining the Samaritans in prison to provide emotional support to other prisoners. Others were members of a prison Violence Reduction Team or a Diversity Team on the wings; others described standing up for prisoners who were being bullied.

For example, Hussain (male, 41, British Asian Pakistani, Born-Muslim, HMP Cherwell, Category C Prison) described a situation in which he intervened to stop a prisoner from attacking a prison officer. A group of prisoners had stood by and watched the altercation without getting involved, but Hussain felt that his religion compelled him to protect the prison officer.

Following his involvement, Hussain became the target of attacks by prisoners and had to be placed in the Vulnerable Prisoners' Unit, and his family outside prison were also threatened. Despite the hardships he faced due to his actions, Hussain was sure he had done the morally correct thing and would be rewarded by God for his actions:

> I never got nothing. I never done it for anything. I'd do it again. My humanity's my humanity. It's my deen [religion] that made me step in. My reward is with Allah, [not with] none of these people.

Suleiman (male, 26, British Black Caribbean, Born-Muslim, HMP Parrett, Category B Prison) described helping other prisoners of all types with low literacy skills:

> Interviewer: So how do you help people?
>
> Suleiman: Even when I was on Induction Wing here and talking to people about their cases, and even if you need help reading or writing, I'll be that person to always help you. ... I met a good brother here, he's not a Muslim. ... I spoke to him, he talked to me about his case saying he caught two Grievous Bodily Harm cases. I said, "Do you know what you can do? Because I know. I've been in jail so I know a bit about cases and what will happen." I said, "Write a letter to the judge." He's like his writing isn't that good. I said, "Tell me what you want, write a little letter of what you want, and I will rewrite it for you." Because I do calligraphy, I make my own cards, etc. So, he wrote out a little two-page, he wrote two pages, and I rewrote it for him, and he sent it to the judge, or his solicitor. About three days later, he thanked me so much, he said, "That made a great difference to my life."

This desire to 'make a difference' in a pro-social way to their own and others' lives was the principal characteristic of prisoners who held the Worldview of **Mainstream Activist Islam**.

Conclusion: The rehabilitative potential of Mainstream Islam

In this chapter, we have seen how, contrary to stereotypes of Muslims in prison as jihad-crazed gangsters and terrorists-in-waiting, **76 per cent** of our characteristic sample of Muslim prisoners held a Worldview of **Mainstream Islam** which was grounded in respect for basic human equality and the spiritual quality of Unity-in-Diversity, including regret for their crime.

Mainstream Muslim prisoners brought the core values of **Mainstream Islam** to life by aspiring to care for and share with other prisoners, to show respect and politeness towards other people of all types and to reconnect lawfully with family and society. For these Muslim prisoners, especially **Converts** and **Intensifiers** with a **Mainstream Activist** Worldview, their Islamic faith strongly encouraged an ethos of moderation, helping others, reconnecting with education and work and the avoidance of future crime.

Islamism and Islamist Extremism in prison

We have seen in the previous two chapters how the large majority – 76 per cent – of our characteristic sample of Muslim prisoners held a Worldview of Mainstream Islam characterised by Unity-in-Diversity and an aspiration to fulfil Mainstream Islamic practices and values which often fed productively into their commitment to rehabilitation.

In this chapter, we document the experiences of the **other 23 per cent**[1] of Muslim prisoners who held **Islamist – 19 per cent** – and **Islamist Extremist – 4 per cent** – Worldviews and show how these Worldviews were enacted and affected prison life.

ISLAMISM

Islamism marks a shift from a Worldview of Unity-in-Diversity and human equality before God to a Worldview of 'Us'/Muslim versus 'Them'/Infidel/ *kafir* in which the 'Them'/Infidel begin to be regarded as lesser human beings.

The Worldview of Islamism (as the -ism suggests) also marks the significant shift from Islam-as-religion to Islam-as-revolutionary-political-ideology which is directed at overthrowing, rather than transforming, existing political structures and replacing them with an Islamic state governed by an Islamist interpretation of Islamic Law. Islamists tend to suggest the incompatibility of Islam with democratic political models and that only the religious laws of Islam (Sharia) are applicable to Muslims (Maududi, 1967; 1975; Al-Banna, 1975).

---

[1] Figures are rounded up or down, which accounts for the fact that these percentages total 99 per cent.

The Islamist prisoners in our sample of Muslim prisoners

Nineteen per cent of our characteristic sample of Muslim prisoners held this exaggerated 'Us'/Muslim versus 'Them'/Infidel/*kafir* **Islamist** Worldview and we have observed in Chapters 3 and 4 how **Converts** and **Intensifiers** were significantly prominent in holding this Worldview. In interviews and through observations Islamist Muslim prisoners accentuated various aspects of it.

'Us'/Muslim versus 'Them'/Infidel/kafir: separation and exaggerated difference

In order to prop-up the idea of 'Us' versus 'Them', **Islamists** often propagate a conspiratorial Worldview that the unbelievers (*kuffar*) – especially 'Infidel' subgroups like 'world Jewry' – are out to trick and subjugate Muslims.

In this respect, Abbas (male, 31, British Asian Pakistani, Born-Muslim, HMP Cherwell, Category C Prison) described to us how he had been discouraged from participating in our research by an Islamist prisoner on his wing on the conspiratorial basis that we were working for a "government agency", although we had explained on multiple occasions that we were completely independent academic researchers:

> Yes, he was like, "Oh these people have come and they're pretending to be researchers and they're pretending that they want to help Islam, but really they're part of some sort of government agency, these lot, they do this type of stuff, they pretend to be part of our community and Muslims but they're not. It's all fake so watch what you say and don't be open because it's going to be used against you," and all that kind of stuff and I was just like, "Oh my God, again with all that [Illuminati] talk. Not conspiracies."

Islamist justification of crime

The exaggerated 'Us'/Muslims versus 'Them'/Infidels/*kafir* **Islamist** Worldview also provided some prisoners with grounds for the spurious 'religious' justification of crimes, such as sex offences.

Bashir (male, 67, British Asian Pakistani, Born-Muslim, HMP Forth, Category A Prison) said that because "white girls" were content to "hang around with Pakistanis and Muslims" he could not have been guilty of rape because

> "If I rape you, would you come back again, and again, and again?"

This notion of the availability and licentiousness of white, *kafir* women was used by several sex offenders in our sample to justify their crimes. For example, one prisoner justified his sex crime on the basis that Muslims today, regardless of the law and of contemporary sexual mores, are entitled to have sex with minors because the Prophet Muhammad was betrothed in marriage to his wife 'Aisha when she was a minor.[2]

THE WORLDVIEW OF ISLAMIST EXTREMISM IN PRISON

The idea of 'Us'/Muslims versus 'Them'/'wrong Muslims'/non-Muslims is taken to an extreme in the Worldview of **Islamist Extremism** in which non-Muslims and 'wrong Muslims' are stripped of their basic human attributes and rights, which leaves them open to harm.

In our characteristic sample of Muslim prisoners, Muslims who populated the **Islamist Extremist Worldview** represented a small minority of **4.4 per cent**.

The Worldview of Non-Violent Islamist Extremism in prison

The Worldview of **Non-Violent Islamist Extremism** takes the Islamist Worldview a stage further and stresses the absolute difference between the 'true' ideological Muslims versus the 'non-Muslim' and 'wrong Muslim' who are afforded a less human or subhuman status but are not explicitly targeted for violence.[3]

---

[2] This Islamist justification disregards the fact that, over the past 1,450 years, sexual mores and definitions of minority have changed and that Islam requires Muslims to obey the laws of today. This Islamist justification also ignores the fact that while Muhammad was betrothed to 'Aisha between the ages of 6 and 12, they did not consummate their marriage until 'Aisha was 15 or 16, which was normal at the time.

[3] It is sometimes referred to as 'Qutbism' after its principal protagonist, Sayyid Qutb (1906–1966 CE).

We witnessed this Islamist Extremist identification of 'wrong Muslims' in prison. For example, Kevin (male, 45, White British, Convert, HMP Severn, Category B Prison) believed that Sufi Muslims (esoteric, inward-leaning Muslims) and Shia Muslims (see Chapter 1) were 'wrong Muslims' who should not be afforded religious rights in prison. Kaiser believed that the governor should only recognise Salafi Islam as the 'true' Islam. To justify this Worldview of **Non-Violent Islamist Extremism**, Kevin used the idea that Shia Islam and Sufi Islam were religious innovations (*bida'*):

> Well, you need to get the correct view and my view is the Salafi way. And basically you just need someone in power just to believe in the Salafi way and be overruled ... so if the Governor here said we would only accept Salafi here everyone else we believe that everything else, if you're pro-bida' [religious innovation], you're an innovator, if you're pro-kufr [Unbelief] you're actually out of the fold of Islam ... and you have problems because in the West you can practise being a Shia and you're protected here.
>
> You are protected. I'm not saying that they should be targeted and slaughtered, but that Islam would refute them, and we would call them enemies of Allah because they are dangerous ... they will confuse people and if someone believes in what they say then they will put someone into the Fire [of Hell].

This belief that 'wrong Muslims' (in particular Shia Muslims) are "out of the fold of Islam" and destined for Hell Fire is characteristic of the Worldview of Islamist Extremism.

Rejecting democracy and lawfulness

For **Non-Violent Islamist Extremists**, all secular laws and all secular governments are, in principle, in conflict with Islam. Non-Violent Islamist Extremists can only support a state that is based on a severe, literalist version of Sharia Law. Non-Violent Islamist Extremists believe that taking part in democratic government through voting constitutes an act of unbelief (*kufr*) that takes the Muslim believer out of Islam.

Kevin also exemplified this aspect of the Non–Violent Islamist Extremist Worldview in his belief that participation in democracy was forbidden for Muslims.

> Interviewer: So, do you think we shouldn't be participating in democracy?
>
> Kevin: No, it's not part of our culture. It's not part of our way to do that. You can't vote that there is this belief, there are opinions about it. So, I follow the opinion that you can't vote, it will take you out of the fold [of Islam]. ... You can't vote. I'm not allowed to. It's not allowed.

Similarly, Kevin believed that only Islamic religious laws could be the basis of a legitimate government:

> Kevin: Yeah, if you want to get into the depths of it, I don't even believe in prison, but I believe in laws, just laws and basically, I don't believe in prison.
>
> Interviewer: So, let's say that prison didn't exist and that you believe in 'just laws'. So, in your mind, how would you enforce 'just laws'?
>
> Kevin: Basically, that the rulers would enforce their laws of the books. So, the laws of Moses, the Sharia Law, that's it.

Jamal (male, 27, British Black Caribbean, Muslim Convert, HMP Cherwell Category C Prison) also rejected the idea of acceptance of non-Muslim laws:

> Well, I don't know. Can anybody bring me a verse in The Qur'an where it says, 'Obey the law of the land'?[4]

Absolute separation and the Doctrine of Loyalty & Disavowal

Non-Violent Islamist Extremist prisoners aspired to enact their Worldview of the absolute separation and difference between Muslims and Non-Muslims (including 'wrong Muslims') by exercising in prison an informal policy of Loyalty & Disavowal (*Al-Wala' wal Bara'*).

The Doctrine of Loyalty & Disavowal forms the backbone of **Islamist Extremism**. It states that Muslims must *prove* their loyalty to Islam and their commitment to the Doctrine of the Oneness of God (*Tawhid*) by shunning, avoiding and, in Violent Islamist Extremism, destroying all non-Muslim peoples, their cultures and their political activities (Bin Ali, 2015; Wilkinson, 2019).

In our characteristic sample, Non-Violent Islamist Extremist prisoners performed The Doctrine of Loyalty & Disavowal by shunning, or pretending to shun, non-Muslim prisoners and prison staff and encouraging other Muslim prisoners to follow suit. In some instances, our interviewees described how they had seen non-Muslim prisoners get bullied out of jobs on the servery or off the wing according to this principle.

For example, Suleiman (male, 26, British Black Caribbean, Born-Muslim, HMP Parrett, Category B Prison) described an example of 'Disavowal':

> I saw a brother, he's called Loco, I don't know his real name, I don't really know him like that, but he was an alright guy. And then, because he wasn't Muslim, they kicked him off, the Muslims on the wing made him quit servery, they started doing a little bit of malice to him and he moved the wing. He was alright with everyone and I see them oppressing him and I didn't like it. I told them, "Why are you lot doing this to him?" [They answered] "He's not Muslim."

Abbas (male, 31, British Asian Pakistani, Born-Muslim, HMP Cherwell, Category C Prison) described how he was reprimanded by Islamist Extremists on his wing for socialising with non-Muslim prisoners.

---

[4] The Qur'an 4:59 says 'O believers! Obey Allah and obey the Messenger and those in authority among you'.

They told him to

> "keep your difference" by "not socialising with kafirs [infidels]".

The 'unserious' nature of Loyalty & Disavowal in prison was described by a Mainstream Muslim prisoner who pointed out its hypocrisy and impracticability in the prison environment. Bashir (male, 33 years, British Asian, Born-Muslim, HMP Cherwell, Category C Prison) said,

> if you're saying, "kafir," "kafir," "Don't speak to them" they're hypocrites because secretly you do talk to them because when you go to work, you converse with them.

In other words, in a prison environment it was impossible to avoid non-Muslim staff and non-Muslim prisoners and pretending to 'disavow' them ended up being hypocritical.

THE WORLDVIEW OF VIOLENT ISLAMIST EXTREMISM

The Worldview of Violent Islamist Extremism is the absolutely divided and antagonistic 'Us' versus 'Them' Islamist Extremist Worldview in which the 'non-Muslim' and the 'wrong Muslim' (those who do not fight to establish a global Islamic state) are construed as eternal enemies of 'true' Islam and are therefore fit to be exterminated.[5]

Violent Islamist Extremists' belief that Islam is in an eternal 'state of war' against Unbelief (*kufr*) is used to justify violence towards anyone who opposes their Worldview.

---

[5] Violent Islamist Extremism is also known as 'Jihadism' or, more academically, as 'Salafi-Jihadism'. The term 'Jihadism' runs the risk of conflating what Islamist terrorists do with the noble doctrines of struggling to please God (*Jihad fiy sabilillah*). 'Salafi-Jihadism' is only one form of Violent Islamist Extremism as this Worldview takes on a wide variety of denominational forms.

The Worldview of Violent Islamist Extremism in prison

Out of our characteristic sample of **279 prisoners, only one prisoner** was classified as a **Violent Islamist Extremist**: a White British Convert at HMP Cherwell, Category C Prison.

This tiny representation of Violent Islamist Extremists in our sample was, we believe, a fair quantitative representation of the small number of Muslim prisoners who are actively committed to Islamist violence. It was also a product of the fact that most Violent Islamist Extremist prisoners chose not to engage actively with our research.

However, we detected and recorded the presence of this Worldview of **Violent Islamist Extremism** in prison:

- from the reports of other prisoners;
- through the reasons that some prisoners offered us for not engaging in our research;
- and through our ethnographic observations of prison events, such as Islamic Studies classes and the Friday Prayer.

Despite the statistically tiny proportion of Violent Islamist Extremists in the Muslim prisoner base, these accounts and observations showed us that Violent Islamist Extremism is propagated in prison, and Violent Islamist Extremists pose an active threat to the lives and minds of other prisoners and prison staff that belies their small numbers.

Legitimising violence

In the **Violent Islamist Extremist** Worldview, the coexistence of non-Muslim societies with Muslim societies is deemed impossible (Qutb, 1964): non-Muslim rulers and their people must be challenged and fought. We witnessed this belief in the total incompatibility of Islam with the System of Unbelief of the **Violent Islamist Extremist** Worldview in prison.

At HMP Forth, Category A Prison, one prisoner told us in passing,

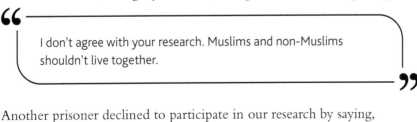

> I don't agree with your research. Muslims and non-Muslims shouldn't live together.

Another prisoner declined to participate in our research by saying,

> When Islam comes, it always comes by force.

The same prisoner expressed the view that

> Shia Muslims are kafir [infidels].

A terrorist offender told us,

> I don't believe in talking. I believe in direct action.

Also, in HMP Forth, Category A Prison, we observed a group of prisoners who refused to pray behind the Muslim prison chaplain because they considered the chaplain, as a government employee, to be an 'infidel' (*kafir*).

In HMP Severn, Category B Prison, a prisoner expressed the view that the stabbing of a 'snitch' during the Congregational Friday Prayer had been legitimate.

Another prisoner in HMP Severn, Category B Prison questioned whether the Congregational Friday Prayer should be conducted at all in 'The Land of Unbelief ' (*Dar al-Kufr*), that is, in a Muslim-minority country. This debate occupied ten minutes of an Islamic Studies class, which made the other Muslim prisoners and the Muslim prison chaplain frustrated and uncomfortable. There were four other occasions during the session when the same prisoner raised the same question 'from the wings', which interrupted the tenor and the teaching of the Islamic Studies classes.

In an interview with a prisoner at HMP Severn, Category B Prison, the participant expressed his support for the leader (at the time) of the so-called Islamic State group, Abu Bakr al-Baghdadi (1971–2019 CE). This prisoner also expressed the view that supporting Islamic State was not an extreme position, and that "the real extremists" were actually on his wing!

At the Friday Prayer and in the Islamic Studies classes at HMP Severn, Category B Prison, we observed that a small number of **Violent Islamist Extremists** sported an exaggeratedly 'Islamic' look: long robes, long beards and shoulder-length hair. These same prisoners were also known by their index offences and other prisoners to be adherents and/or sympathisers of Islamic State.

We noted that during Islamic Studies classes, this group dominated discussions by challenging the views of the Muslim prison chaplain. Furthermore, we noted during Association following the Congregational Friday Prayer that this group exhibited a higher than usual degree of authority and charisma among other prisoners.

Extremist radicalisation

As well as becoming aware of pockets of Violent Islamist Extremist prisoners through observations of prison life, our interview with Hussain (male, 41, British Asian Pakistani, Born-Muslim, HMP Cherwell, Category C Prison) illustrated the potential for Violent Islamist Extremist prisoners to radicalise others.

In a previous prison, Hussain had been gradually convinced that terrorist violence, such as the 9/11 attacks, were permitted (halal) in Islam as he **shifted** from **Mainstream Islam** towards a **Violent Islamist Extremist** Worldview:

> I was saying I can't get my head round that brother al Farhad. They [the 9/11 attackers] killed 3,000, 4,000 people, man. What if there was Muslims in 9/11 that went down as well?' [He replied], "Brother, they're going to Jannah [Heaven]. The operation that the brothers done was a beaut', it was halal, there's fatwas, halal, we're in a state of war, you can go and do it." So much so that I was encouraged to, when I get out, go and commit an atrocity myself. He asked, "How do you think you could do one, brother Hussain?" I said, "Well, I've got access to guns." [He replied] "That's beautiful, that's beautiful. I can introduce you to a few good brothers, if you can get the guns, all you have to do, brother, is go to Piccadilly Circus Saturday night and don't do a bomb. If you're worried about suicide bombings and that, although I'm giving you a fatwa, that's halal" because I'd accept it if was halal, yeah. He said, "How you do it then, you get your guns, get your little team together, roll up into Leicester Square on a Saturday night and pick you targets. The ones in skirts, the ones that are drunk, pick your targets. Police will get the armed squad out, there'll be a firefight, you'll die on the battlefield. Alhamdulillah you complete the mission." Boom, my head started turning, as it goes, that's right, he's right.

As this quote clearly shows, using the religious language of Islam such as *fatwa* and halal, Violent Islamist Extremist prisoners encouraged and justified actions that are strictly forbidden in Islam: suicide, murder and causing civic destruction.

Eternal separation with lethal consequences

Hussain (male, 41, British Asian Pakistani, Born-Muslim, HMP Cherwell, Category C Prison) also described how, as part of the process of radicalisation, the Islamist Extremist Doctrine of Loyalty & Disavowal (Al-Wala' wal-Bara') began to 'embed' the Violent Islamist Extremist Worldview in his head:

> My hatred started coming towards me. He said, "Look at these Jews! Look at these Christians!" He said nothing but division and hatred. Teaching how to hate everyone with Islamic law behind him. Picking and choosing parts of The Qur'an, "Look what it says here, 'Terrorise them everywhere you see them.'" Wow, that is what The Qur'an says? But I never opened my mind to study the whole Qur'an myself. Let me see what else it says as well. No, these chapters are embedded in my mind now. This ideology's embedding itself in my mind now. I'm one of your operatives.

As well as the Doctrine of Loyalty & Disavowal, other core themes and behaviours associated with **Violent Islamist Extremism** also found expression in prison.

THE ACT OF SEEKING MARTYRDOM (ISTISHHAD)

Violent Islamist Extremists teach that the most sought-after religious ideal is seeking death through martyrdom by fighting the *kuffar* and the 'wrong' heretical Muslim (Azzam, 1987; Bonner, 2006).

Hussain, who, as we have just seen, was radicalised by a notorious Terrorism Act (TACT) prisoner, described how his entire Worldview shifted to the point where he felt the sole purpose of his life was to seek Martyrdom:

> I'm coming up the pack. Slowly, slowly, I'm one of the brothers now.
> Gifts are coming to me. Everything's coming to me. Wow! Book after
> book after book from the House of Saud is also coming. But I'm noticing
> these little things. My hatred towards everyone who's not Muslim is
> increasing, increasing, increasing. Now I'm following an agenda. I've got
> tunnel vision.
>
> Now what I want is Jannah [Paradise], I don't want This World.
> I don't want nothing. I want to die. I want to kill one of these
> people in the process.

THE TYRANT

The idea of the Tyrant (*Taghut*, pl. *Tawaghit*) is a **Violent Islamist Extremist** trope which means 'the corrupt', 'the evildoer' or 'the deviant'. Muslim regimes and rulers who are deemed not to govern according to Islamic Law are often referred to by Islamist Extremists as 'Tyrants'.

Nicolas (male, 32, White French, Convert, Hauterive, Category B Prison) explained that he joined Al-Qaeda in Syria to "oppose a tyrant". Nicolas explained that his journey to join Al-Qaeda in Syria was a religious obligation and that he did not regard himself guilty of any crime because he considered himself to be following his beliefs. While he accepted his conviction, he refused to participate in a penal system which he denied possessed any legitimacy.

THE APOSTATE (MURTAD)

Another **Violent Islamist Extremist** trope is the idea that anyone who does not fight to impose an 'Islamic' state has left (apostatised from) Islam. This idea also found expression on the prison wings.

Ethan (male, 43, White British, Muslim Convert, HMP Forth, Category A Prison), whose case we will follow more fully in Chapter 7, said that anyone who was in opposition to the 'Muslim' leaders on his wing was considered an 'apostate' or an 'oppressor', and acts of violence against these 'oppressors' were considered to be a way of pleasing God.

The Islamist Extremist gang

Ethan also described the way in which the Islamist Extremist Muslims on his wing had formed a gang, with a hierarchy in which the senior leaders remained hidden and exercised their power through "enforcers".

> Oh, yes, every wing will have an [Amir]. In some cases you might even have a couple of [Amirs]. Yes, because what happens here, you've usually got what's called the 'Public' [Amir], the one that the staff thinks are doing whatever. And then, you've got the person who is standing back, telling him [the 'Public' Amir] what to do and say. So, you understand that now, yes, none of the Public [Amirs] are really [Amirs]. And then, you've got the enforcers. So, you've got the likes of [Janner] over there. You know, I could mention 20 or 30 different ones, like. Some of them are horrific. Mohammed, he's one of the most brutal. He's the one that loves giving young buggers lashes and stuff like that.

Despite enforcing a skewed version of a moral code on the wings, Islamist Extremist gang leaders were usually associated with an 'unserious' practice of Islam: they enforced extreme religious practices on others while continuing to be involved themselves in crime and practices that are forbidden in Islam, such as viewing pornography. As Ethan said:

> Unfortunately, you've got a lot of people that read hadiths, even quotations from books like, 'Fortress of the Muslim' and stuff like that, and they will say, "Look, you've done this. You must be punished." It's power. And they're telling you with the right hand that you must obey them and obey the rules of Islam and this, that and the other. But, with their left hand, they're selling cocaine, drugs over there, using phones and looking at dirty magazines and stuff like that.

Other prisoners bore witness to Islamist Extremist prisoners policing other Muslim prisoners by pointing out their deficiencies of faith, and where they were getting Islam wrong, often on totally spurious grounds. For example, Bashir (male, 33, British Asian Pakistani, Born-Muslim, HMP Cherwell, Category C Prison) said:

> You get these other people, they're just reading the book, every day, every day, every day, every day. So everything is, "Your haircut is wrong." and "You're this and you're that. You should be walking in sideways to the mosque." They're just making up things.

The fear of Islamist Extremists and their danger to Shia Muslims

The fear generated by Islamist Extremist gangs was particularly directed at Shia Muslims. Hussain, for example, felt that being a 'wrong' Shia Muslim in prison was more dangerous than being a non-Muslim (*kafir*) and that particularly vicious forms of Loyalty & Disavowal were directed towards Shias. Hussain hid his Shia affiliation from other Muslim prisoners because Shia Muslims were prone to violent attack:

> They're [Islamist Extremists] like, "Oh, he claims to be Muslim, but we don't accept he's Muslim." They're not classifying him as Muslim. So that person, he doesn't just get that sense of no acceptance, everyone spreads words around of, "He's a Shia. Don't go next to him. Don't go in his cell." Or "Don't help him out" or this and that.
>
> For example, [in my previous prison] someone was Shia and I told him, I said to him, "Just do taqiyya [pretend that you are not Shia] and say that you're Sunni so you don't have to say you're Shia. You have your own beliefs in your heart." He said, "No, I'm proud to be Shia." He got beaten up by ten guys. He got rushed. He got jumped and they beat him up badly.

Zaki (male, 40, British Asian Pakistani, Remainer, HMP Cherwell, Category C Prison), who was tolerant of Shia Muslims and non-Muslims, also felt threatened by the small group of Violent Islamist Extremist Muslims in HMP Cherwell:

> So I'm friends with two of the Shias on my wing. They're the only two Shias in this prison, I think. But because I'm friends with them and I say, "Asalaam alaikum" ... to them and they say, "Asalaam alaikum" to me, people try to challenge me. When I say 'people', [it's] the Salafi group [that] tries to challenge me, especially the reverts [Converts]. ... Yes. Not to mention, if I am too outwardly about my tolerant views about other religions and other people, the Salafis will attack me and this is not a speculation. I have seen this happen ... it's not a big group per se, there's a few of them. But the thing is, the attack never comes from the group, they can hire anybody to attack you. So, if somebody has a problem with my case, they can hire a drug addict to say, "Look, we'll promise you so and so drugs if you cut my man's face."

Zaki's observation that "the Salafi group" were most likely to hold and enact Islamist and Islamist Extremist Worldviews was backed significantly by our statistical data ($p = 0.045$). Those prisoners who identified as 'Sunni Salafi' constituted:

- 12 per cent of our total sample, but
- 20 per cent of Islamists and
- 30 per cent of Islamist Extremists.

We have already noted in Chapter 4, the over-representation of **Converts** in these two categories of Worldview.

As Zaki claimed, while the Violent Islamist Extremists were "not a big group", they nevertheless had the capacity to produce violent and damaging effects on prison life. This was consistent with our findings that even a tiny minority of Islamist Extremists caused trouble to prison chaplains and other prison staff and generated an atmosphere of fear and mistrust among other prisoners that belied their small numbers.

Conclusion: Islamist Extremists comprise a small, but vicious minority

In this chapter, we have shown how **19 per cent** of our characteristic data sample of Muslim prisoners held a divided 'Us' versus 'Them' **Islamist Worldview**, which included distancing themselves from non-Muslim prisoners, rejecting democracy as 'un-Islamic' and sometimes justifying their crimes on spurious 'Islamic' grounds.

We also encountered a small number of **Islamist Extremists** – both **Non-Violent Islamist Extremists** and **Violent Islamist Extremists** – who represented **4 per cent** of our characteristic sample of Muslim prisoners. These prisoners believed that Islam was eternally and violently opposed to Unbelief (*kufr*) and supported terrorist groups. Some **Islamist Extremists** were eager to conduct themselves violently against other prisoners, supposedly in the name of Islam.

In these cases, their religion, such as it was, was criminogenic: they were prone to disrupt Muslim chaplaincy activities and they engaged in criminal behaviour such as drug dealing and violent feuds with other prisoners.

According to other prisoners, these **Islamist Extremists** were prone to organise themselves into gang hierarchies which drew in vulnerable prisoners, especially **Converts**, and generated fear among prisoners of all types and trouble for prison staff, which belied their minority status.

The lives of Muslim prisoners: opportunities and risks

In this chapter, using **seven short case studies**, we give voice to the often intense experiences of the different types of Muslim prisoner that we have outlined in the previous chapters: **Converts**, **Intensifiers**, **Shifters**, **Remainers** and **Reducers**, who hold different types of Islamic Worldview.

We tell the stories of these prisoners to illustrate the opportunities for rehabilitation and the risks involved in significant religious change in prison, as well as the complexity and diversity of Muslim prisoners' lives.

The Converts

Converts we have defined as those prisoners who chose to follow Islam for the first time from another faith or from no faith in prison. Converts represented **21 per cent** of our data sample.

As we discussed in Chapter 3, the largest proportion of **Converts** were in **English prisons** (27 per cent). In Switzerland and France, it was far less common to choose Islam for the first time in prison.

We have also seen how **Converts** are likely to exhibit strong **Attitude to Rehabilitation**, as well as being prone to some risk of Islamism and Islamist Extremism.

Case study 1: Chris, 'Convert', HMP Cherwell, Category C Prison

Chris is an example of a slow reflective process of religious conversion and rehabilitative change in prison. Chris had turned to Islam with a Mainstream Worldview to help him give up his dependence on drugs and to achieve emotional balance. This rehabilitative change was supported by engagement with Muslim prison chaplains and caring relationships with other Muslim prisoners.

Biography

Chris is a 47-year-old, White British Convert to Mainstream Islam in prison from Anglican Christianity (Church of England). Coming from a "strict" Anglican upbringing which involved going to Church and Sunday School every week and being "taught right from wrong" by his grandmother, conversion to Islam had been a slow and reflective process for Chris.

Chris's journey towards Mainstream Islam was eased by the fact that he had close family members who were also Muslim. Chris's parents had split up a few years before his arrest. His mother remarried a Moroccan and she herself converted to Islam after her marriage. Chris's brother had also been sentenced to prison and he too had converted to Islam during his sentence.

Type of change and Worldview

When Chris started his prison sentence, he described himself as "off the rails" and addicted to drugs and alcohol. He was seeking to reform his life and to find a way to fulfil himself. In prison, Chris found the Muslim prisoners a kind influence: when he became emotionally distressed as a result of his offence (murder), Muslim prisoners were supportive of him and they looked out for him.

Significantly, while Chris was in prison, his grandfather died. Although Chris considered himself Anglican Christian at that time, it was the Muslim prison chaplain who gave him the news of his grandfather's death and he felt the Muslim prison chaplain really supported him. Chris appreciated that, even though he was not Muslim, the Muslim prison chaplain had treated Chris as a "brother".

As a result, Chris began exploring the religion more deeply. He read The Qur'an in English and had discussions around faith with different Muslim prison chaplains and with different prisoners. Chris's interest in Islam was also supported and encouraged by his mother and brother, both Muslim Converts. Chris, however, did not want to rush into changing his religion:

> I wanted to make sure that I was pure in my heart, that I was 100 per cent behind it, that I wanted to take up Islam.

After a long period of reflection and learning about Islam over ten years, Chris slowly built up his knowledge of Islam. This slow process of reflection and searching for knowledge, whereby a person may initially reject their previous beliefs and then, after several years, embrace Islam, is common in the stories of Converts to Islam both inside and outside prison (van Nieuwkerk, 2006; Hermansen, 2014).

The fact that Chris arrived at Islam slowly, taking his Christian background into account, reading a lot, asking a lot of questions and processing feelings of remorse for his crime, resulted in Chris taking up a Mainstream Islamic Worldview of Unity-in-Diversity (see Chapters 4 and 5).

For Chris, the Mainstream Islamic ethos of the importance of family was central to his new Worldview. He maintained a close relationship with his father and siblings who remained with the Church of England, and with his Muslim Convert mother and brother:

> it makes a lot more better for everyone really if we're all, like, in the same sort of, got the same faith.

Chris used the similarities between the Bible and The Qur'an as an important mechanism to connect with both sides of his family.

Rehabilitation

Chris felt that conversion to Islam had given him a new start to life and a second chance:

> Yes, it's like I've got a fresh start, basically, like the pages haven't been written yet and I'm able to set my life out different now rather than my past, like being the way I was in the past.

This sense of a new beginning and a fresh chance to move away from a criminal past is an important aspect of conversion in prison and often enables prisoners to take on a law-abiding identity (Maruna et al, 2006). After his conversion to Islam, however, Chris felt that the prison staff were more suspicious of him.

This sense of suspicion emerged regularly in the interviews of prisoners and especially of **Converts**, who felt that their religious change made them receive more negative attention from prison staff. For some prisoners, this can lead to an antagonistic relationship with prison staff. Chris, however, felt that he was able to respond calmly to any provocations. He felt that Islam helped him control his emotions, that he became calmer, and he moved away from substance abuse to taking control of his life:

> I mean, I've done a lot of reflecting on my past. I mean, I'm in for murder. I killed one of my friends eleven-and-a-half years ago now. But I was in a bad place then.

> That's why, taking up this faith as well, it's learning me to control, it's learning me to be in control of my life. Basically, I'm not going to stray off or nothing like that because I want to do everything right. So, guiding, it's guiding me as well.

The role of religion in avoiding altercations and managing guilt inside prison has been noted in previous research (Clear et al, 2000).

This reflective appraisal of a past which includes processing many painful memories, coupled with feelings of remorse over past actions and a resolve to build a better future, was a common trope in the conversion narratives of many prisoners.

For Chris, this resolve to move away from the mistakes of his past was buoyed by the company of Muslim 'brothers' on the wings, which, as we have seen in Chapters 3 and 4, was a common experience of **Converts**. The 'brothers' were an important emotional support for Chris, and he felt that his new friendships played a crucial role in keeping him committed to his faith and away from crime:

> They [other Muslim prisoners] see me going in the wrong direction, they sort of like pull me back, distract me for about five seconds and then my mind's all clear again.

On the wings, Chris prayed his Obligatory Daily Prayers with a fellow Muslim prisoner. Another 'brother' was teaching him the Arabic alphabet. The time, effort and patience of these Muslim 'brothers' and their desire to help and support him in his journey were inspirational for Chris.

Chris had three and a half years left of his sentence and he wanted to use his time in prison to carry on reading The Qur'an both in Arabic and English and to build up his knowledge of Islam.

Using time in prison to gain religious knowledge was an important way of finding purpose and meaning in life inside for many prisoners.

Aspirations for life after release from prison

Chris chose to convert just before being transferred to an open prison. After his release, he wanted to start applying his knowledge of Islam to lead a crime-free life and to live close to a mosque so that he could be part of a Muslim community and continue to perform the Obligatory Daily Prayers.

Summary

Chris's conversion to Islam with a Mainstream Worldview was a 'a slow burn' which had developed both through a long period of inner reflection, including deep remorse for his crime, education and through relationships with family, Muslim prison chaplains and fellow Muslim prisoners. Mainstream Islam had provided him with a stable and hopeful platform to move towards a crime-free life.

Case study 2: Kadir, 'Convert', HMP Parrett, Category B Prison

In contrast to Chris, whose conversion to Islam took the form of a gradual journey of discovery, Kadir's conversion took place in sudden fits and starts, both inside and outside prison, and was largely the result of relationships with other people rather than as the result of a process of study and inner reflection.

Kadir's story illustrates the ways in which processes of identity development during adolescence, including religious identity, can be heavily influenced by the Worldviews of prisoners' peers (Head, 1999).

Biography

Kadir is a 19-year-old, male, British Black Caribbean, who converted outside prison from Catholicism to Islam.

Kadir was brought up by his grandmother while his father was serving a prison sentence. His grandmother was a practising Catholic and would take him to Sunday Mass. However, he did not feel any connection to the Catholic Christian faith as "it just didn't grab me."

Kadir's father converted to Islam in prison and although soon after his release he stopped practising Islam. Kadir recalls a childhood memory of his father taking him to the mosque for the Friday Prayer where they prayed together. As Kadir saw little of his father, this remained a significant memory.

Kadir became interested in Islam at the age of 11 because a neighbourhood friend had converted to Islam while in custody and they would go regularly to the mosque together. While his friend was involved in crime, he continued to attend the Friday Prayer. Despite the apparent contradiction, Kadir was intrigued by his friend's mix of crime and spirituality: he found this mix appealing.

On Kadir's first visit to the mosque, he met other Muslim 'brothers', who encouraged him to convert to Islam. On his second visit to the mosque on a Friday, Kadir decided he was ready to convert and make the Declaration of Faith (*Shahada*):

> Either way, do it now or I don't do it at all.

So after the Friday Prayer, and without any prior induction or education, Kadir made the Muslim Declaration of Faith (*Shahada*) with the Mosque Imam. Shortly after his conversion to Islam, Kadir had a falling out with his friend and, as a result, his Islam "faded":

> The person that took me on that journey, took me for my Shahada, we fell out, so we no longer spoke, so it kind of left me in a weird place with my religion.

Type of change and Worldview

After being convicted and sentenced to prison, Kadir reconnected with Islam. Initially Kadir was incarcerated in a Young Offenders Institute where he started attending the Friday Congregational Prayer. However, he found the Friday Prayer a volatile place: he had a fight with one of the inmates and was consequently banned from the Friday Prayer and so he again stopped practising Islam.

Later, Kadir was transferred to the adult prison estate, where he again started to engage with his Islam and where he tried to become more regular in performing the Obligatory Daily Prayers. However, he felt that his practice was still inconsistent and he still felt that he had not found his purpose in life.

In the adult estate, Kadir became more solitary in his practice of Islam; he wanted to explore Islam for himself and to discover his purpose in life:

> I'm never follow someone; I always want to do it my own way. Always want to do my own thing.

This desire to explore religion for himself marked a new inward departure which paid spiritual dividends to Kadir: Islam now made Kadir feel spiritually and physically clean, and this was very important to him. He also felt a connection to God and a sense of inner peace. Praying, especially the Friday Congregational Prayer, became important to Kadir:

> Yes it [prayer] brings my spirit peace all the time.

For Kadir, religion had transformed from being largely a matter of copying influential others into a personal journey through which he had reframed his life in terms of worshipping God and seeking to go to Heaven.

> For me to be a Muslim, it means being clean, number one. Number two, it means worshipping Allah, which is God, and it means finding peace within yourself and, one day, hopefully, can be at the inshallah [if God wills] go to Jannah [Heaven].

Aspirations for life after release from prison

For the duration of his sentence, Kadir hoped to become regular in his practice of Islam and he aspired to leave prison with the skills to look after himself and his future family:

> The way I practise my deen [religion], I would just like to insha Allah [God willing] pray five times a day, someday, all the prayers ... wake up to Fajr [Dawn Prayer] every morning and get my religious routine on point.
>
> I would love to do that. But my plans for the future? Insha Allah one day have a family, get married.

Summary

Kadir was a young man who, while liking to feel independent, as a teenager has been highly dependent on his peer group for his religious choices and habits. After a stop-start relationship with Islam, the Obligatory Daily Prayers had begun to represent a break from his chaotic life and a way of finding inner peace and purpose within a Mainstream Islamic Worldview.

The Intensifiers

Intensifiers represent **48 per cent** of our characteristic sample.

Intensifiers are born Muslims who become significantly more devout in prison in terms of performing the Obligatory Daily Prayers more regularly and in finding their religion 'more important' than before they went to prison.

As we have observed in Chapters 3 and 4, our data evidenced the positive relationship between **Intensification** and **Attitude to Rehabilitation**, especially when accompanied with advice and guidance from trusted Muslim prison chaplains within a Mainstream Activist Worldview.

Case study 3: Faheem, 'Intensifier', HMP Severn, Category B Prison

Faheem is a 38-year-old, male, British Pakistani, Born-Muslim serving a life sentence, whose case illustrates this positive relationship between **Intensification in Islam** and **strong Attitude to Rehabilitation**.

Biography

Faheem explained that growing up in England he had experienced a religious upbringing and that until the age of 15 he had attended Islamic Studies classes at the mosque. Although Faheem's family was observant of Islam, in his teenage years he had moved away from Islam as he became heavily involved in crime:

> Obviously when I was young, I used to go to the mosque to learn The Qur'an, but when I got to the age of about 14 or 15, you know, things started to change for me.
>
> I stopped reading The Qur'an and so I forgot a lot of things, Allah forgive me, basically I forgot how to do Wudu [ritual cleaning in preparation for prayer], I was just basically ... I would still be a Muslim, but I wasn't a practising Muslim and then to be honest, for me, at that time things just started to get very bad, you know. I started to dwell [delve] into things that I shouldn't be dwelling [delving] into, you know, I started to obviously be involved with bad groups of people, I started to obviously take drugs, I obviously started to drink alcohol. I started to basically be involved in illegitimate relationships out of marriage, yes, and basically all sorts of crime basically, just a crime-filled life.

When he was 30, Faheem was convicted with a group of friends and he received a three-and-a-half-year sentence. During his imprisonment, Faheem was convicted and sentenced for further historic offences, which meant that, at the time of our interview, Faheem was serving a life sentence.

Type of change and Worldview

Faheem had reconnected seriously with Islam in prison in terms of praying regularly and finding his faith an important component of his life.

At the time of his arrest, Faheem started to reflect on his life outside prison. His involvement in crime had created a distance between him and his family. Yet, despite this, his mother reached out to him in prison and suggested that he use his imprisonment as a time to reflect and turn towards God.

As Faheem was registered as Muslim, the Muslim prison chaplain also reached out to him and registered Faheem for the Friday Congregational Prayer. Faheem said that initially he was embarrassed to attend the Friday Congregational Prayer because he had forgotten even the basic teachings of Islam:

> Yes, it's an embarrassment. You claim to be someone, or you claim to be part of something, but you don't know what you're doing with it, you know?

Despite this initial embarrassment, Faheem decided to copy the actions of other prisoners and continue attending the Friday Congregational Prayer. He also found the Muslim prison chaplain's sermons inspirational as they offered Faheem a way to interpret his criminal past as driven by attractive temptations from Satan (*shaytan*) and his sentence as a God-given opportunity to reform his behaviour:

> There's some good Imams in prison *masha'Allah* [as God wishes]. They can understand the obstacles out there for young people ... for young Muslims and how the shaytan [Satan] can make them look nice to you, like honey. You know, for example, lucrative businesses, drugs, etc, you know, the lifestyle of that. You read about the rap stars and how they enjoy their lives and so he was taking some of that and bringing it into Islam and you know, why Islam says "no" and why if you [had] protected yourself from

> all of them, you wouldn't be where you're sat today, you know. *Alhamdulillah* [Praise be to God] Allah has brought you in here. Now reform yourselves, better yourselves, learn about Islam.
>
> **99**

The Muslim prison chaplain's sermons had inspired Faheem to find meaning in his prison sentence: Faheem had begun to see his sentence as part of God's destiny for him to improve his life. This was a turning point for Faheem. To turn his life around, Faheem aspired to reconnect with his family and his religion:

> It's quite a strange moment in my life. I'll be honest, I'm doing quite a big sentence, you know, so when I sit here, I think to myself, "Allah, I've been taken away from outside society, from my family." I would love to be with my family now, you know. *Alhamdulillah* [Praise be to God] you know, Allah's put me in a place where at least in here, *Alhamdulillah*, I've bettered myself, I've probably increased my chances of living longer, *in sha Allah* [God willing], you know.
>
> **99**

As for our **Convert** Chris, and indeed for two thirds of our sample who either 'always' or 'sometimes' sought advice about Islam from other prisoners, the company of other Muslim prisoners had been instructional for Faheem: his Muslim cellmate had retaught him the basics of Islamic practice including how to perform the ritual washing (*wudu*) before the Obligatory Daily Prayers and how to perform these Prayers. Faheem also joined the Islamic Studies classes in prison and he reacquired his childhood knowledge of reading The Qur'an in Arabic.

In prison, Faheem developed a Worldview of Mainstream Activist Islam which meant that he explicitly connected his renewed faith with his involvement in prison initiatives to support other prisoners: Faheem was on the Violence Reduction Team; he became a Listener for the Samaritans, an Equality Representative, and a Ramadan Representative; and, on being made a Store Orderly by prison staff, he became a Trusted Prisoner. This is how Faheem described his Mainstream Activist Worldview:

> For me to be a Muslim means, *insha Allah* [God willing] to be law-abiding, to be caring, to be respectful, to live within the Sharia of Islam and to try to follow the Sunna of the Prophet. ... And basically, to follow the Islamic way of life and basically, you know, respect all humankind, even take care of animals as well, you know.

Rehabilitation

Turning to Islam had helped Faheem reflect on his crimes and plan a purposeful life, which he felt was a significant change from his attitude in the past:

> I didn't think for the future. I just lived for the moment.

On the advice of the Muslim prison chaplain, Faheem had also joined rehabilitation courses and he felt that Islam had provided him with a framework to think more about the consequences of his actions and to respond in a more positive way to the provocations in prison:

> Obviously, someone can get angry very easy in prison. And how to behave in such a way, you know, because obviously if you get angry as well it's just going to make the situation worse. And so sometimes, being a Muslim, you think to yourself, "You know what? ... I need to think straight away. I'm a Muslim and I need to resolve this before it escalates."

Faheem had also faced significant personal setbacks in prison: he had begun with a six-year sentence, hoping to be out of prison in three years. However, he received two further convictions and had time added on to his sentence for historic crimes, which resulted in a life sentence with a minimum 12-year tariff.

He said that his faith in God and his Islamic values had helped him cope with the distress of these setbacks:

> You've been tried and tested three times and you're still, *Alhamdulillah* [praise be to God], you're still praying, you're still smiling and you're still helping people. I said, "Brother, I'm not even arguing, All I know is Allah's has blessed me with *sabr* [patience], and that *sabr* has only come from prayer."

This use of religious beliefs to frame and to cope with the challenges of the prison environment was described by many of our characteristic sample of prisoners, which enabled them to feel a sense of freedom and self-control while imprisoned (cf. Sykes, 1958; Clear et al, 2000).

Aspirations for life after release from prison

Faheem still had 12 years left of his sentence. He said that he wanted to focus on taking care of his family after his release from prison:

> If I get chance to get out again, I'm just going to wipe my mother's feet with water, *insha Allah* [God willing] and I'm never going to upset her again. I'm going to respect my wife. I want to stay home and I'm not going to get involved with all the haram [forbidden] that I did.

Faheem intended to continue his voluntary work and to continue to be involved with charities and in helping others.

Summary

Faheem was a typical example of a born, previously non-practising Muslim prisoner who reconnected strongly with his faith in prison and intensified his Islamic Worldview.

This reconnection with faith had led to a significant shift in his Worldview to that of Mainstream Activist Islam, which was reflected in his acknowledgement of the damage caused by his crimes to himself and others and in his active commitment to serving others. The role of the Muslim prison chaplain in supporting and encouraging this rehabilitative change was crucial to Faheem's development.

The Shifters

Our qualitative data showed that the nature of prisoners' religious Worldviews could change dramatically in prison, especially through engagement with the prison chaplaincy and under the influence of other prisoners. We have classified such prisoners as 'Shifters'. Shifts in religious Worldviews can occur positively towards Mainstream Islam as well as negatively towards Islamist Extremism and can occur on multiple occasions in a single prison sentence. We discuss both types of shift through the following two case studies.

Case study 4: Ethan, 'Convert-and-Shifter', HMP Forth, Category A Prison

Ethan is a 43-year-old, White British male Convert of Irish heritage.

Biography

Ethan grew up in the north of England, where he described his life as "tough" and "full of hardship". As a child, Ethan received some degree of a religious education, but he turned away from religion as a result of being abused by his mother's violent boyfriend. At a young age, he became involved with drugs and crime. Ethan's first prison sentence was for robbery and drug possession, for which he served a four-year sentence.

Type of change and Worldview

We have categorised Ethan as a Convert-and-Shifter because he had moved from no-religion to Mainstream Islam, to Violent Islamist Extremism, and then gradually back to Mainstream Islam.

During his time in prison, Ethan had experienced a wide range of the risks as well as the rehabilitative benefits of religious conversion and change. During Ethan's first prison sentence, he became interested in religion as his cellmate was a practising Muslim. Ethan became intrigued by the constancy of his cellmate in performing the Obligatory Daily Prayers (see Chapter 3 for further details).

Ethan and his Muslim cellmate began discussing religion and they developed a respectful friendship. This friend introduced Ethan to the Muslim prison chaplain and the three began discussing religion together. Over time, Ethan became increasingly interested in Islam and he asked the Muslim prison chaplain for some literature so that he could explore it more on his own. Through these discussions and through his own reading, Ethan converted to Islam.

During this first prison sentence, Ethan was diagnosed with a mental health disorder and he was released from prison under the Mental Health Act. After his release, Ethan stopped practising Islam and he returned to taking very strong drugs. With increased drug use, Ethan's mental health deteriorated further and he became increasingly paranoid. During a psychotic breakdown, Ethan murdered two people, for which he received a life sentence.

At the time of his second prison sentence, Ethan's mental health was fragile: he was deeply remorseful about his crimes and he was struggling to cope with what he had done. At this time, he was approached by some Muslim prisoners on his wing who saw his vulnerable state and started to look after him. Ethan did not realise it at the time, but these prisoners who had volunteered to support him were in fact grooming him into a Violent Islamist Extremist Worldview. These prisoners gradually convinced Ethan that the only way he could be forgiven for his crimes was if he killed the enemies ("oppressors") of Muslim prisoners in prison for the sake of God:

> He [an unnamed fellow Muslim prisoner] used to bring me food, and he used to come in and talk to me and cuddle me and hold me and say, "Listen, I love you." ... And, other brothers used to come in and say, "Listen, trust me. We've got a plan for you, brother. The sorrow that you feel, we know how to take this sorrow away." I said, "How is that?" And he said, "Listen, the only way that you can get any justification for killing those two innocent people is if you kill one of our oppressors ... in the melee you might even, you're a big strong brother, yes, you might get two or three more, and then all your sins will be wiped away for that, and then you will definitely be accepted into Paradise." And the problem is, at one stage, they turned my head. I actually was starting to believe them.

Under the influence of these prisoners with Violent Islamist Extremist Worldviews, Ethan himself adopted a Violent Islamist Extremist Worldview and became part of their gang hierarchy as "an enforcer". Ethan described beating up many prisoners on the orders of their *Amirs* ('leaders').[1] When Ethan joined the Violent Islamist Extremist gang, he was also told to stop following the Muslim prison chaplain because

> They [the gang leaders] don't like him [the Muslim prison chaplain]. They think he works for the government.

---

[1] For further details, see Chapter 6.

After a while, Ethan started becoming disillusioned with the gang: he noticed that the *Amirs* enforced very strict rules on junior members but did not follow the rules themselves. When the *Amirs* then told Ethan to kill a Muslim prisoner who was smoking "Spice",[2] Ethan felt that this was wrong and he refused. The Violent Islamist Extremist gang started to pressurise him and then turned against Ethan. Ethan then suffered another mental breakdown during which time he attacked and badly injured the gang *Amir*. After Ethan's attack on the *Amir*, the prison authorities moved Ethan to the Segregation Unit for his own safety.

Rehabilitation

During Ethan's second prison sentence, his emotional distress over his crimes and the fear of being attacked made him feel completely hopeless and he tried to kill himself. His guilt over his crimes became overwhelming for him and he continued to self-harm to punish himself and to prevent himself from suicide. Encouraged by a prison chaplain, his prayers focused on seeking forgiveness from God and he used his belief that he was created by God with a body "on loan" from God to dissuade himself gradually from self-harm and suicide, as he slowly shifted away from Islamist Extremism back to Mainstream Islam:

> This body is not mine. It's on loan to me and anything that I do to it, I have to justify when I go before Allah. Yes, I know that this body is on loan to me but here's the thing: I hurt myself now only to prevent me from killing myself. And here's the thing: I know both of them are sins but when you're faced with two choices, take the lesser one every single time. And then when you're stood before or knelt before Him [God] and you're explaining yourself, you say, "Look, they were my choices at the time." And I'm hoping He will forgive me for that.

The Muslim prison chaplain supported this process by suggesting that Ethan interpret his failed suicide attempt as a sign that God was giving him a second chance:

> [The Muslim prison chaplain said], "See it for what it is: a miracle. See it for what it is: that you're here now as a miracle. There's

---

[2] 'Spice' is a prohibited New Psychoactive Substance (NPS), which is illegal to possess in prison in England and Wales per the Psychoactive Substances Act 2016.

> no reason for you to die right now, other than there's still a plan for you."

In prison where it can be challenging to access long-term mental health support, prison officers also became a source of moral support and pastoral care for Ethan and he came to rely on the good relationships with caring prison officers:

> A lot of them [prison officers] care and want to help, and help people like me that are suffering, and they want me to try and get over it.

Summary

Ethan was a Vulnerable Prisoner with severe mental health difficulties, crippling guilt about his crimes and a tendency to act violently. His vulnerability had been preyed upon by Violent Islamist Extremist prisoners.

Ethan's fragile mental health made his relationship of trust with the Muslim prison chaplain critical: at times, this relationship had made the difference between life and death.

As a 'Convert-and-Shifter' who had moved from no-religion to Mainstream Islam to Violent Islamist Extremism and then was shifting gradually back to Mainstream Islam, Ethan had experienced both the intense risks and the rehabilitative, pro-social benefits of religious conversion and change in prison.

Ethan's shift in Worldview from Violent Islamist Extremism to Mainstream Islam is also highlighted in the story of Nadim.

Case study 5: Nadim, 'Intensifier-and-Shifter', HMP Forth, Category A Prison

Nadim is a 45-year-old, British Asian Pakistani, Born-Muslim, who had been convicted of terrorist offences.

Nadim is an example of a prisoner whose Worldview had shifted dramatically in prison from Violent Islamist Extremism to Mainstream Activist Islam. Through this change, Nadim had accrued a wide variety of spiritual and rehabilitative benefits.

Biography

Nadim had grown up in England and, although he had been given a religious education at a mosque near his home, he felt that it was difficult for him to gain "any real purpose or anything or understanding" from his early religious education.

In particular, Nadim had struggled to communicate with the mosque Imams due to language barriers: the mosque Imams spoke Urdu and although Nadim comes from a Pakistani background, as a British-born Muslim he found it difficult to understand Urdu and he became disengaged from the Imams at his local mosque.

Later, lacking any clear religious understanding, Nadim became influenced by Violent Islamist Extremist preachers outside prison and participated in a significant terrorist plot. His conviction was for terrorist offences with a life sentence.

Type of change and Worldview

Nadim is an **Intensifier-and-Shifter**: with the guidance and instruction of Muslim prison chaplains, he had learnt about Islam inside prison and he had experienced a significant change of Worldview from that of Violent Islamist Extremism (as a convicted terrorist offender) to Mainstream Activist Islam.

The Muslim prison chaplain's detailed explanations around the contradictions in Violent Islamist Extremist interpretations of religious belief – for example their use of weak or fabricated sayings of the Prophet Muhammad to justify terrorist violence – were crucial in helping Nadim shift to a Mainstream Islamic Worldview.

Nadim felt that, through his learning with and trust of the Muslim prison chaplain, over time he had developed enough knowledge to assess critically a variety of religious opinions, including understanding that it was wrong simply to pronounce something as forbidden in Islam (*haram*) without proper knowledge:[3]

These things like "What is a *bida*' [religious innovation]?" and "What is forbidden?" these things, on the road, or before prison, certain people who speak Arabic, they might say something and then, just because they speak Arabic or they've got more knowledge of The Qur'an or Hadith [sayings of the Prophet Muhammad] and then they tend to be followed or

---

[3] See Chapter 3, The Islamist risk in conversion to Islam.

> blind-followed without any questions being asked of them. Now you can see there are differences of opinions, there are certain conditions that have to be met, so it's not just clear cut, you know, as some people just say, "Halal" or "Haram" even you know it's not right. Unless it's in The Qur'an, in the Hadis [Hadith], you shouldn't just on your own back say, "This is haram" just [a] clear cut fact when it's not really, And, on the road that seems to be a big problem.

Unlike his childhood religious education at a local mosque, which Nadim had felt was disconnected from his daily life, the Muslim prison chaplains in HMP Forth were good at connecting religion to everyday issues facing Muslim prisoners. With their advice, Nadim liked to apply his knowledge of Islam to his daily life and to his daily interactions. In doing this, Nadim felt that his faith had become serious and sincere.

Rehabilitation

For Nadim, the shift of Worldview to Mainstream Islam had given him inner peace, an inner happiness and a purpose to lead a peaceful life in the community:

> Well, the peace within myself, I feel calm, I feel relaxed, I feel happy and I feel at peace. And then, also, the purpose is that when you read the *hifz* [a section of The Qur'an] and when you read the scripture, The Qur'an, and then knowing that if you live a peaceful life without causing harm to anybody and being good with your community, then the end goal will be peaceful, as well.

Gradually, after a bumpy start, Nadim began to develop good relationships with the prison officers. Nadim felt that he had moved away from the mentality of the 'Us'/prisoners versus 'Them'/prison officers and that he had begun to respond more calmly to the provocations of the prison environment.

For example, Nadim had seen a copy of The Qur'an thrown into a dustbin, possibly by a prison officer. Following the example of the Prophet

Muhammad that he learnt about in prison, Nadim moderated and channelled his behaviour into a legitimate form of protest by submitting a formal complaint to the prison authorities, in answer to which he received a formal apology from the Prison Service.

In this way, Nadim became a **Mainstream Activist Muslim**: to promote tolerance and respect between peoples he learnt Braille and started transcribing Islamic books into Braille for blind prisoners.

Aspirations for life after release from prison

Nadim was serving a long sentence but on release he wanted to continue to find opportunities to help others through translating more Islamic texts into Braille.

Prison had given Nadim time to reflect on the effects of his crime and his incarceration on his family, for which he had experienced deep feelings of shame and remorse. Processing these feelings had strengthened his determination to avoid future crime. His faith inspired him to want to become a role model and leader in his family after his release:

> I'm going to do what's right for myself and what is right for my family and, at the end of the day, what is right for my Islam.

Summary

Nadim is an **'Intensifier-and-Shifter'** whose change of religious Worldview had been brought about in large part through the sustained deconstruction of the Worldview of Violent Islamist Extremism by a knowledgeable and engaged Muslim prison chaplain using the primary sources of Islam.

Nadim's reconnection with his religious faith helped him make sense of his strong feelings of remorse for his crime and helped him develop an emphasis on rehabilitation through service to others. He was confident that his transformed faith would help him return to society successfully and peacefully post release.

The Remainers and Reducers

Moving from examples of prisoners who *increased* their religious practice in prison, we turn to examples of Muslim prisoners whose faith remained unchanged in prison – the **Remainers** – or who *reduced* their commitment to Islam in prison – the **Reducers**.

Both groups predominated in Switzerland and France and among female prisoners. As we have seen in Chapter 3, statistically, **Remaining** and **Reducing** were both connected with weak **Attitude to Rehabilitation**.

Remainers, whose understanding and commitment to their faith remained broadly the same in prison as before, represented **23 per cent** of our total data sample.[4]

Case study 6: Badia, 'Remainer', La Citadelle, Category A, Female Prison, Switzerland

Badia is a 26-year-old, female, Black African Catholic Convert to Mainstream Islam, whose understanding of and commitment to her faith had remained the same in prison.

Biography

Badia converted from Catholicism to Islam outside prison with a group of friends at her place of work. She explained her decision to convert:

> I was missing something ... it made more sense for me to be Muslim than to be Catholic simply.

Badia felt that conversion to Islam had given her unstable life outside prison a measure of inner stability and peace:

> My life is not really what one calls a stable life, ... I mean that from time to time, I'm homeless from time to time, I'm in a home [hostel for the homeless] so it's not really a life. It's a life that we often need God, for my part in any case and that's what he [the Prophet Muhammad] brings me. The Prophet brings me a lot of love, I have a lot of gratitude in him.

---

[4] Remainers represented 52 per cent of Muslim prisoners in Switzerland, 41 per cent of Muslim prisoners in France and 13 per cent of Muslim prisoners in England.

Before prison, religion was an important part of Badia's life, which is similar to the experiences of a majority of respondents in our Swiss and French samples.[5]

Type of religious change and Worldview

In prison, Badia's understanding and practice of religion had not changed and therefore we have classified her as a '**Remainer**':

No, it [my religion] hasn't changed. No, no, it's the same.

Badia spent some time in prison reading The Qur'an and other religious books and, when she felt the need, she prayed:

Not every day. From time to time. I would like to pray every day, but I do not. Maybe I do not need or feel it. I do not yet pray every day.

Like the majority of our female prisoner participants (**73 per cent**), Badia held a Mainstream Muslim Worldview and, like a lot of the respondents, Badia felt that in prison she had more time to pray, especially because she spent a lot of time alone in her cell (Wilkinson et al, 2021). At these times, Badia felt that Islam gave her a sense of peace, love and support:

When I'm alone in a cell, unfortunately it's [the] examples where you're often alone. ... When, for example, you're in a group or in a community [outside prison] you feel supported. So, for my part, it's when I'm alone in my room. I need to think, I need a certain peace, a certain feeling, a certain love, so that's it.

---

[5] Our questionnaires showed that more than 80 per cent of respondents in Switzerland and France felt that religion was 'quite important' or 'very important' in their life before prison, compared with 60 per cent in England.

In contrast to the experiences of **Converts** and **Intensifiers** in **England** described earlier, in her Swiss prison, Badia did not have access to the Friday Congregational Prayer nor was she provided with regular contact with a Muslim prison chaplain:

> I saw him once [a Muslim prison chaplain]. Unfortunately, I had the opportunity to see him only once because we do not often have the opportunity to see him. But I asked again to see him but, for now, I have not had any news.

Badia wished that she had access in prison to Islamic Studies classes and to communal religious services such as the Friday Congregational Prayer and the *Taraweeh* prayers during Ramadan.

Badia had not met the Christian prison chaplains and she said that she felt uncomfortable going to the Christian religious services. This lack of access to Muslim prison chaplaincy is similar to the experiences of a majority of women whom we interviewed, especially in Switzerland, and was one of the underlying factors that made prison a more 'reducing' religious environment for Swiss prisoners and especially for Swiss women.

Aspirations for life after release from prison

Badia was looking forward to reconnecting with her family:

> Yeah, to see my family: that's it.

Badia does not anticipate any changes to her religious practice, and her prison does not offer her any formal or informal opportunities to deepen her religious understanding.

Summary

Badia is an example of a **Remainer** whose practice and understanding of religion had not changed significantly in prison. In prison, with little access to support from a Muslim prison chaplain or any opportunity to engage with communal religious activities, Badia's commitment to Islam remained the same as outside prison. Badia's religiosity was expressed personally and individually, rather than as part of a collective experience or identity. As we have observed in our statistical data, this lack of deepening of religious understanding produced a weakening effect on **Attitude to Rehabilitation** and therefore increased prisoners' chances of reoffending post release.

Case study 7: Hani, 'Reducer', Hauterive, Category B Prison, France

Hani is a 28-year-old, male, French National, Born-Muslim of North African heritage in Hauterive, Category B Prison, France.

Biography

During his childhood in France, Hani was taught the basic beliefs and practices of Islam and he attended Arabic school. Although Hani presented himself as a secular non-practising Muslim, he possessed a foundation of religious knowledge and belonged to a religious family. Despite this religious knowledge, he considered himself to be a non-practising Muslim and perceived himself as belonging to a religious community that "got lost":

> We were taught the basics of religion, and then it is everybody according to his degree of faith. You see, everybody has their own degree of faith. ... For me, Islam is a religion in which one is aiming at something else after death. ... Islam is always a religion of peace, that encourages peace. It's the opposite of what we do. I'm telling you honestly. We got lost.

At school, Hani had got involved in some "crap" and he said that he experienced racism. He left school without completing his education and became involved in using and dealing drugs, as well as theft.

Hani is characteristic of many young adults imprisoned in France: he came from a deprived neighbourhood where he admitted to consuming a lot of hashish, even after going to prison.

During our interview, Hani seemed intoxicated: he was often mumbling, had difficulty finding his words, and was staring blankly. Hani was angry and seemed disconnected and hopeless about his future. His story is consistent with the descriptions of the 'nihilist generation' of young French Muslims described by Olivier Roy (Roy, 2016).

Type of change and Worldview

Hani was a Mainstream Muslim who described his religion as follows:

> For me, being Muslim is to be submitted to God, but from one's own free will, and through worshipping and not through force, but worship and love.

Hani's religious Worldview had remained the same in prison:

> Islam before prison or after prison, it's the same.

Hani, when asked about his religious practice, described how in prison his practice of his faith had decreased:

> My practice changed in the bad sense. I'm not lying: since I am in prison, I practise less. It's sad to say, but it is the truth: at the moment my heart is too black to think about Islam.

By "my heart is too black to think about Islam", Hani meant that he did not feel he could follow his Islam as he was now involved in behaviour, including in prison, that went against Islam's religious teachings and so he could not live up to the values of Islam:

> I am not going to lie to you: here, we are too tempted by bad things. I am telling you honestly: here we are more tempted by things that are not ok with Islam. ... Like smoking a joint. Or if somebody talks to me in a bad manner or insults my mother, I react badly, and I hit him. And that is opposite to Islam.

Since arriving in prison, Hani had stopped praying entirely:

> Since I put a foot in here, I did not pray at all.

For Hani,

> It is not easy to be in prison, frankly. I have not seen my family for a long time. It is not easy.

Hani explained that he felt lonely and that he did not really enjoy friendships with the other prisoners. He did not discuss religion with other prisoners because

> [I do not want] to be assimilated to some people [that is, terrorist offenders].

This fear influenced his decision not to practise his religion in prison, and Hani avoided meeting with the Muslim prison chaplain or attending any of the Muslim chaplaincy services.

Hani's experience was typical of the fact that, in France, prisoners feel that talking about religion is often quickly linked by the authorities and other prisoners to terrorism. On many occasions, Hani said things that showed that he had more religious education than he wanted to admit in our interview. This was probably linked to his fears of being regarded as an extremist in prison.

Rehabilitation

Hani felt that if he had followed his religion outside prison he would not have ended up in prison:

> When you end up in prison, normally, it's not because you followed Islam. If you follow Islam correctly, you don't end up in prison.

Whereas Converts and Intensifiers, especially those with regular access to Muslim prison chaplains, often interpreted their prison sentence as an opportunity from God to make a fresh start, Hani as a reducer interpreted his imprisonment as a punishment from God:

> I've not been a good Muslim in the sense that I didn't do good deeds, but I did a lot of bad ones and God punished me. But I'd rather have the consequences of my acts on earth than in the afterlife.

However, despite this remorse, Hani was pessimistic about being able to make any type of positive change in his life and was sure he would end up in prison again.

Aspirations for life after release from prison

Hani was pessimistic about his chances of resettling successfully in society after leaving prison:

> Honestly, I don't see myself settling down after [this prison sentence]. I will come back here. I have a criminal record.

For Hani, the biggest challenge was finding employment with a criminal record: he felt that he would not be able to fulfil his role as a provider for a family without securing proper work and therefore he felt unable to move on in his life and get married.

Summary

Hani provides a typical example of a French Muslim prisoner. Although Hani had had a religious education as a child, he was reluctant to discuss his religious beliefs and he avoided participating in communal religious activities in prison because of a fear of being regarded by the prison authorities as an extremist. Hani's dependence on drugs and his general pessimism about his future is representative of a nihilist Worldview among French Muslim prisoners which has been described in previous research (Roy, 2016).

Hani's sense of hopelessness and his turning away from religion due to a fear of being regarded as an extremist prisoner is similar to the experiences of some of the women in our research, a quarter of whom were **Reducers**.

Like Hani, many of the women had experienced multiple traumas and had found it difficult to take responsibility for their crimes or engage with their faith. Hani's fear that practising his Islam in prison would lead to discrimination and suspicion was also a concern for many of the women, who, to avoid being targeted in prison, did not overtly express their faith (Schneuwly Purdie et al, 2021).

Conclusion: The lives of Muslim prisoners exhibit rehabilitation, risk, volatility and change

The seven case studies we have presented here of different types of Muslim prisoner illustrate both the significant opportunities for rehabilitation presented by following Islam in prison, as well as the risks of being drawn into Islamist Extremism and/or being tarred with the Extremist brush.

We have highlighted the multiple changes in religious Worldview and identity in different periods of the seven participants' lives, which illustrate how prisoners' religiosity is often in a state of flux and change.

The role of the Muslim prison chaplaincy in supporting or failing to support the religiosity of prisoners has been highlighted in all seven case studies as a significant factor in the levels of prisoners' engagement with their faith and its knock-on effects in terms of rehabilitation.

In the next chapter, we discuss in more detail the significant role of Muslim prison chaplains in prisoners' experiences of their faith.

Caring for Muslim prisoners: Muslim prison chaplaincy

In the previous chapter, we evidenced the pivotal role of chaplaincy in many of the positive rehabilitative changes in the lives of Muslim prisoners, such as the discovery of meaning and purpose in life, and that the absence of effective chaplaincy can contribute to a reduction of faith, to extremism and to nihilistic despair. We have also seen in Chapter 3 how the factor **Engagement in Chaplaincy** was a significant predictor of strong **Attitude to Rehabilitation**.

In this chapter, we describe in detail how chaplaincy and institutional aspects of Islam in prison make a difference to Muslim prisoners' lives. We do this in order to provide some guiding principles for best chaplaincy practice in supporting the rehabilitation of Muslim prisoners.

History of prison chaplaincy

Historically, the role of religion, and especially Protestant Christianity, was central to the development of the modern prison (Ignatieff,1989). In the 18th and 19th centuries, non-conformist Protestants such as the Quakers believed that religious values should penetrate the heart of social and political life. This belief led them to be active in social and economic reforms.

One particular concern was the reform of the punishment of criminals: through reflection and hard work, reformers sought alignment between the punishment of criminals and the religious values of forgiveness and personal reform. This prison reform movement resulted in a gradual shift from corporal forms of punishment to the establishment of prison regimes that would lead to the moral reform of offenders. Thus, the locus of punishment shifted from punishment of the body, to control and reform of the mind (Foucault, 1979).

In consequence, prisons were built upon ideas of collective control and with a focus on moral education; regimes were established on discipline, hard work and an austere lifestyle (Ignatieff, 1989). In order to oversee this process of religious and moral prisoner transformation, since the 19th century prison chaplaincy has, to varying degrees and in different ways, formed an integral part of European prison regimes.

Statutory Duties, professional roles and experience

In England and Wales, the role of Anglican Christian prison chaplains is legally prescribed and is integrated into prison management.[1] Over the last two decades, prison chaplaincy in England has also experienced significant diversification and a shift to a pluralistic multi-faith approach (Tipton and Todd, 2011).

While prison chaplaincy is still centred upon faith provision for prisoners and staff, by virtue of their job descriptions and PSIs, prison chaplains are also obliged to undertake a wide range of Statutory Duties (Ministry of Justice, 2016).

In England and Wales, the Statutory Duties of prison chaplains include:

- visiting new arrivals to the prison within 24 hours of reception;

- checking on the formal registration of faith or no faith of newly received prisoners;

- daily visits to the Segregation Unit and recording their visits;

- visiting the Health Care Unit to speak with and check on the welfare of prisoners in the unit.

More recently, PSIs and prison policy have emphasised the role of prison chaplains and other prison staff in managing extremism in prison (Ministry of Justice, 2011).

---

[1] Prison Act 1952, s 7(4).

In short, in England and Wales prison chaplains are integrated into the core functions of prison.

The development of Muslim prison chaplaincy in England, France and Switzerland

Over the last two decades, *Muslim* prison chaplaincy in Europe, and in England and Wales in particular, has experienced significant development and professionalisation (Gilliat-Ray et al, 2013).

The development of Muslim prison chaplaincy in England and Wales

Since 2001, these developments have included the:

- appointment of a dedicated Muslim Advisor to HMPPS;

- establishment of full-time professional Muslim prison chaplains;

- coordination and support from the Muslim Chaplains' Association and the Community Chaplaincy Association.

As of March 2017, these developments have meant that in England, HMPPS employed:

- 23 full-time Muslim prison chaplains at management grade;

- 71 Muslim prison chaplains (37 full-time; 34 part-time) below management grade;

- sessional and volunteer Muslim prison chaplains, for which records are not kept centrally by the Ministry of Justice (Ministry of Justice, 2017).

The development of Muslim prison chaplaincy in France

In France, the right to exercise prison chaplaincy is recognised for six faith groups (*cultes*):

- Catholic Christianity

- Protestant Christianity

- Judaism

- Islam

- Buddhism

- Jehovah's Witnesses

The structure of each faith's prison chaplaincy is similar and includes:

- a national prison chaplain;

- regional prison chaplains;

- local prison chaplains working in their local prisons.

However, in accordance with the principle of *laïcité* (secularity), which outlaws the influence of religion over public life and state policy, as well as guaranteeing freedom of private religious belief and practice (Martínez-Ariño and Zwilling, 2020), prison chaplains do not have direct access to prisoners.

- Prison chaplains may only meet prisoners at their express request. In this way, prison chaplains in France are significantly less integrated into the core statutory functions of prison life than they are in England and Wales.

- In addition to their pastoral duties, French prison chaplains organise religious celebrations and sometimes religious classes and discussion groups.

- There are approximately 190 Muslim prison chaplains working in the French prison system (Sénat, 2016).

The development of Muslim prison chaplaincy in Switzerland

In Switzerland, prison chaplaincy is a prerogative of the Roman Catholic and the Evangelical Reformed Churches. Their prison chaplains adopt a 'universalist' approach to prison chaplaincy, which means that they visit and support all prisoners regardless of their religion. For a Muslim prison chaplain to conduct the Friday Prayer or to run an Islamic Studies class, a Muslim volunteer must be found from the local community (Schneuwly Purdie, 2011).

In Switzerland, there is currently only one professional Muslim prison chaplain, who is based in a Category A prison in the Canton of Zurich. At all other Swiss prisons, the collective rituals, such as the Friday Prayer, Eid al-Adha and Eid al-Fitr, are organised by Christian prison chaplains or by community volunteers.

Therefore, despite the increasing marginality of historical forms of organised religion in contemporary Western society, prison chaplaincy continues to maintain a presence within European prison systems, if only to guarantee the inmates' freedom of religion (Tipton and Todd, 2011).

Building on what is already known about prison chaplains, we sought to understand the role of the prison chaplaincy in influencing rehabilitative religious change among Muslim prisoners.

Prisoner 'Engagement with Chaplaincy'

The strong and significantly rehabilitative effects of prisoners' engagement with prison chaplaincy have been borne out in previous chapters:

- Statistically speaking, the factor **Engagement with Chaplaincy** was a significant ingredient for transforming prisoners' religiosity into a productive rehabilitative force.[2]

---

[2] 'Engagement with Chaplaincy' was strongly and significantly associated with (0.420; $p = 0.000$) positive prisoner 'Attitude to Rehabilitation'.

- From the seven case studies in Chapter 7, we saw how **Engagement with Chaplaincy** could make a vital contribution to rehabilitative shifts of Worldview by prisoners from Islamist Extremism to Mainstream Islam.
- We have seen in the cases of individual prisoners how developing relationships of mutual trust and respect with prison chaplains from their own faith and from other faiths can be life changing in a positive sense, when, for example, chaplains conveyed to prisoners a sense of hope that God had not abandoned them and that a path to a successful future was still available.

Muslim prisoners' generally positive experiences of engagement with Muslim prison chaplaincy were also strongly borne out in further analysis of our questionnaires (see Figure 8.1).

In **England, Switzerland and France**, our data sample showed that:

- **53 per cent** of our sample of Muslim prisoners had a '**high**' level of **Engagement with Chaplaincy** in terms of regularly attending chaplaincy events and 'often' or 'always' seeking the religious advice of chaplains;
- **10 per cent** of our sample of Muslim prisoners had a 'low' level of **Engagement with Chaplaincy**.

Figure 8.1: Engagement with chaplaincy

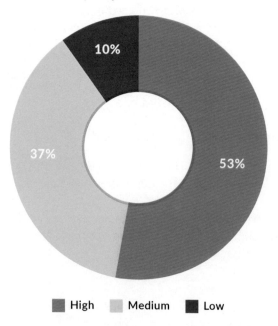

This positive experience of Muslim prison chaplaincy was echoed in our interviews:

- **86 per cent** of our sample of Muslim prisoners mentioned their relationship with a Muslim prison chaplain in **appreciative terms**.
- **14 per cent** of our sample of Muslim prisoners mentioned their relationship with a Muslim prison chaplain in terms of **conflict or tension**.

Supporting rehabilitation

Muslim prison chaplains themselves saw assisting prisoners' engagement with rehabilitation and desisting from crime as a core pastoral component of their work. For example, a female Muslim prison chaplain at HMP Parrett, Category B Prison explained,

> As I said to you, to see the residents as human, I think it's also my challenge. ... How far can I reach with this person? That this person starts liking and loving herself or himself and then says, "Actually, it just makes sense that, yes. I could do it that way and actually, I will benefit from that."

As we have seen in Chapter 6 in the case of Nadim, Muslim prison chaplains focus on supporting rehabilitation by providing a sustained religious education in Islam, which can nudge prisoners away from extremism and towards Mainstream Islam. For example, a male Muslim prison chaplain in Switzerland (Fontgrise, Category B Prison) felt that helping prisoners adopt a Middle Path in balancing their faith was an important part of his role:

> As soon as I start, I try to show the Middle Way of religion, the way that we should all take, the one that the Prophet [Muhammad] recommended to us. This obligatory Middle Way, avoiding the extremes. ... So, my goal is really to bring that Middle Path. I try on my side, and he tries on his side until he's on that Middle Path.

These largely positive and rehabilitative experiences of **Engagement with Chaplaincy**[3] were generated by the mechanisms of:

1. the Friday Congregational Prayer and other acts of collective worship;
2. Islamic Studies classes;
3. pastoral care, both through Statutory Duties and through informal visits and encounters.

FRIDAY CONGREGATIONAL PRAYER

The Friday Congregational Prayer (Salat al-Jumu'a) is the only regular Muslim prayer obligatorily performed in congregation.

It consists of a brief Friday Sermon (*khutba*) delivered in prison by the Muslim prison chaplain in the role of the Imam.

This brief Friday Sermon (*khutba*) is followed by an Obligatory Prayer of only two cycles of prayer (*rakats*) of standing, bowing and prostrating (rather than the usual four cycles of prayer of the Midday Prayer (*dhuhur*)) because listening to the Friday Sermon (*khutba*) stands in place of two cycles of prayer.

Therefore, listening to the Friday Sermon in silence is an obligatory act of worship.

Friday Congregational Prayer

A core requirement for Muslim prison chaplains in England and Wales and in France is leading the Friday Congregational Prayer (*jumu'a*).

In England, some prisons hold two Friday Congregational Prayers: one for Vulnerable Prisoners (usually sex offenders) and another for all other prisoners. In some prisons, this requires two Muslim prison chaplains to lead two Friday Congregational Prayers.[4]

---

[3] Together, the factors 'Religious Intensification' and 'Engagement with Chaplaincy' could successfully predict 30 per cent of the variance underlying prisoners' 'Attitude to Rehabilitation'.

[4] In our sample of prisons, the main group of Muslim prisoners was always larger than the vulnerable prisoner population. In the Category A Prison, HMP Forth, Muslim prison chaplains were confronted by a further challenge presented by a small group of Muslim prisoners housed in the Close Supervision Unit (CSU). The Muslim prison chaplains

Notwithstanding some of the logistical challenges presented by large congregational gatherings in prison, the Muslim prison chaplains emphasised the social and spiritual benefits of the Friday Congregational Prayer for prisoners. For example, a male Muslim prison chaplain at HMP Severn, Category B Prison emphasised both its social and spiritual benefits for prisoners:

> It [the Friday Congregational Prayer] gets them together, they enjoy that. They get a message of course. We do get feedback from them as well to say it's good, the subject that we deliver, they learn from it. Yes, I think it's a good thing for them.

The prisoner experience of the Friday Prayer

Dedicated mosques and dedicated spaces for Friday Congregational Prayer

The quality of the space allocated for the Friday Congregational Prayer and congregational Prayer was generally perceived by Muslim prisoners as an important marker of respect (or lack of respect) for their faith and we observed a strong, significant[5] association between our variable that measured prisoners' perceptions of **Religious Provision** in their prison and the variable that measured respect between prison staff and prisoners. For example, the Governing Governor of HMP Cherwell, Category C Prison had authorised a dedicated mosque space and this decision had won her affection and trust in the eyes of many Muslim prisoners (see Image 8.1).

Overall, in **England, Switzerland and France, 80 per cent** of prisoners were satisfied with the place allocated for the Friday Prayer and were appreciative of the spaces that were allocated for Muslim events (see Images 8.1, 8.3, 8.5 and 8.7).

In prisons with dedicated mosques, trusted prisoners could become mosque orderlies and we noticed that they took considerable pains and pride in the upkeep of these dedicated mosques. For example, the dedicated mosque at HMP Stour, Category D Prison is a converted classroom with a prayer 'niche' (*mihrab*) jutting out into the garden beyond (see Image 8.3).

---

tended to rotate leading the Friday Prayer for this small group of prisoners, or to enable one prisoner to lead the others prisoners in the absence of the Muslim prison chaplain.

[5] $p = 0.08$.

Image 8.1: The dedicated mosque at HMP Cherwell

At HMP Stour we found a prisoner methodically painting the mosque, using masking tape to keep straight lines. The mosque orderly felt pride in keeping this mosque spotlessly clean. Another male Muslim prisoner at HMP Stour, Category D Prison, who regularly attended this dedicated mosque told us,

“

This mosque is the best thing about this prison.

”

We noticed that this dedicated mosque was an oasis of calm, with prisoners popping in and out to pray, rest for a few minutes or to read from a well-stocked library of Islamic books (see Image 8.3).

The differences in the institutional recognition of Islam in prison and in Muslim prison chaplaincy in England, Switzerland and France were reflected in differences in the prayer spaces allocated for the Friday Prayer.

The English prisons referred to earlier all contained dedicated mosque spaces and ablution (*wudu*) areas (see Images 8.2, 8.4, 8.6 and 8.7). In comparison, in Swiss prisons, multi-purpose, undedicated areas which doubled as a computer room (Prison de Doriath, Image 8.8) and a sports hall (Prison de Fontgrise, Image 8.9) served as the spaces for Friday Congregational Prayer.

These differences were symptomatic of the different levels of dedicated Muslim chaplaincy provision in England and in Switzerland: in England at

Image 8.2: The ablution (*wudu*) area at HMP Cherwell

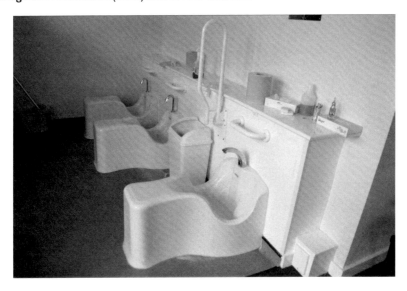

Image 8.3: The dedicated mosque at HMP Stour

the time of research there existed 94 professional Muslim prison chaplains, both full-time and part-time, whereas in Switzerland there was just one.

Learning through the Friday Congregational Prayer

For **Converts and Intensifiers**, the Friday Congregational Prayer was often the first occasion on which they (re)engaged with religious learning.

Image 8.4: The ablution (*wudu*) area at HMP Stour

Image 8.5: The dedicated mosque at HMP Severn

Image 8.6: The ablution (*wudu*) area at HMP Severn

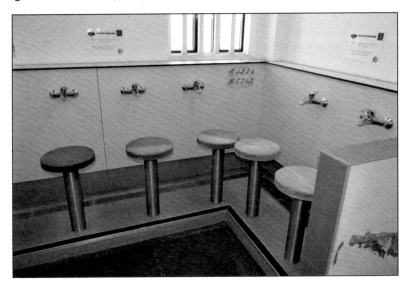

Image 8.7: The Multi-faith Prayer Hall ready for the Friday Prayer during the Covid-19 pandemic at HMP Parrett

Image 8.8: The computer room that is cleared for the Friday Prayer at Prison de Doriath, Switzerland

Image 8.9: The sports hall that is used for the Friday Prayer at Prison de Fontgrise, Switzerland

For example, Suleiman (male, 26, Black British, Convert, HMP Parrett, Category B Prison) said that he had learnt the basic practices of Islam by attending the Friday Congregational Prayer.

> The actions of prayer, as well, I learnt that very quickly from being in Jumu'a [Friday Congregational Prayer].

Arash (male, 25, Turkish, Intensifier, HMP Cherwell, Category C Prison) described relearning the basic teachings of Islam from the Muslim prison chaplain by attending the Friday Prayer:

> I think that was the icebreaker: attending prayers, attending Islamic gatherings, learning the basic, basic things of Islam such, as you know, the Five Principles, Five Pillars and how to pray. What's to make or do, to make *ghusul* [major ablution]. Those sort of things, you don't know. So, when you do start to do those things and you start to pray five times a day or four times a day, however many, gradually it all adds to your *Iman* [faith] increasing.

Gary (male, 34, British White, Convert, HMP Cherwell, Category C Prison) described how important it was for him to repeat his Declaration of Faith (*Shahada*) at the Friday Congregational Prayer and to feel accepted by the congregation:

> I said [to the Muslim Prison chaplain], "Could we do my *Shahada* [Declaration of Faith] again, but in the full congregation?' [He replied], "No problem." And on that Friday, when that Friday came, he called me out, sat there, took my *Shahada* with me, and then the eruption with all the brothers, and it was beautiful, it was absolutely beautiful, it's not a feeling that you ever forget.

The Sermon (Khutba)

The sermon (*Khutba*) lies at the heart of the Friday Congregational Prayer. In and of itself, the sermon provided a significant opportunity for Muslim prison chaplains to preach around the core rehabilitative values of Mainstream Islam. The themes of the need for prisoners to develop the virtues of mindfulness of God (*taqwa*), repentance to God (*tawba*) and reliance on God (*tawakkul*) constituted the key messages of the 12 sermons that we attended.

For example, at HMP Cherwell, Category C Prison, the Muslim prison chaplain explained that:

> the root of *taqwa* [mindfulness of God] is to build a barrier against the anger of God.

At the Friday Prayer for Vulnerable Prisoners [mostly sex offenders] at HMP Severn, Category B Prison, during Ramadan, the Muslim prison chaplain explained with obvious rehabilitative undertones that

> Ramadan is the month of seeking forgiveness. The blessed Prophet said, "Woe to the one who does not find forgiveness in the month of Ramadan." The condition of *tawba* [making repentance] is that you resolve never to repeat that sin again.

We observed that prisoners were almost universally respectful of the rulings and protocols around the correct observance of the Friday Congregational Prayer, including showering (*ghusul*) beforehand, dressing smartly, and listening attentively and without interruption to the sermon.

Participants tended to confirm their serious attitude to the Friday Prayer at interview. Suleiman said,

> I can say I'm following the *deen* [Islam]. I take Friday seriously, when I'm praying, very seriously. And the *masjid*, I wouldn't say that I pray *Salat* every day, that's something I need to work on in myself. But I respect that, I respect Allah so much … when I come to *Jumu'a* [the Friday Congregational Prayer] every week, you will only see me in the front row. I don't like to conversate [*sic*] with people, … I know the etiquette of being in *Jumu'a*. So when you see me in *Jumu'a*, I'll only be in the front row, never talking.

Prisoners' dissatisfaction with the Friday Prayer

For many of the prisoners, attending the Friday Congregational Prayer was an important part of their religious practice and, as the chaplain at HMP Severn had observed, their normal experience was to gain spiritual, social and rehabilitative benefits from it. With fewer distractions inside prison than in the outside world, they felt they could attend the Friday Congregational Prayer more regularly.

Nevertheless, the Friday Congregational Prayer also became a focus of dissatisfaction among some of the prisoners. For example, a Shia Muslim prisoner at HMP Cherwell, Category C Prison felt that the Sunni Muslim prison chaplain did not pay enough respect in his sermons to the family of the Prophet Muhammad.

Also, as we have seen in Chapter 4, issues of the amount of time allocated in the prison regime to enable prisoners to shower (take *ghusul*) before Friday Prayer was also a point of contention: some prisoners felt rushed and disrespected by prison officers, who, they felt, did not understand the importance of this practice of preparing oneself to attend the Friday Congregational Prayer.

Muslim prison chaplain avoidance of addressing contemporary issues

One prisoner spoke about how the sermons of the Muslim prison chaplains at HMP Severn, Category B Prison were cyclical and could therefore get boring. This repetitive element was probably exacerbated by the fact that – as a Muslim prison chaplain explained to us – HMPPS Chaplaincy Headquarters had advised Muslim prison chaplains to steer clear of commentating on contemporary affairs, which traditionally is part of the sermon at the Friday Congregational Prayer.

This advice was adhered to on all the occasions that we observed, except once: after the murders of 51 Muslim worshippers by a far-right terrorist in Christchurch, New Zealand in March 2019. On this occasion, the Muslim prison chaplain preached,

> As you know 49 people were made *shuhada* [martyrs for God] in New Zealand today. This shows how much people hate Islam.

Afterwards, the Muslim prison chaplain clearly realised that, in a fit of anger and emotion, he had overstepped the mark in this sermon because the following week, the same Muslim prison chaplain said in his sermon,

> The events of Christchurch have shown us that a minority of people have hatred; but the solidarity that has been shown to Muslims by the people of New Zealand has been moving. This is because we are all human.

Thus in his second sermon, the same Muslim prison chaplain stressed the shared humanity of all human beings. Therefore, our observation of one foray by one Muslim prison chaplain into addressing a contemporary affair showed us why Muslim prison chaplains have been advised to steer clear of contemporary issues.[6]

---

[6] We were also told of an occasion when a Muslim prison chaplain asked his congregation to pray for the British soldier, Fusilier Lee Rigby, who had been murdered on 22 May 2013 by two Muslim Converts, Michael Adebolajo and Michael Adebowale. The Muslim prison chaplain received death threats from prisoners.

Nevertheless, this silence on contemporary affairs is not ideal: it means that controversial topics are not addressed in a direct, mature manner by an educated Muslim prison chaplain and therefore the topics can come out 'sideways' in prisoner conversations on the wings. For example, we were present at HMP Forth, Category A Prison observing the Friday Congregational Prayer in the immediate aftermath of a BBC documentary which exposed 'temporary' or 'pleasure' marriage endorsed by rogue Shia clerics in Iraq in a way which amounted to prostitution.[7] After the programme, the Muslim prisoners were discussing the matter a lot and, on the way to the prison Friday Congregational Prayer, we overheard a couple of prisoners making violently anti-Shia Muslim comments. However, in the sermon, the Muslim prison chaplain made no reference to what so many of their congregants were discussing, when it might have been constructively addressed.

Disruptions to the Friday Prayer

Some of our research participants also spoke of disruptions to the Friday Congregational Prayer by prisoners who came to the Friday Prayer to socialise, to settle grievances or to deal drugs. For example, we were told of an occasion when, at the same time as the Muslim prison chaplain at HMP Severn, Category B Prison led the Friday Congregational Prayer, a prisoner led a parallel Friday Congregational Prayer in the same room, which caused mayhem in the congregation.[8]

During three Friday Congregational Prayers – at HMP Forth, Category A Prison, HMP Severn, Category B Prison and HMP Cherwell, Category C Prison – we witnessed prisoners dealing drugs with apparent impunity at the back of the mosque, which bore out the accounts of other prisoners about abuse of the Friday Congregational Prayer by a small minority of prisoners.

---

[7] *Undercover with the Clerics: Iraq's Secret Sex Trade* (BBC, 2019).

[8] Some prisoners described the different strategies that Muslim prison chaplains used to deal with disruptive prisoners:
- some Muslim prison chaplains banned disruptive prisoners from attending the Friday Congregational Prayer;
- some Muslim prison chaplains halted their sermons and respectfully told disruptive prisoners prisoner/s to stop their behaviour;
- some Muslim prison chaplains ignored disruptions in the Friday Congregational Prayer and carried on.

    None of the strategies was entirely successful and chaplains acknowledge that it is a challenge inside prison to handle disruptions to Friday Congregational Prayer.

The format of the Friday Congregational Prayer

The particular format chosen by the majority of Muslim prison chaplains for the Friday Congregational Prayer also leaves the occasion more open to disruption than necessary.

In eight of the 12 sermons that we observed, 15–20 minutes of the first of the customary two sermons was entirely in Arabic, only then followed by a shorter explanation (*bayan*) in English.

Some Muslim prison chaplains reversed this order: just before the Friday Congregational Prayer itself, they gave the full sermon in English, followed by the summarised sermon in Arabic. To our mind, this format is better suited to the prison environment because it allows congregants to absorb the important messages of the sermon to which they are obliged to listen, without getting bored or distracted. Thus, this format better fulfils the purposes of the Friday Congregational Prayer to remind congregants of their obligations before God.

Religious festivals and other events

The Muslim chaplains also took a lead role in the provision of other religious events and festivals such as the two Eid Holidays. In English and Welsh prisons, the issue of celebrating Muslim festivals – such as Eid al-Fitr after the month of Ramadan, and Eid al-Adha after the *Hajj* (Pilgrimage) – has for many decades been appropriately addressed.

While the specific way in which Eid is celebrated may vary from prison to prison, Muslim prison chaplains in all jurisdictions stressed the importance of the congregational prayers and the sharing of food as a way of commemorating Eid in prison.

By contrast, due to security issues, at HMP Severn, Category B Prison, the privilege for prisoners to gather to share food at Eid had been curtailed because of a disruptive incident at a recent Eid celebration. Therefore, at HMP Severn celebrating Muslim festivals had become a source of considerable tension and mistrust between the Muslim prison chaplains and prisoners, which was latched onto by Islamist prisoners to corroborate their story that the Muslim chaplains were merely government stooges.

In addition to overseeing the weekly Friday Congregational Prayers and their routine Statutory Duties, during our research the Muslim prison chaplains occasionally received requests to officiate marriage ceremonies for prisoners. For example, in HMP Cherwell, Category C Prison, our research team had the opportunity to attend a prison Muslim wedding ceremony. The managing prison chaplain explained that in most cases he would discourage prisoners from having a wedding ceremony in prison and would suggest that a prisoner wait until they were released. However, in this case the prisoner was serving a life sentence and he was being visited by his fiancée. The prisoner felt uncomfortable when his fiancée visited owing to their physical closeness and he asked the Muslim chaplain to marry them so that they could be intimate with each other in a permitted (halal) way. The ceremony was held in the prison administrative offices with members of the prisoner's family, some prison officers and Muslim prison chaplains in attendance. The prisoner himself catered the reception that followed.

This event illustrates the degree to which Muslim prison chaplains are prepared to operate flexibly within the institutional confines of prisons in order to balance the welfare of prisoners with the rules and customs of Islam, sometimes coming up with unique solutions to uniquely prison-based situations.

Islamic Studies classes

In all of our English prisons there were significant Muslim prisoner populations and, in addition to leading the Friday Congregational Prayer, Muslim chaplains regularly convened weekly or twice-weekly Islamic Studies classes. Some classes focused upon Qur'anic reading and recitation, while others incorporated a broader remit which included Islamic history, religious principles, and life lessons.

We observed how beneficial these classes could be in terms of prisoner well-being and interest. This observation was consistent with our statistical data, which showed that the variable **'I have learnt about Islam from classes with Muslim prison chaplains'** was positively[9] and significantly[10] correlated with the factor, **Attitude to Rehabilitation**.

Qur'an classes

We have seen in Chapter 3 that The Qur'an forms the centrepiece of much Islamic education in prison, and we observed how Qur'an recitation classes in prison are often imbued with a tranquil sense of the sacred (Otto, 1958). Creative chaplaincy helps generate this tranquillity, which is also conducive to learning.

For example, at HMP Cherwell, Category C Prison, the Muslim prison chaplain in his Qur'an recitation classes had instituted a mentoring system whereby the more accomplished reciters helped him teach the beginners. This not only facilitated the progress of a group of around 20 regular learners, but also built relationships of trust, which meant that learning to read and recite

---

[9] r = 0.386
[10] p = 0.000

in Arabic could carry over to the wings. On two occasions, we observed how this system helped prisoners retain their concentration on their reading tasks for extended periods of an hour before chit-chat finally broke out.

Similarly, at HMP Severn, Category B Prison, the calm and consistent Qur'an teaching of an experienced Muslim chaplain in his weekly Qur'an recitation class, which was attended by 12 Vulnerable Prisoners, had generated a strong sense of brotherhood and a shared commitment to learning. This chaplain was insistent that, along with the recitation in Arabic, his students should study and understand the English meaning of what they were learning to recite. He told one student:

> Very good. Have you looked at the meaning? You can always ask me any questions in the class. It's important that we learn to memorise and understand the meanings.

Tarbiyah *classes*

Since 2011, instruction in the basic beliefs and practices around Islam in English prisons has been structured around the 'Iman to Islam' Tarbiyah (education) course. The 'Iman to Islam' Tarbiyah course has been embroiled in controversy for apparently legitimising armed jihad (Iqbal and Titheradge, 2016). We observed the 'Iman to Islam' Tarbiyah course in action on two occasions: at HMP Severn (Category B Prison) and at HMP Forth (Category A Prison).

Both on the syllabus and in action we found that the 'Iman to Islam' Tarbiyah course broadly presents a standard version of Mainstream Islam (see Chapter 4). For example, this course clearly delineates the Greater Struggle (jihad) as the 'struggle with the self' rather than any direct or violent action. However, the course did exhibit other problems. For example, a Muslim prison chaplain at HMP Forth, Category A Prison explained that, due to a political controversy, only 12 of the 36 weeks of the curriculum had ever been developed. Moreover, each of those 12 sections that had been developed seemed to us overly long, requiring more than two hours of concentrated learning, and the topics often did not pertain to issues raised by prisoners, such as ablution in cells.

Furthermore, it was clear to us that Muslim prison chaplains had received no pedagogical instruction and no teaching tools to make the course interesting. Hence, they uniformly talked from the syllabus and then answered questions. This talk-and-questions method was often both boring for prisoners and open to abuse, as prisoners sometimes brought a range of obscure questions 'from the wings' to classes, which interrupted the flow of the classes. These questions usually did not pertain to the taught topic and were sometimes designed to challenge aggressively the authority of the Muslim prison chaplain.

For example, we observed at HMP Severn, Category B Prison a prisoner taking ten minutes of class time probing an obscure topic about whether the Friday Congregational Prayer was permitted in Dar al-Kufr (A land of Unbelief), which was clearly designed to unsettle the Muslim chaplain and his teaching of the 'Iman to Islam' Tarbiyah course, as well as to cast aspersions on the conduct of the Friday Congregational Prayer in prison.

As a result of its unwieldy substance and pedagogy, at over half the Islamic Studies classes, we observed Muslim prison chaplains using their own informal syllabus and not the syllabus of the 'Iman to Islam' Tarbiyah course. Sometimes this more spontaneous approach led to exciting discussions. For example, at HMP Forth, Category A Prison, we observed a discussion about why the so-called Islamic State group was not Islamic. However, this discussion also meandered into apparently irrelevant territory for prisoners, many with life sentences, on the detailed Islamic legal rulings about marriage!

Nevertheless, even given these limitations and the fact that these sessions were often prone to interruption and disruption, it was clear that many prisoners appreciated time spent being instructed in their faith by qualified professional Muslim prison chaplains, often for the first time, since the classes were well attended and prisoners almost always engaged with their learning avidly.

Their value to Converts and Intensifiers

Islamic Studies classes were an especially valuable resource for **Converts** to and **Intensifiers** in Islam since they provided an opportunity to be inducted into their new faith in an organised way. For example, Idrees (male, 29, British White, Muslim Convert, HMP Parrett, Category B Prison) explained:

> To know that there is such a course was a bit of an eye opener for me and a bit of an attraction. It is taught to you when you enter Islam to try and live your life as the Prophet did in his footsteps. So, inspire in his life. So, to have that opportunity to study the course was an opportunity that I would not miss.

For **Converts**, much of their religious education happened on the wings through interactions with other prisoners. **Sixty-three per cent** (n = 177) of our characteristic data sample were prone either 'sometimes' or 'always' to '**turn to other prisoners for religious advice**'. In this environment of informal prisoner-to-prisoner learning, Islamic Studies classes with Muslim prison chaplains performed the important function of clarifying interpretations of Islamic texts or issues that arose in these discussions on the wings.

Muslim prison chaplains also felt that Islamic Studies classes were an opportunity for prisoners to raise legitimate queries about scripture or about particular positions in Islam. A female Muslim chaplain at HMP Parrett, Category B Prison explained:

'You've got different ... people believe in different background School of thought, so you have to respect that, this is the way I have learnt it and that's the way I'm coming from again.

When prisoners challenged certain religious positions such as how to perform prayers, chaplains attempted to make it clear that they were a legitimate source of religious authority in the prison. For example, a male Muslim chaplain at HMP Severn Category B Prison explained:

OK then again we will talk about it, that's your view and I respect it but I'm here and I know what I'm doing, so you have to make them clear that you are the authority here at the moment.

Muslim prison chaplains acknowledged challenges about deciding at what level of reading ability to pitch their Islamic Studies classes. For example, one chaplain explained that he tended to use children's texts with colourful illustrations to introduce prisoners to the basic principles and interpretations of The Qur'an. A female Muslim chaplain at HMP Parrett, Category B Prison had also found this a good solution:

I like to use children's books ... and they [the prisoners] like it.

In another English prison, the Managing Christian Chaplain emphasised the importance of a sequential, structured and meaningful syllabus for religious education classes for all the faiths he oversaw:

> " I want a syllabus. You must work by syllabus and not just come in and say, "Today, we'll look at the weather." No, no, no. What are you teaching them? You must teach them in a sequence because if you don't, if you can't tell me what you do in a process, you don't know what you're doing. You must do it systematically ... you feed them the scripture and that scripture will sit in you. "

Books and libraries

As well as Friday Congregational Prayers and Islamic Studies classes, libraries are another potential institutional source of knowledge about Islam in prison over which Muslim prison chaplains have influence.

Prisoners' perspectives[11] on the availability and quality of useful books about Islam corresponded broadly with our own observations: the library provision of books around Islam tended to be 'good' but also exhibited plenty of room for improvement.

For example, at HMP Forth, Category A Prison, we observed that there was a sophisticated and broad collection of canonical primary source books on Islam, such as the Hadith Collections of Sahih Muslim and Bukhari. However, while it was well stocked with introductory books on Christianity, there were no similar introductory books on Islam.

By contrast, at HMP Parrett, Category B Prison, there were only three library books about Islam, all written from a distinctively Sufi point of view, which might alienate some prisoners.

The prison library staff that we encountered were dedicated to providing the best religious books that they could for prisoners despite hurdles in procurement. For example, the librarian at HMP Forth, Category A Prison

---

[11] Across our characteristic sample:
- 20 per cent of prisoners thought that 'the books and information about Islam in the library' were 'excellent';
- 43 per cent of prisoners thought that 'the books and information about Islam in the library' were 'good';
- 17 per cent of prisoners thought that 'the books and information about Islam in the library' were 'not very good';
- 21 per cent of prisoners thought that 'the books and information about Islam in the library' were 'poor'; and
- 56 per cent of prisoners wanted 'access to better books about Islam' in order to follow on from their Islamic Studies classes and to continue to learn on their own.

was noticeably and movingly concerned to provide the prisoners – "the lads" – with books of all types which would improve their learning:

> I love the job. In here there are people with a good mix of characteristics … you have a static population. You personally can make a difference … the lads appreciate what you do for them.

Her impressions of the prisoners dovetailed with what we observed in Islamic Studies classes in that many prisoners seemed genuinely grateful to the people who taught about their faith regularly, often for the first time, and who were concerned more generally about their education.

While the prison libraries where we researched seemed mainly to provide books that broadly speaking represented Mainstream Islam, we did also encounter some distinct outliers. For example, the library housed in the mosque at HMP Stour, Category D Prison housed an eclectic mix of upwards of 200 Islamic books and 100 CDs. These books ranged from the classic Hadith Collections of Sahih Muslim and Bukhari to the complete Qur'anic Commentaries of Ibn Kathir and Mainstream Islamic translations of the 14th-century Damascene jurist Ibn Taymiyya.

The collection also included more divisive Islamist texts such as *The Clash of Civilisations* by Bilal Phillips (Philips, 2007) and *The Music Made Me Do It* by Dr Gohar Mushtaq (Mushtaq, 2011). This last book essentially equates all types of music with the work of Satan.

Other books which raised our eyebrows included *Religious Extremism in the Lives of Contemporary Muslims* (Luwayhiq and Al-Mutairi, 2001), which contained a section expanding on the virtues of the Islamist Extremist Doctrine of Loyalty & Disavowal (*Al-Wala' wal-Bara'*):

> Disassociation with non-Muslims is a matter that is established in Shareeah. … Allah has prohibited in the strongest terms the believers from entering into any form of loyalty to the disbelievers rather than to believers. (Luwayhiq and Al-Mutairi, 2001: 247)

The presence of unsuitable books offering Islamist views such as these in this library seemed at odds with the fact that we also came across at HMP Parrett, Category B Prison a list of proscribed Islamic books from the UK Ministry of Justice. This list included a standard introductory book on Islam called *The Lawful and Prohibited in Islam* by Yusuf Qaradawi (Al-Qaradawi, 1994), which explicitly advocates a Middle Way and the avoidance of extremes.

The variable quantity and quality of books on Islam that were available to prisoners suggested to us that, rather than the authorities merely vetting Islamic literature upon unknown criteria, more thought needs to be given to provide a consistent provision of varied and well-recognised books on Islam across all prison libraries. The Muslim prison chaplains would clearly be best placed to develop such consistent library provision.

Pastoral care

Pastoral care by Muslim prison chaplains, both in the form of official Statutory Duties and informal counselling and chatting, played an important role in reducing tensions, helping prisoners cope with the deprivations and setbacks of prison life and generating hope in the Mercy of God.

In an informal pastoral role, a Muslim chaplain can provide the following support to prisoners:

- talking to the prisoner if they are experiencing difficulties or missing their families;
- praying with a prisoner in crisis;
- helping the prisoner to see a way out of the criminal life and reform themself;
- providing books or other sources of religious knowledge;
- liaising with prison staff or management to raise prisoner concerns.

The Muslim chaplains whom we interviewed and observed had clearly developed a strong ethic of engagement with prisoners and other prison staff. Those prison chaplains who frequently walked on the wings and checked in on prisoners in their cells and in their workplace tended to have developed a good rapport with most prisoners and to have gained their trust.

On the whole, this mirrored the prisoners' perspectives on the approachability of and pastoral value of chaplains. For example, at HMP Forth, Category A Prison, we observed how the presence of the Muslim prison chaplain in the Segregation Unit had a soothing influence on a prisoner (Ethan; see case study in Chapter 7) who was regularly self-harming.

The Christian Prison chaplain at Fontgrise, Switzerland, Category B Prison and Doriath, Switzerland, Category A Prison explained how he viewed his role and interaction with prisoners:

And this guy, the first time I saw him, he asked for an interview, we were about five minutes together, the only thing I could do with him was give him my hand. All he did was cry. At the interview, I gave him my hand, that's all, held my hand, that's all. And it lasted five minutes and it was long. And it was hard. But today, he has come a long way and he says that he's not alone. It's paradoxical.

Prison allows personalities, I wouldn't say to blossom, but to expand so that when these guys get out, if they find the balance they can find a strength that is incredible. They're incredible people. I still maintain a relationship with an inmate who got out a year ago. It's amazing. He is a gentleman who has completely rebuilt his life, he has a strength, a presence.

99

The female Muslim prison chaplain at HMP Parrett, Category B Prison explained her non-judgemental approach to her work:

My passion is just to be there for people. ... As I've said, I'm not here to judge, whether it's right or wrong, but in the moment where they are in such a devastated moment, to be there as a support. On the top of this, working from the faith aspect, to help them to improve and become better and also to hope and pray that once they leave prison, they can turn their life around.

99

These forms of informal, patient, non-judgemental pastoral support were regarded by prisoners as crucial to their well-being. For example, Arash (male, Turkish, Intensifier, HMP Cherwell, Category C Prison) saw the chaplains as father/uncle figures for prisoners and as a shoulder to cry on, and voiced his wish

to see them [Muslim prison chaplains] more on the wing. People become conscious about their father or uncles has just arrived, and that in itself makes them behave better. Turns down the music, makes them feel embarrassed, ashamed or at times, "Oh I'm not allowed to be doing this, Imam's here," you know? Or a moment of "I have this question to ask," and "Imam, can you answer this question?" Or I'm feeling really down, I need to speak to someone. Imam is here, "Oh Imam can you spare a minute of

> your time?" So, when he's off for two weeks, there's no one in replacement for him. So, a bereavement can take place, you've got no one in place, you've got an individual willing to ask a question or want to help or something, there's not one in place. 〝

This wish for the Muslim prison chaplains to be a more visible and a more regular presence on the wings was expressed by **47 per cent** of our male participants, who agreed that they 'would like more visits from the Muslim prison chaplain'. This wish was echoed by the Muslim chaplains themselves, who were uniformly frustrated at the volume of their administrative duties, which too often kept them away from their pastoral work on the wings.

Women's deficient experience of chaplaincy

In Chapter 3, we have seen that prison impacts differently on the religiosity of Muslim male and female prisoners. Whereas the religiosity of Muslim men tended to intensify in prison, the religiosity of Muslim women tended to reduce in prison. We illustrated this in Chapter 7 through the case study of Badia, a Remainer at La Citadelle, Category A Prison, Switzerland.

We have outlined the complex reasons for these differences in the religiosity of men and women in prison in more detail elsewhere (Schneuwly Purdie et al, 2021). Here we discuss the ways in which the provision of Muslim prison chaplaincy services for Muslim women was weaker and less aligned with their specific needs than it was for Muslim men.

Our questionnaires showed that the women in the sample engaged with chaplaincy much less than the men.[12] We also found that Muslim women prisoners were more dissatisfied with chaplaincy provision that the men.[13]

At interview, Muslim women prisoners often expressed the fact that their spiritual needs were insufficiently met by chaplains. For example, Maya (60, Asian, Born-Muslim, HMP Parrett, Category B Prison) was critical of the

---

[12] • 41 per cent of women had a 'High' level of 'Engagement with Chaplaincy' compared with 54 per cent of men;
 • 27 per cent of women had a 'Low' level of 'Engagement with Chaplaincy' compared with 9 per cent of men;

[13] • 82 per cent of female Muslim prisoners wanted more religious classes compared with 54 per cent of male Muslim prisoners;
 • 64 per cent of female Muslim prisoners wanted more collective prayers compared with 50 per cent of male Muslim prisoners;
 • 73 per cent of female Muslim prisoners wanted more visits from Muslim prison chaplains, compared with 47 per cent of male Muslim prisoners.

Muslim prison chaplaincy at HMP Parrett. When we asked if following Islam was helping her cope in prison, she answered:

> I thought having my own religion would mean that I could rely on the chaplaincy and on the chaplaincy leaders. But they are rubbish in every sense, they are nonsense. They actually have too much work to do, too much pressure, they're too overloaded with too much pressure that they actually cannot be bothered. They don't give you any one-to-one, they don't treat you as if you matter. It's like you can just fumble your way through where you're not really getting the help but you want to be able to concentrate on your own religion because that's where you think you'll get the help but you're not getting it.

These unfulfilled needs were indicative of great disparities not only between Swiss and British Muslim prison chaplaincy provision, but also between the Muslim chaplaincy provision for Muslim women and men within each country.

There were important differences between religious services provided by the chaplains for men and for women. For example, in HMP Parrett, Category B Prison, no Friday Congregational Prayer was held for women,[14] where debates among the female Muslim prisoners about the Islamic legality of a woman leading the Friday Congregational Prayer – led in particular by a vocal terrorist offender – had prevented the female chaplain from providing the Friday Congregational Prayer and so the women never prayed together on Friday. The chaplain, although she was pastorally accomplished and respected, did not feel that she had the religious education to challenge the terrorist offender on theological grounds.

In Switzerland at the time of our research, in the female wing of La Citadelle, Category A Prison, the volunteer Muslim chaplain had suggested the possibility of visiting the women once a month after one of the male Friday Congregational Prayers. However, due to a lack of time or to miscommunication between him and the prison, this opportunity for interaction with the women had not taken place.

---

[14] While the Friday Congregational Prayer is not obligatory for women as it is for men, it is highly encouraged for women.

Indeed, Camilla (43, French Moroccan, Remainer, La Citadelle, Switzerland, Category A Prison) said that she had registered for the volunteer Muslim prison chaplain's last visit, but apparently he:

> saw the men, and I think he didn't have time for us afterwards.

This experience was highly indicative of the notion observed in previous research of women in prison: that because of their small numbers in relation to the male estate, women are an 'afterthought' in prison management (cf. Becci and Schneuwly Purdie, 2012). The particular spiritual needs of female offenders who may be dealing with multiple experiences of trauma and abuse, and who often feel that they are primarily victims of crime rather than offenders, requires more carefully directed chaplaincy attention (Schneuwly Purdie et al, 2021).

Conflict and improvements to Muslim prison chaplaincy

Although a *majority* of the participants emphasised the positive significance of Muslim chaplains' pastoral role in providing emotional support and being the source of religious knowledge, there were *some* notes of dissension and conflict between prisoners and chaplains, and in the febrile prison environment mutual trust could quickly fragment or break down.

Breakdown of trust

For example, a damaging breakdown of trust between prisoners and prison staff can occur if staff members do not follow through on something that they have agreed to do. The same applies to chaplains. Mahdi (male, 31, British Black African, Convert, HMP Parrett, Category B Prison) described how he stopped trusting the chaplain when he saw how unreliable he was at honouring commitments:

> It was a time when I witnessed in the block my next-door neighbour ... and I've heard other people tell me stories as well, but I witnessed it myself this time. Basically, my next-door neighbour kept asking [the Muslim chaplain] for the prayer times. He [the chaplain] said, "Yes, don't worry I will get one sent down for you." It didn't happen, but he's asked for it three times.

As well as following through on requests and keeping promises, our research participants often expected the chaplain to be an ally who would advocate on their behalf if they experienced discrimination or faced any issues in prison.

Azim (male, 39, Asian, Born-Muslim, HMP Severn, Category B Prison) was frustrated by the chaplains' reluctance to advocate for Muslim prisoners:

> Chaplain says he's been here for a long time and here and there, and he's done this, and he's done that for people, but he never helps, for example, if a law is broken, PSI, PSO [Prison Service Order], forget the Muslim part we expect some sort of help from somebody.

Being present on the wings, listening to the concerns of prisoners and supporting them were key to building trust. If the Muslim chaplain was inconsistent in carrying out these duties, it raised questions about their general trustworthiness. Of course, sometimes prisoners had unreasonable expectations about what chaplains could achieve for them.

Balancing security with pastoral care

Contemporary prisons require Muslim chaplains to perform a balancing act of carrying out their responsibilities of pastoral care and faith provision, while maintaining prison rules around security and the Preventing Violent Extremism Duty (Williams and Liebling, 2018). This was a source of tension between prisoners and Muslim chaplains that could lead to a breakdown of trust.

Karim (male, 34, British Mixed Heritage, Born-Muslim, HMP Cherwell, Category C Prison) described how, after a conversation he had had with a chaplain, his name had been put on an Extremism Watch List. This had made him distrustful of all chaplains and it meant that critical conversations around controversial issues such as jihad were no longer conducted with a person with sound religious authority but tended to occur covertly among prisoners.

Karim thought that a breakdown of trust between a prisoner and a chaplain could contribute to a prisoner adopting an Islamist Extremist Worldview:

> I know certain Imams [Muslim Prison chaplains] ... a brother has gone to prison Imam one time and said, "Imam, I'm selling drugs, is this money halal?" The next day, the brother got spun. So,

> rather than give the Imam the opportunity to rectify the brother's behaviour, they'll start going to the authorities and that's what creates extremism. ... He's [the Muslim Prison chaplain] part of them, part of the *kuffar* [unbelievers] and you hear it. No one wants to go and talk to an Imam about jihad, "Imam, what does jihad mean? Can we talk about what's going on in the world right now?" The reason being 'cause of the situation that I've ended up in. And a lot of people are aware that chaplains will go and tell the authorities and we're gonna have. ... I'm gonna have a TACT marker over my head for the rest of my life now.

As we have already shown, there were several other examples of participants who were being discouraged by other prisoners on the wings from trusting the Muslim chaplains as legitimate religious authorities. This was a particular concern for Converts who possessed less Islamic knowledge and were more likely to be misled.

For example, Liam (male, 31, White British, Convert, HMP Cherwell, Category C Prison) said that he did not trust one of the Muslim prison chaplains because the chaplain "was a Sufi". When pressed to explain what "Sufi" meant and why a "Sufi" could not be trusted, Liam had no knowledge of what it meant to be a Sufi. He had been told by prisoners on his wing that "Sufis cannot be trusted" and he had assumed that to be a commonly held legitimate Muslim attitude.

Another example was Bobby (male, age unknown, White British, Convert, HMP Forth, Category A Prison), who had stopped going to the Friday Congregational Prayer because of what prisoners on his wing were saying about the Muslim prison chaplain. However, he had no clear idea of why he was supposed not to trust the chaplain:

> I don't know, to be honest. I think what's happened is, I think I've allowed people to plant them little seeds of doubt of the Imams.

Bobby felt as a result of "these seeds of doubt",

> I've allowed people to, kind of, pollute my mind.

Problems and challenges faced by chaplains

Too much documentation and bureaucracy

These issues that could lead to a damaging breakdown of trust between Muslim chaplains were symptomatic of the challenging emotional and logistical role that chaplains play in prison life. The (mainly Christian) Managing Chaplains, for example, relayed a sense of the increasingly administrative burden which comes with their role.

For example, the Managing Chaplain at HMP Cherwell, Category C Prison said:

> Being the Managing Chaplain, I have noticed, and this is only relatively recently that I've taken that on, that I am increasingly sitting at my desk and doing admin in order to run the Chaplaincy. ... I've already noticed, in the couple of months that I've been doing it, that I am increasingly tied to my desk.

Muslim chaplains have traditionally served as part-time volunteers in English prisons. The appointment of full-time professional Muslim prison chaplains since 2003 has been accompanied by increasing Statutory Duties which require adhering to various administrative protocols and bureaucracy.

Therefore, an unintended consequence of the professionalisation of Muslim chaplaincy is that Muslim chaplains feel they now have less time for pastoral duties. For example, a Muslim chaplain at HMP Severn, Category B Prison expressed his frustrations at not being able to spend more time with pastoral work and teaching:

> I'm here three days a week. I've been only on one wing today, but that's because it's Friday. I've been busy with the kitchen, busy with morning meetings and attending to certain individuals who come to actually see me, seeing the group go up and clean the mosque. ... So my time is like this. Two classes on Thursday, *Jumu'a* [Friday Congregational Prayer] on Friday with meetings, Saturday is Statutory Duties, so really my time is full already without anything else. ... There are two of us in here, one full-time and one part-time chaplain, but there is not the time to really [dedicate] more effort on educating these guys. Even the other week, I could easily hold the class during the week individually, but there isn't time, there isn't time.

Managing extremism

As previously mentioned in this book, prisons are under increased scrutiny to monitor and challenge extremist behaviour, whether that is from prisoners or from staff.

As our research has illustrated, prisoners holding Islamist Extremist Worldviews represent a small proportion of the total. Nevertheless, they have the capacity to impact disproportionately upon prison life. Muslim prison chaplains find themselves at the forefront of challenging Islamist Extremist behaviour, although the extent to which they can successfully perform this role varied.

The Muslim chaplains themselves acknowledge the corrosive nature of Islamist Extremist Worldviews and the challenges they present. For example, a Muslim prison chaplain at HMP Forth, Category A Prison said:

> I know there have been difficulties, talking to my colleagues here, that they've experienced difficulties at times with more extremist prisoners. It's a difficult one, because it does need to be addressed, as increasingly prisoners will probably come back from Syria at some point and the system needs to gear up to that. I think we're probably better prepared in terms of having a large number of Muslim chaplains in this country than some others. And, we probably have a responsibility to help deradicalise those that have been indoctrinated. I think the mission here to teach and to challenge [extremist ideas] is a very challenging one for Muslim chaplains.

In England, some full-time Muslim prison chaplains undertook deradicalisation intervention work, sometimes at the request of other prisons.

Undermining of authority: 'Scholars for Dollars'

In our focused observations at HMP Forth, Category A Prison, we witnessed the challenges that Islamist Extremist prisoners posed when they openly declared their opposition to the full-time appointed Muslim prison chaplain. A group of prisoners refused to pray directly behind the full-time appointed Muslim chaplain and instead established their own small clusters of prayers while the Obligatory Daily Prayers were being offered. The Muslim chaplain expressed his anxiety about this practice but also reflected upon his relative impotence to challenge it.

For some prisoners, the Muslim chaplain's position as a civil servant offered a pretext to level accusations that Muslim prison chaplains were not 'real' Muslim Imams but were actually *kuffar* (infidels). As one chaplain put it, "[they call us] Scholars for Dollars."

The accusation of infidelity (*kufr*) to Islam had been levelled on multiple occasions to one experienced and knowledgeable Muslim prison chaplain at HMP Forth, Category A Prison, who was himself a Convert to Islam. This Muslim chaplain had needed to develop a thick skin to an allegation that was nasty, false and potentially even dangerous and that was clearly designed to undermine his religious legitimacy.

Some suggested principles for improvements in practice

Based on our data from prisoners reported earlier, and on our interviews with and observations of Muslim prison chaplains, we have developed some suggested principles of best practice through which Muslim prison chaplains can further improve their care of Muslim prisoners.

Avoidance of exaggerated difference

With a multi-faith, multi-ethnic prisoner population, we found many examples of the ways in which multi-faith chaplains supported each other's work and catered to the diverse needs of the prison population. However, in England, while chaplains of different faiths were committed professionally to cooperating with each other, they were almost universally reluctant to engage in inter-faith practices and events. This highly siloed aspect of prison chaplaincy sometimes led to chaplains exaggerating differences between faiths.

For example, at a Muslim Conversion Shahada (Declaration of Faith) we observed the prison chaplain adding his own words to the universally accepted *Shahada*. As well as "There is no god but God and Muhammad is the Messenger of God", the chaplain asked the prisoner Convert to repeat

> I testify that Jesus Christ is not the Son of God, but the son of Maryam [Mary].

This caused surprise and discomfort to the prisoner, Chris (male, 47, British White, Convert, HMP Cherwell, Category C Prison), who was converting from Christianity to Islam and whose case we followed in Chapter 7.

Later, the chaplain explained that he had added these words to the Shahada in order to give Chris, as a former Christian, doctrinal clarity about the new faith. However, this sort of exaggerated difference was counterproductive to promoting relationships of respect between prisoners in a multi-faith context and was also an incorrect addition to a standard Islamic practice.

We also observed that Muslim chaplains occasionally had developed stricter rules for Muslim prisoners than was strictly necessary in Islamic Sharia, for example, by declaring that certain haircuts and that all types of music were *haram* (forbidden), which, as we noted in Chapter 2, caused some prisoners, especially **Converts**, unnecessary guilt and anxiety.

Development of inter-faith experiences

Relatedly, when we raised the possibility of inter-faith events or discussions in the English prisons HMP Cherwell (Category C Prison) and HMP Parrett (Category B Prison) we encountered great resistance from chaplains of all types bordering on hostility at the idea of inter-faith exchange:

- The Anglican prison chaplain at HMP Cherwell (Category C Prison) feared that theological differences between faiths might become a source of conflict.
- The Muslim prison chaplain at HMP Cherwell (Category C Prison) could see "no point in people praying together" and thought that the fact that the rituals of the different religious are different presented an obstacle to meaningful exchange.
- The Anglican prison chaplain at HMP Parrett (Category B Prison) thought that it would be "too challenging" to organise such events in prison and that there was "no need" for them.

Nevertheless, in Switzerland we observed an inter-religious service organised by the chaplains at Mitheilen (Category A Prison). This inter-religious service took place in a pleasing purpose-built multi-faith space (Image 8.10) that was suitable for Muslim, Christian and other forms of worship.

At this inter-religious service – which regularly happens twice a year – the theme was 'The Divine Light of the Truth' and it was attended by all 11 chaplains[15] and around 22 prisoners, including ten Muslim prisoners. During the service, each chaplain read from the Holy Scriptures of their own traditions and made informal prayers around the chosen theme. These readings and prayers were directed to God but did not include any denominational complexity beyond that.

---

[15] Two Catholic Christian; two Protestant Christian; three Muslim; three Orthodox Christian; and one Hindu.

Image 8.10: The Multi-faith Space at Gefängniss Mitheilen, Switzerland

The event was well received by the prisoners. For example, Abe (male, 45, African Heritage, Remainer, Mitheilen, Category A Prison, Switzerland) said that he enjoyed the inter-religious services because they represented rare occasions to meet all the chaplains at the same time:

> That is the only chance we have to hear different things, a little bit of all the imams.

Abe also thought that they

> should try to thank the Prison Director who give us this chance to meet and perform prayers together.

After the event, prisoners shared baklava and tea and they clearly enjoyed socialising with each other. The event had served as a forum to build religious literacy and to challenge prejudice (Moore, 2016), facilitated by the space at Mitheilen, which, to our minds, was a model of a clean and creative space for worship in prison.

Therefore, notwithstanding the great respect that we developed for chaplains in England and the fact that there may be grounds for some of their fears, we would beg to differ that there is no need for or benefit from inter-religious exchange in prison.

The fact that **20 per cent** (n = 57) of our characteristic sample of Muslim prisoners **'disagreed'** that **'wisdom can be found in many religions'** suggests that there exists a tendency for prisoners of different faiths to club together around exaggerated notions of difference from those of other faiths that needs to be addressed.

We do not deny that there exist genuine and sometimes deep differences of belief and practice between different traditions of faith. Nevertheless, the inter-religious experience that we observed at Mitheilen Category A Prison in Switzerland suggests strongly that if an inter-religious event were constructed carefully by professional chaplains, it could be spiritually and intellectually enlightening for prisoners. Furthermore, it would create a forum for friendships to develop between prisoners of different faith traditions, to build a learning community of religious literacy for life post release (Moore, 2007) and to help dispel prejudices.

The need for an appropriate Islamic Studies curriculum

We have outlined in great detail the positive rehabilitative benefits for prisoners of engaging with their faith through the Muslim prison chaplaincy, along with the risks of radicalisation in the unmanaged prison environment.

To support rehabilitative change and to manage the risks of radicalisation in prison it is critical, as the Managing Chaplain of HMP Forth noted, to have a systematised and appropriate Islamic Studies curriculum.

Prisoners, such as Arash (male, Turkish, Born-Muslim, HMP Cherwell, Category C Prison also noted:

> I think it's vital for the Muslim population in prison to have more classes for learning about Islam, the correct way from someone that is put in a position of leadership and has knowledge on the *deen* [Islam] instead of having their own interpretation of it.

Earlier in this chapter, we observed that the 'Iman to Islam' Tarbiyah course that is currently used in England exhibits pedagogical shortcomings and is structured to be completed in 36 weeks, despite prisoners remaining only six weeks on average in any local prison. This means that the course is often a source of frustration to both Muslim chaplains and to prisoners.

A more systematic and appropriate curriculum is needed in order to provide a sound knowledge of Islam that is relevant to the particular circumstances and spiritual and emotional needs of prisoners, including preparing prisoners to practise their faith post release and to use it as a protection against further crime.

Conclusion: Prison chaplains are agents of rehabilitation

Our research has highlighted the crucial and challenging role played by Muslim prison chaplains in supporting Muslim prisoners. Engagement with Muslim prison chaplaincy was pivotal for offenders, including terrorist offenders, to undergo transformative pro-social shifts of Worldview; it resulted in their engagement with rehabilitation in the form of education and work and acted as a barrier against despair.

Well-educated and empathetic chaplains also counter the influence of extremist prisoners by deploying both a forensic knowledge of Islamic texts and a sustained attention to building productive relationships with offenders over time. Chaplaincy was a lifeline for Converts and Intensifiers to take on productive and safe forms of Islam and to supplement and counter some of the ad hoc religious teaching that took place on the wings.

Our comparison of prison chaplaincy provision between the three different jurisdictions shows that Muslim prison chaplaincy in England has professionalised to a higher level than its Swiss and French counterparts. This is manifest in the wider range of duties performed by chaplains in England, their integration into prison management and dedicated spaces for Islamic worship in English prisons. These differences relate to the macro-level differences in the prison policy context and the legal status of religion within each country.

In Switzerland, where Muslim chaplaincy was underdeveloped and amateur in comparison to both England and France, we also encountered a model example of an inter-faith service which allowed people of different faiths and no faith to interact and learn about and from each other. Such inter-faith events were missing from the more professionalised and siloed prison chaplaincy in England, where the fact that chaplaincy culture lacks any significant inter-faith component occasionally plays into a more Islamist Worldview of exaggerated 'Us' versus 'Them' difference.

Managing Muslim prisoners: treading a middle path between naïvety and suspicion

We have seen in the previous chapter how **Engagement with Chaplaincy** was a key factor in a positive **Attitude to Rehabilitation** among Muslim Prisoners.

Our questionnaire results also showed that the factor **Prison Environment**, which included **Treatment by prison officers**, was strongly and significantly positively associated with **Engagement with Chaplaincy**. We interpreted this to mean that if Muslim prisoners felt that prison staff, and especially prison officers, treated them fairly and respectfully and that they were safe in prison, they were then more likely to engage with the prison chaplaincy and more likely to increase their commitment to work and education.[1] In other words, the perception that prison staff were fair and respectful – or not – significantly impacted on the religiosity of Muslim prisoners.

In light of this influence of prison culture and staff interaction on religious outcomes in prison, this chapter presents our findings about how prison officers and prison governors interacted with Muslim prisoners. By highlighting examples of good practice and when things went wrong, we suggest some practical *Principles for Engagement* with Muslim prisoners, mindful of the fact that we are outsiders to the challenging role of being a prison officer. These Principles for Engagement[2] identify flashpoints and describe three types of possible response from prison staff:

- a *naïve* response;
- a *suspicious* response;[3]

---

[1] Scholars of procedural justice have also emphasised as key factors that determine the success of offender management the importance of legitimacy of authority, process fairness and group engagement (Kaiser and Holtfreter, 2015).

[2] While we draw upon policy documents such as Prison Service Orders on religion in England and Wales, our Principles for Engagement will have wider applicability for European and other international contexts.

[3] In this chapter, we use the term 'suspicion' to describe an unfair or disproportionate attitude towards aspects of prisoner behaviour or practices.

- a *balanced* response that charts an informed and fair Middle Way between naïvety and suspicion.[4]

The views of prison staff about Islam and Muslims in prison

The prison officers whom we interviewed[5] universally expressed an aspiration to deal with Muslim prisoners fairly and professionally.

Some prison officers, for example an officer at HMP Cherwell who was a former British serviceman who had served in the Middle East, were informed and sensitive to the religious and cultural practices of Muslims, including the wishes of prisoners to perform their Obligatory Daily Prayers and their desire to express their Muslim-ness by, for example, wearing Islamic-style clothing to the Friday Congregational Prayer.

Prison staff often expressed a mature attitude to religious faith and religious conversion generally. For example, a nurse (female, British White, HMP Cherwell, Category C Prison) described a typically frank discussion with some opportunistic Converts to Islam:

> I, from over the years in the prison service ... I said to them, "Why have you converted?" ... And a few of them, they said, "To be honest, Miss, I just go with the flow and with the Muslims in the prison. They get more benefits than us, so that's why I converted." And I said to him, "Well, that's not a reason to convert." So I said to him, "So you're not really a Christian and you're not really a Muslim. In other words, you are using religion to suit you." ...
> And I said to him, "Well, it doesn't matter what faith you have," I said to him, "As long as you do it for the right reasons, to benefit yourself, not materialistically but also to actually become a better person. Because with your addiction, if you use religion to benefit, it's a good thing. But if you are using it to gain material stuff, then you've lost again.

---

[4] Some academic readers may be critical of our moving from an 'is' to an 'ought'. However, since this book is intended to inform the practice of frontline professionals it is hoped this chapter suggests some effective ways of ameliorating, lowering or removing the causes of tensions and misunderstanding between Muslim prisoners and staff.

[5] These included some Muslim prison officers who had experienced both racism from their colleagues and suspicion from Muslim prisoners.

Also, prison staff acknowledged the difficulty that they faced in making judgements about a prisoner's religious faith. For example, a Governing Governor (female, British White, HMP Cherwell, Category C Prison) said:

> And with faith and with religion, it's very difficult to monitor and manage and therefore it can be treated in custodial settings, as sometimes taken with a pinch of salt. Is this person's conversion to faith or finding their faith, is it genuine?

The fact that Muslim prisoners often do un-Muslim things – including dealing drugs or behaving violently – had influenced many prison officers to develop a degree of cynicism towards a prisoner's choice to follow Islam. In the minds of some prison officers, a prisoner's choice to follow Islam had become linked to a strategic shift to gain privileges or to gang membership. For further details, see Chapter 3 and the 'cynical view'.

In addition to a suspicion of prisoners' motives for choosing Islam, some prison officers felt nervous around issues of diversity and inclusion when dealing with Muslim prisoners. For example, a prison officer (male, British White, HMP Forth, Category A Prison) explained:

> The Muslim faith is classed as a hot potato. People are scared to talk about it because you get lambasted as racist, bigot. And then that frightens staff off from doing their jobs.

These anxieties centred around being considered racist or ignorant, and also around the potential for retaliation from 'gangs'. The combination of these anxieties, together with a lack of training around religion, meant that dealing with Muslim prisoners often caused prison officers significant professional stress and feelings of being under threat. The prison officer explained:

> As an officer, I feel I sometimes, if I'm honest, I feel intimidated. I can feel a bit on edge. I feel particularly nervous. More so because I feel that if I was to say anything. Obviously, I'm aware of saying something which could be perceived as anti-religious or maybe racist. You're extra aware, obviously, in this climate. But you're also aware that if you upset one of them then the

> likelihood is that they're all going to gang up and you're going to deal with a big situation. **"**

This nervousness and a fear of being perceived as Islamophobic could be lethal. For example, at HMP Severn Category B Prison, we were told of an occasion when a group of Muslim prisoners had persuaded prisoner officers for the Friday Prayer that under no circumstances whatsoever must they step on the prayer carpet in their shoes. At the Friday Congregational Prayer, a prisoner was stabbed by a fellow prisoner, but prison officers were slow to help because they were hesitant about crossing the prayer carpet wearing their shoes.

'Gangs', coerced conversion and extremism

The pro-social effects of Mainstream Islamic practice described in Chapters 3, 4 and 5 often did not come to the attention of prison staff. Those prison officers who took a jaundiced view of conversion to Islam had often been forced to deal with the unpleasant and dangerous pockets of Islamist Extremism that we described in Chapter 6. While emanating from small numbers of Muslim prisoners, the antisocial effects of Islamism and Islamist Extremism caused problems for prison staff and generated many effects disruptive to the smooth running of prison regimes. To illustrate, a Governing Governor (male, British White, HMP Parrett, Category B Prison) expressed surprise to hear that our measurement of **prisoners' Worldviews** was as follows:

- **76 per cent** of Muslim prisoners hold a **Mainstream Islamic** Worldview;
- **19 per cent** of Muslim prisoners hold an **Islamist** Worldview;
- **4 per cent** of Muslim prisoners hold an **Islamist Extremist** Worldview.

"
> I might have thought that it would be the other way around! **"**

Prison staff often spoke about 'Muslim' gang activity, coerced conversion and extremism as interconnected issues; they did not often refer to the positive facets of conversion to or intensification in Islam, such as piety and emotional coping, that we identified in Chapter 3.

For example, a prison officer (male, British White, HMP Severn, Category B Prison) noted the negative effects of prisoners resisting pressure to convert to Islam:

> It [conversion to Islam] can be through subtle manipulation. It can be through, "If you join us, we can make sure you have this. We can make sure we look after you. We can provide you sort of protection on the wings so that others don't harm you." It can also, I have experienced it, not often, but it has happened, where it has led to violence, where because people haven't converted, they found themselves quite under threat or being branded racist because they haven't converted. And then that has a knock-on effect.

Another prison officer (male, British White, HMP Parrett, Category B Prison) was of the opinion that many prisoners converted to Islam to find safety in numbers:

> So, there's always the little groups. And it's mainly the same ethnicity or same religion and then they do try and get [someone to convert to Islam] and sometimes people, if they're scared, they'll convert because they know that they'll have the safety of that group because it's a big group. So, it's the intimidation.

Another prison officer (male, British White, HMP Forth, Category A Prison) said that Muslim prisoners were notorious for forming "the strongest gang". Interestingly, this view was received through second-hand reports from prisoners, rather than held by direct experience:

> When you talk to a prisoner about moving on from HMP Forth, they might say, "I'm not going to HMP X." And you say, "Why aren't you going to HMP X? Why don't you want to go to HMP X?" And it will be because of their gang. Or they perceive it to be more racist there. HMP X among the prisoners is perceived to be a racist prison. So, they don't want to go somewhere where they believe they're going to come up against more racist staff. Or where they're going to come up against where the Muslims aren't the main gang. In HMP Forth, in my opinion and in the Government's opinion, I would imagine the biggest gang, the strongest gang is the Muslim gang.

Other staff, such as the Governing Governor at HMP Parrett (male, British White, HMP Parrett, Category B Prison), were clear that gang culture and authentic religious culture were not the same:

> 66
>
> I can't call it a religious culture. It's more of a gang culture. I think what they do is they try to give it a name, "It's Muslim." It's not. It's actually a gang culture where the Tottenham boys are fighting with the, you know, they look like they're Muslims but then I've seen two rival gangs but they've both been Muslims with black lads.
>
> 99

Therefore, a key challenge faced by prison staff was to differentiate fairly and accurately between common Muslim practices and norms and Islamist Extremist views or behaviour.

It was important for prison staff to be able to differentiate between Muslim 'leaders' and 'elders' on the wings, whose influence might be benign or malign.

We found that *benign* 'leaders' and 'elders' on the wings were those who with kindness encouraged Muslim prisoners to perform their Obligatory Five Daily Prayers and to engage productively with the Muslim prison

SIGNS OF ISLAMIST EXTREMISM

Signs of Islamist Extremism that we have outlined and evidenced in Chapter 6 include:

- being antagonistic towards prison staff;
- avoiding non-Muslim prisoners;
- policing other prisoners to stop doing supposedly 'forbidden' things such as listening to music;
- actively opposing Muslims befriending non-Muslim prisoners;
- refusing to pray with the Muslim prison chaplains.

chaplaincy and with work. Benign Muslim leadership might also, on occasion, encourage Muslim prisoners to take a stand for something that they needed to have or needed to do, such as showering before the Friday Congregational Prayer.

Malign 'Muslim' leadership discouraged engagement with the prison authorities or any non-Muslims. In the worst cases, malign leadership propagated violence and vendettas on spurious religious grounds, such as the Doctrine of Loyalty & Disavowal (see Chapter 6).

This extract from an interview with the Prison Director (female, French White, HMP Hauterive, Category B Prison, France) illustrates the problems staff faced when trying to distinguish between cultural norms, genuine religious practice and Islamist Extremism:

> I didn't know. For example, the Calls to Prayer are in fact everywhere. They are broadcast on the radio. And, in fact, when we don't know, we immediately get alarmed. We say to ourselves, "Well, he's making a Call to Prayer to pray with everyone." Whereas it's in his culture. In fact, I mean, frankly, I couldn't tell if he's radicalised or not. But there's a young person I know that when I go out at night, I do the rounds, there's always Muslim background music. So, I could say, "Maybe it's an [extremist] … you know?"

The task of making fair and informed distinctions between genuinely religious Worldviews and extremist Worldviews was complicated by the fact that Islamist Extremist Worldviews were not confined to Muslim prisoners.

A Muslim prison officer (male, British Asian, HMP Parrett, Category B Prison) explained how he had encountered Islamist Extremist Worldviews in fellow Muslim prison officers:

> Muslim prison officer: I've known officers to brainwash prisoners.
>
> Interviewer: Do you mean Muslim prison officers?
>
> Muslim prison officer: Yeah. Mainly told them things that, when a prisoner is low, mentally low, drained, and nothing going for him, you tell him anything, just to up their spirit. They'll do it.
>
> Interviewer: And do you challenge them or …?

> Muslim prison officer: Straight away, because the prisoners know me more. So, I told them, I said, "Look, whatever he said it's not all true. Twenty percent of it is true. The rest, 80 percent he's telling you, is a bit extremist."

Lack of training

In this complex landscape of different types of religious expression, the prison officers we interviewed acknowledged that their training in diversity, especially around religion in general and Islam in particular, was inadequate to make sense of the religious complexity of prison life.

For example, in his Prison Officer Entry-Level Training (POELT) a prison officer (male, British White, HMP Parrett, Category B Prison) recalled the inadequacy and superficiality of the training in religion:

> Training in religion. I think it was just an hour, two-hour slot where they just talked about different religions. The only thing I can remember concerning Islam was 'servery'. And they just asked you a question, "Can Muslim servery workers, like prisoners, serve bacon?" Basically, that's it really.

Another prison officer (male, British White, HMP Forth, Category A Prison) explained:

> I did very little training [about religion and Islam] in basic training, I've done very little really. I mean, you know, the basics. However, I did an extra week prior to going into the Separation Unit.

The absence of training of our prison officer participants in religion in general, or Islam in particular, was consistent with our review of all 60 modules of the POELT Core Curriculum (Her Majesty's Prison & Probation Service, 2018) in which there is not a single mention of the words 'religion', 'chaplain' or 'Islam', nor of any other faith.

In this way, in the POELT training, religion in general, and Islam in particular, constituted a powerful 'absent curriculum' which added confusion and danger to officers' professional experience (Wilkinson, 2014).

In addition, in England prison officers observed that a lack of effective religious education in school, and of religious literacy more widely in British society, contributed to leaving them bereft of the types of religious awareness necessary for their job. This lack of Religious Education meant that officers were likely to receive their religious awareness through stereotypical media narratives. A prison officer (male, British White, HMP Cherwell, Category C Prison) explained:

> If I say to my 23-year-old [son] now, "Repeat the Lord's Prayer to me", he wouldn't have a clue. He'd say, "What are you talking about, Dad?" You know, he wouldn't have a clue. They don't do that anymore. And that's the same with any society now, within that, it doesn't happen anymore. Media dictates what goes on now. All the stabbings going on in London, they generalise that into one particular sect or group. Do you see what I'm saying? And then we look at this sort of, I mean, it's the crazy place we're in at the moment.

In summary, among individual prison staff, attitudes to Islam and Muslim prisoners varied hugely from prison staff who were alive to the rehabilitative and protective potential of faith, to those who thought that Islam was only ever an expression of gang culture, and that Islam was essentially synonymous with extremism.

Prison officers whom we interviewed were universally of the opinion, though, that they required more targeted training about religion in prison.

Using this data, we can summarise the range of views of prison staff towards Islam as follows:

Naïve response

■ To pretend that no coercive and/or extreme religious attitudes and behaviour exists in prison or is propagated on the wings.

■ Being oblivious to the fact that on prison wings, gang-like groups do exist with their own hierarchies of authority and power and with the means of enforcing their authority through both physical and psychological violence.

Suspicious response

■ To interpret any Islamic-sounding conversation, group or request as symptomatic of potential extremism.

■ To believe that the practice of Islam is likely to represent deviant behaviour.

Balanced response

■ To be aware that the majority – our study suggests around three quarters – of Muslim prisons aspire to learn and practise their faith in a way that allows them to make productive and peaceful use of their sentence and to cope in prison (see Chapters 4 and 5).

■ To be aware of the vulnerabilities and risks of choosing to follow Islam for the first time (see Chapter 7).

■ To be aware that a small but influential minority of extremists seek to justify their antisocial, violent, criminal and/or bullying behaviour on spurious religious grounds.

Guidance on flashpoints

Following this general account of the attitudes of prison staff to Islam and Muslim prisoners, we next identify some particularly contentious areas of interaction between prison officers and Muslim prisoners and suggest some Principles for Engagement.

Handling and searching

Here we explain the sensitivities Muslim prisoners may feel around how they are physically searched and how their belongings are handled by prison staff.

Before the Friday Congregational Prayer at several prisons, we observed prisoners being searched. We are mindful of the vital necessity of these searches given the offending history of some Muslim prisoners and the obvious potential for violence at such gatherings. Because searches are by their nature invasive and involve touching, we offer some guidance that prison officers may find helpful.

Searching an individual

It may be helpful for prison officers to be aware that, other than in cases of necessity, a Muslim is only permitted to be naked in front of their spouse; they are prohibited from being naked before any other person, even a person of their own gender.

In Islam, **rub-down searches** by a member of the opposite sex are not usually acceptable, and security protocols in the English & Welsh Prison Service have, where practicable, accommodated this sensitivity for several years.

For the safety of prison staff, the prisoner and the wider prisoner population, the **strip searching** of Muslim prisoners has been deemed compliant with Islamic Law to stop the concealment of weapons, narcotics or other prohibited items.

At the same time, HMPPS with Muslim legal experts in England have approved the manner in which a strip search of a Muslim prisoner should be undertaken. This guidance suggests:

- at no time should a Muslim prisoner be totally naked;
- the strip search must not be undertaken in the presence of a member of the opposite sex.[6]

---

[6] Prison Service Instruction 07/2016: 'Searching of The Person', Full Searches of Muslims – Annex D2.

Belongings with sacred *or* sensitive *significance*

In Islam, the Arabic text of The Qur'an holds a sacred value (see Image 9.1; The Qur'an, 56:79): it cannot be touched unless the individual is in a state of ritual ablution, in other words, unless the individual has done *wudu*.

Image 9.1: An Arabic-English copy of The Qur'an

HANDLING THE QUR'AN

Muslims regard The Qur'an as the literal word of God, as revealed by the Angel Gabriel to the Prophet Muhammad (see Chapters 1 and 2). According to Islamic tradition, the revelation was made in the Arabic language, and the recorded text in Arabic has not changed since the time of its revelation, more than 1,400 years ago. Although modern printing presses are used to distribute The Qur'an worldwide, the printed Arabic text of The Qur'an is still regarded as holy and has never been changed in any way.

'THE PAGES'

The Arabic text of The Holy Qur'an is known as the *mushaf*, literally, 'The Pages'. There are special rules that Muslims follow when handling, touching or reading from the *mushaf*.

■ The Qur'an itself states that only those who are clean and pure should touch the sacred text: 'This is indeed a Holy Qur'an, in a book well-guarded, which none shall touch but those who are purified' (The Qur'an, 56: 77–9).

■ The majority of Islamic scholars interpret this verse to refer to a state of purity, which is attained by making ablution (*wudu*). Therefore, most Muslims believe that only those who are purified through formal ablutions should touch the pages of The Qur'an.

THE 'RULES' OF HANDLING THE QUR'AN

As a result of this general understanding, the following 'rules' are usually followed when handling The Qur'an:

■ One should perform ablution (*wudu*) before handling The Qur'an.

■ One who needs major ablution (after ejaculation or menstrual bleeding) should not touch The Qur'an until after bathing.

■ Those who are unable to handle The Qur'an based on these reasons should either avoid handling The Qur'an completely or, if absolutely necessary, hold it while using some sort of barrier covering the hand, such as a cloth or a glove.

■ When one is not reading or reciting from The Qur'an, it should be closed and stored in a clean, respectable place. Nothing should be placed on top of it, nor should it ever be placed on the floor or in a bathroom.

- Acceptable ways of disposing of a damaged copy of The Qur'an include wrapping in cloth and burying in a deep hole, placing it in flowing water so the ink dissolves, or, as a last resort, burning it so that it is completely consumed.

- In summary, Muslims believe that The Qur'an should be handled with the deepest respect. However, God is All Merciful and we cannot be held responsible for what we do in ignorance or by mistake.

Information from Huda, 2020.

Other items – such as Books of Prophetic Sayings (*hadith*) (see Chapter 4), prayer mats, prayer beads or hats worn for prayer – do not possess a sacred value in Islam in the sense of necessitating ritual purity. Yet for many Muslim prisoners, such items take on a special sensitivity in prison because Muslim prisoners connect these items with their faith (see Image 9.2 and Chapter 3).

It is also likely that many Muslim prisoners will not know which object in Islam is actually sacred – the Arabic text of The Qur'an – and which objects have taken on a sacred worth in their mind due to their association with worship, such as prayer mats.

Our research contained many examples of good practice by prison officers with regard to the recognition of sacred and sensitive objects. Most prison officers had developed these good practices on the job rather than through training. For example, a prison officer (male, British White, HMP Parrett, Category B Prison) explained:

> I learn from asking questions from residents [prisoners] and chaplaincy how to search The Qur'an. If I needed to, if I had a suspicion that I needed to, which is an inevitable part of my job, I would ask the residents [prisoners] to open it for me.

We also observed prison officers checking religious attire with due sensitivity in order to alleviate any tension that may arise, including the caps of prisoners attending the Friday Congregational Prayer.

Image 9.2: Sensitive objects for Muslim prisoners: a prayer mat, remembrance beads (*tasbih*), robe (*thawb*) and prayer cap (*kufi/taqiyah*)

Source: Getty Images

The methods by which sacred and sensitive objects are touched, searched or stored all have potential for increasing conflicts between prison officers and between Muslim prisoners in shared cells.

When undertaking cell searches for drugs, the use of sniffer dogs where sacred and sensitive items are stored can be a particularly contentious issue for Muslim prisoners: some Muslim prisoners may perceive that the spittle of a sniffer dog has 'defiled' an item.[7] A clear solution for prison environments is the use of passive drug dog on a lead with a handler rather than active drugs dogs. HMPPS amended their policy to reflect this issue in **Prison Service Instruction, 07/2016, Annex D5**:

> It is good practice to make available protective clothing for Muslim visitors, staff and prisoners attending the Friday Prayer to wear when being searched by a passive drug dog and to provide instruction previously contained within the Religion Manual that washing/changing facilities must be made available should they be touched by a dog during the search.

Naïve response

▢ To believe that all objects connected with Islam are sacred and therefore cannot be touched or moved.

Suspicious response

▢ To assume that Muslim prisoners are concealing prohibited items in religious artefacts as an abuse of the system; or that they are seeking some perk or benefit by requesting that searches be more compliant with their religious beliefs and practices.

Balanced response

▢ To train all staff who interact and search Muslim prisoners about sacred and sensitive belongings and protocols for searching persons and strip search.

▢ For staff to permit prisoners to handle sacred objects and sensitive objects when conducting cell searches wherever possible.

---

[7] In the different Islamic Schools of Law, there are a variety of different opinions about this. See Chapter 4.

Whenever possible, prison officers should permit prisoners to leaf through texts and to handle sacred objects during cell searches or when conducting on-the-spot searches. To avoid causing feelings of disrespect, copies of The Qur'an should not be placed on floors or with shoes or underwear **(see Information Box on p 234)**.

Worship and religious gatherings

We observed the presence and interaction of prison officers with Muslim prisoners around core weekly religious events – such as the Friday Congregational Prayer – and also during Islamic Studies classes.

The respect and sensitivity afforded by prison officers to searching persons would be well extended to physical places of worship, including dedicated prison 'mosques', multi-faith areas or chaplaincy spaces.

During religious classes and congregational worship, it would be conducive to mutual respect for staff to keep noise to a minimum, including from personal radios or loud conversations.

We noted tensions building at HMP Forth, Category A Prison, where the prison officers' room was adjacent to the Multi-Faith Room and loud voices, shouts and laughing frequently interrupted the Friday Congregational Prayer.

In addition to the Friday Congregational Prayer, Muslim prisoners should be permitted to perform individually the Obligatory Daily Prayers, which are obligatory in Islam (see Chapter 4).

We would recommend that occasions are made above and beyond the Friday Congregational Prayer where daily prayers can be done in congregation with appropriate security measures in place. We observed this happening at HMP Cherwell (Category C Prison) and HMP Forth (Category A Prison) where it created goodwill between prisoners and respect between prisoners and prison staff.

Where the Obligatory Daily Prayers are done in a cell, staff should be sensitive to interrupting prisoners while they are praying, which usually only takes a matter of a few minutes.

Given the fact that the Friday Congregational Prayer and other congregational events have been observed, on occasion, to facilitate disruption and violence, in our opinion, rather than staying outside the room, prison officers should be based in prayer spaces – as discreetly as possible – but in positions from which they can easily and quickly intervene.

At HMP Severn, Category B Prison, prison officers had been persuaded to sit outside the mosque and were not quickly on hand when an incident of disruption involving one of our researchers and the Muslim prison chaplain occurred. In fact, officers seemed oblivious to what was happening and remained out of the room until the disturbance was far advanced.

As we have reported earlier, we also were told at HMP Severn, Category B Prison of an incident when prison officers did not intervene quickly in a stabbing that occurred at the Friday Congregational Prayer because they had been persuaded that they could not step on the prayer mat in their shoes.

For the avoidance of any doubt, the most important value in Islam is the preservation of human life (Kamali, 2008): if there is violence at the Friday Prayer, Islamically speaking as well as through professional duty, prison officers would be expected to intervene as quickly as possible with or without shoes!

Naïve response

☐ To assume that congregational prayers and sessions of religious education are free of the threat of violence and/or disruption.

Suspicious response

☐ To consider religious attendance necessarily as an opportunity for prisoners to exchange prohibited items or to evade work.

☐ To consider that congregational events are necessarily dangerous.

Balanced response

☐ To be aware of sensitivities around spaces used for worship and the value of prisoners engaging in religious education and worship while safeguarding against associated security risks, including the exchange of prohibited items, which sometimes occurs during worship.

☐ To be alert to the slim but real possibility of violence at congregational events.

Ablution (wudu) and 'cleaning' oneself

We have noted in Chapter 5 the significance for prisoners of both doing ablution before the Friday Congregational Prayer and being able to keep clean for their Five Daily Obligatory Prayers and that ignorance of this need by staff can be a cause of conflict.

- Ritual washing (*wudu*) is a core part of Muslim personal hygiene and readiness for prayer.
- Muslims need to wash their private parts with water after using the toilet.
- Simple jugs of water (or integrated bidet systems in toilets) would fulfil these needs.
- A lack of facilities for *wudu* is often a point of conflict in prisons.
- Access to showers for major ablution (*ghusl*) in good time before the Friday Congregational Prayer would relieve potential tension and generate goodwill.

The prisons in our research represented a wide contrast in terms of accommodation and washing facilities.

- At HMP Cherwell, Category C Prison and at HMP Parrett, Category B Prison, there were limited showering facilities.
- HMP Forth, Category A Prison was better equipped with showering spaces.

There were also contrasts between the *dedicated* ablution spaces provided in the *dedicated* mosque spaces and in the multi-faith centres in our sample: some were without hot water, such as HMP Severn, Category B Prison or were inadequate for multiple worshippers to use efficiently ahead of the Friday Congregational Prayer. See Image 8.4.

We also learnt of incidents of prisoners having wet dreams and then having to wait for long periods to take a shower. Notwithstanding the fact that in prison there are many legal and social complications over special privileges, prison staff need to be aware that prisoners cannot perform their Obligatory Daily Prayers or the obligatory Friday Congregational Prayer in a state of ritual impurity (*junub*) (after any form of sexual ejaculation) and that they require to shower quickly after a wet dream **(see Information Box on p 238)**.

Ramadan and fasting

Ramadan is the holy month of fasting for Muslims and, as we described in Chapter 3, fasting is regarded as one of the Obligations of Islam. We also described in Chapter 3 how at HMP Stour, Category D Prison, the careful

Naïve response

To assume that Muslims need to be ritually abluted at all times.

Suspicious response

To be ignorant of the need for Muslim prisoners to have access to washing facilities before the Obligatory Daily Prayers and to equate access to washing as a special privilege or as something superfluous to Islamic worship.

Balanced response

To acknowledge the need for access to washing as part of the religious rights of Muslim prisoners and to accommodate these where practicable, using suitable facilities such as low sinks or ablution bays as in HMP Cherwell. See Image 8.2.

and sensitive attention to Ramadan by kitchen staff generated real goodwill among prisoners.

The facilitation of Ramadan in prison presents several logistical challenges:

- prisons are institutions which are run according to detailed timetables, yet the Islamic calendar follows the lunar cycle which shifts by ten solar days each year;
- therefore an adjustment to the typical daily prison regime is required to facilitate the meal at dawn and the breaking of the fast at sunset;
- in England and Wales, owing to decades of practice and liaison between HMPPS and the Office of the Muslim Advisor to HMPPS, Ramadan is not seen as a particularly problematic period for prison staff.

In fact, prison staff were often highly respectful of the determination of prisoners to observe Ramadan by abstaining from food and drink from sunrise to sunset. A prison officer (male, British White, HMP Parrett, Category B Prison) explained,

> I'm very mindful of it [Ramadan]. Because obviously, when someone's fasting, especially in this heat and fasting a long day, I have a lot of respect for people that are willing to follow that because I personally am not strong enough to do that. Not for any length of time.

A related concern of some individual prisoners was how they were perceived by prison staff if they only fasted some days during the month of Ramadan. Similarly, prison officers were concerned about prisoners who claimed to be fasting the month of Ramadan but who were then observed eating or drinking between sunrise and sunset. This inevitably led to accusations of abuse of the Ramadan process in prison.

There was a tendency among some prison officers to assume that prisoners who were not perfect in their observance of Ramadan or who took the occasional 'day off' were playing the system or were insincere about the fast. However, as Mike, the Head Chef at HMP Stour, Category D Prison, observed,

> even if one day they are seen eating during the day, since ... doing the fast in prison and out of prison are not the same; in prison they may have had a bad telephone call or something has not gone right. So, if they say at lunch, "I want some chips," I give it to them. Then they go back to the Fast the next day.

Mike continued,

> Ramadan in prison is like running two separate regimes: it's difficult.

Nevertheless, despite the difficulties, Mike was adept at liaising with key trusted Muslim prisoners to see that Ramadan was observed to everyone's satisfaction. Mike's approach generated appreciable trust and good feeling between prisoners and staff.

Notwithstanding the fact that some prisoners do abuse the month of Ramadan to gain the privilege of breaking the fast, we believe that Mike's generous and flexible attitude to fasting was appropriate to prison circumstances.

Naïve response

To be unaware that a minority of prisoners may change their faith to 'Muslim' around Ramadan to gain the perceived privilege of better or extra food to break the fast.

Suspicious response

To consider those Muslims who fast the month of Ramadan as necessarily seeking some benefit or perk.

To equate Muslims who fast intermittently as abusers of the system.

Balanced response

To acknowledge that observant Muslims will correctly regard fasting the month of Ramadan as obligatory and may also choose to fast on other days, such as the Day of Arafat during the Hajj Pilgrimage.

To accept that Muslims make a pledge to fast each day and there are a range of reasons why a Muslim may fast on one day and not another, including issues of physical or mental illness.

Staff should be aware that Muslim prisoners can 'make up' any missed days of fasting after Ramadan within the following 11 months or pay some charity in compensation. It is wise to liaise with the Muslim prison chaplains to check any abuse.

Music

We have noted a potential antagonism produced by music in prison because of how music is perceived by some Muslim prisoners (see Chapter 2).

- In workshops, the issue of music arose when supervisors permitted Muslim prisoners to perform their Midday Prayer in a nearby office or similar space while leaving the rest of the prisoners to continue working with loud music playing through the workshop speakers: requests to lower the volume for the duration of the short Midday Prayer were met with hostility from fellow prisoners.
- Elsewhere, Muslim prisoners were regularly told by other prisoners and some Muslim prison chaplains that music in Islam is forbidden (*haram*). In our interviews, prisoners said that this view caused them some psychological distress because music was routinely played in cells, association rooms and gyms. Indeed, on the Segregation Wing at HMP Forth, Category A Prison, prison staff often played rock music at excessive volumes in what seemed to us and to the prisoners that we interviewed as a deliberate attempt to provoke a hostile response from them.

Naïve response

To be unaware that some Muslim prisoners may use the issue of music as a pretext to cause trouble with prison staff and non-Muslim prisoners.

Suspicious response

To be ignorant of the sensitivities and potential negative impact for Muslim prisoners of music upon prayer and reading scripture.

To view objections to loud music from some Muslim prisoners as unreasonable or as a sign of an extremist position.

Balanced response

To be aware of the sensitivities of some Muslim prisoners to music being played, especially near congregational prayers or where religious learning is taking place, and to lower the volume as practicable.

Never to use music as an 'anti-Muslim' weapon.

To appeal to prisoners of all types to be considerate of others when playing music.

- In short, in different sites across the prison estate, music was a potential flashpoint through which Muslim prisoners and non–Muslim prison staff sometimes chose to express aggressively and inflexibly their religious or anti-religious identities **(see Information Box on p 241)**.

Halal diet

We also described in Chapter 2 how a frequent cause of conflict between Muslim prisoners and staff is the availability or storage and cooking of religiously permitted (halal) food.

Flashpoints can arise in terms of:

- the authenticity of halal products available for prisoners to purchase;
- the storage of halal produce;
- whether 'cross-contamination' has occurred by a lack of separate utensils and trays.

The importance of food culture for a prisoner's identity and their relationships, in addition to their general well-being, should not be underestimated (Smoyer and Minke, 2015).

- A report into the significance of food in prison highlights that ethnic minority prisoners may utilise cooking as both a resistance to institutions but also as a means of providing themselves with dignity and resourcefulness (Ugelvik, 2011).
- In England, the Office of the Muslim Advisor to HMPPS produced guidelines over two decades ago for the preparation of food for Muslim prisoners and the procedures for Ramadan (Botterhill and Gora, 2000).
- Consideration should be given to the sourcing and authentication of halal food which is delivered to prisons.
- The way the food is handled and stored as well as issues of contaminated cooking equipment, ingredients and shared cooking all require careful consideration. Prison staff would also do well to communicate to Muslim prisoners how contamination is being avoided.
- In England, these detailed provisions are located in Prison Service Orders, which are regularly updated and overseen by the Muslim Advisor to HMPPS **(see Information Box on p 243)**.

Cultural diversity among Muslim prisoners

Our Worldview approach has painted in broad brushstrokes the characteristics, outlook and behaviours of Muslim prisoners, which are as diverse as those of Muslim populations outside prison in terms of ethnicity, country of origin, languages, sects and doctrine. This diversity was recognised by prison staff.

Naïve response

To be unaware that some prisoners may manipulate the provision of halal food for non-religious purposes.

Suspicious response

To view dietary requests and objections to contamination as hyper-sensitivity or indications of extreme or unreasonable requests.

Balanced response

To be aware of the religious rights for Muslims to have access to *halal* food.

To acknowledge sensitivities around how *halal* food is stored and served, whether in formal prison kitchens/serveries or where produce is available for self-catering.

- Some Muslim prisoners may identify as Muslim in a cultural sense rather than in a religious sense, which may then impact on the degree to which they view particular rights as necessary or important to them.
- The relationships of prisoners with Muslim chaplains and a prisoner's interest (or not) in formal worship will reflect a wide spectrum of religious commitment.
- Our data sample also captured differences in the religious provision and religious experiences of a small yet unfortunately growing population of female Muslim prisoners.[8]
- Our data illustrates that Muslims in continental European prisons tend to have a more secular, less religiously observant Worldview than those in the English prisons.

---

[8] See Schneuwly Purdie et al (2021).

Naïve response

To assume that all Muslim prisoners will wish to practise or articulate their faith identically to other Muslims.

Suspicious response

To assume that variations in religious practice, such as diet, are the product of a prisoners inventing the rules of their faith to cause trouble.

Balanced response

To acknowledge that there are fundamental commonalities among all Muslims and, at the same time, there exist denominational, doctrinal and cultural, and educational variations that may impact upon how a particular Muslim prisoner will follow their faith in prison.

Liaising with Muslim chaplains and the prison chaplaincy team

In England, the prison chaplaincy teams have undergone significant changes to incorporate a multi-faith approach to their work. As we saw in Chapter 8, HMPPS has appointed many Muslim prison chaplains on a full-time basis, and other Muslim prison chaplains have been employed part time and over many years.

During our research, we noted that Muslim prison chaplains are proactive members of the prison chaplaincy teams, performing both statutory and pastoral duties; they are security aware and are frequently called upon for reports and assessments on any behaviour of concern among their prisoner population.

Prison officers in England often described how they enjoyed good working relationships with their prison chaplaincy teams. For example, one prison officer (male, British White, HMP Parrett, Category B Prison) explained,

> Personally, I couldn't do this job without them [the prison chaplaincy team]. I'll put my hands up. I have a very, very good relationship with them. They have supported me my entire career, front to back.

> Not being biased, I've always been able to knock on their door, and they've always had time for me wherever I have worked. **99**

Other prison officers identified how their pastoral care for prisoners was significantly facilitated by their strong professional relationship with the prison chaplaincy teams. For example, another prison officer (male, British White, HMP Parrett, Category B Prison) said,

> To be honest, I think, yes, we've got a really good chaplaincy team. Really open, really friendly.
>
> Regardless of what the face, or whatever, really, really, just open and I believe anyone can speak to anyone. From what the prisoners say, the male and the female, really good feedback from everyone with regards to them guys. So, we've got a good, yes, definitely a good relationship at work. **99**

Naïve response

　To consider prisoners to be the primary source of knowledge about their religious practice and rights.

Suspicious response

　To discount the importance of the input of multi-faith chaplaincy teams as colleagues in the management and rehabilitation of offenders.

Balanced response

　Because a combination of empathetic prison chaplains coupled with fair and informed prison officers is critical for positive prisoner rehabilitation, it is essential that the prison chaplaincy teams and the prison officers consider one another partners in the effective management and rehabilitation of offenders.

Conclusion: Prison staff affect the experience of Islam in prison

In this chapter we have seen that the quality of a prisoner's relationship with prison staff, especially prison officers, had a significant influence on their experience of their faith.

- Prisoners felt nudged towards programmes of work and education when they had a sense of being treated fairly and respectfully by prison officers and when prison officers engaged with the prison chaplaincy teams.
- Conversely, negative, suspicious behaviours from prison officers could play into the 'Us' versus 'Them' Worldviews of Islamism and Islamist Extremism; they exacerbated the Islamist Extremist idea that the *kuffar* (unbelievers) are out to get Muslims.
- We have relayed the varied views among staff with regard to their perceptions and interactions with Muslim prisoners:
    - at one end of the spectrum, we witnessed an informed openness to Muslim prisoners and an acknowledgement of the pro-social behavioural impact of the practice of Islam upon many prisoners;
    - our research also captured prison staff feeling nervous and suspicious about Islam and Muslims and a deep-rooted cynicism about conversion to Islam.
- A key message from prison staff centred on an acknowledgement of the shortcomings of training about religion in general, and Islam specifically, to help inform their interaction with and management of Muslim prisoners.
- Prison officers universally felt under-trained to deal with the religious complexities of life in contemporary prisons, especially around Islam.

This chapter cannot cover all the scenarios pertinent to prison practice and policies but instead has highlighted some principles to dial down flashpoints between Muslim prisoners and prison staff as reflected in our research.

Our suggestions for ameliorating or dealing with these potential flashpoints have been guided by a call for a balanced professional ethos which treads a balanced, informed Middle Way between unrealistic naïvety and unfair suspicion.

Conclusion: The Virtuous Cycle of Rehabilitation and Avoiding the Vicious Cycle of Extremism

Here we summarise our findings and set Islam in prison in a broadly reflective context.

We will identify gaps in prison provision around Islam that urgently require plugging in order to develop the rehabilitative potential of Islam in prison and to reduce the criminogenic risk of Islamism and Islamist Extremism.

Chapter 1: Where does Islam come from and who are Muslim prisoners?

We described:

- how Islam came into the world;
- how Islamic civilisation developed, contributed to other civilisations and declined;
- how, against a backdrop of post-colonial migration and a century of conflict in the Muslim-majority world, Muslims have come to be a significant presence in prisons throughout Europe;
- a broad socio-demographic portrait of our characteristic sample of 279 Muslim prisoners who, when compared to the general European prison population, exhibited:
  - higher levels of education;
  - higher levels of pre-prison employment;
  - longer prison sentences;
  - more reoffending/reconviction.

Chapter 2: What is Islam in prison?

We outlined:

- the essential elements of Islamic belief: the Articles of Faith, the Pillars of Islam and the Permitted (halal) and Forbidden (haram);
- how, in prison, these basic elements of Islam are living realities that brought structure and meaning to the lives of many prisoners;

- how the levels of belief and practice of Muslim prisoners fluctuated greatly;
- how Islam was part of the cultural heritage of many Muslim prisoners, especially in France and Switzerland, rather than constituting a commitment to religious practice and belief.

Chapter 3: Finding their faith: why do prisoners choose Islam?

- Religious conversion was defined as 'any significant change in type or intensity of religious Worldview'.
- We provided a typology of Muslim prisoners as: **Converts**, **Intensifiers**, **Shifters**, **Remainers** and **Reducers**.
- Using this broad typology, we discovered that prisons in Europe are places of intense conversion activity both into and within Islam – 77 per cent of our prisoner sample had experienced a significant change in their religious Worldview in prison.[1]
- We observed that **male Muslim prisoners** tended to be **Intensifiers**.
- We observed that **female Muslim prisoners** were more likely than men to be **Reducers**.
- We found that prisoners are *more likely* to convert to or intensify in Islam for reasons of faith, emotional coping and good company than for perks, privileges and protection.

Chapter 4: What types of Islam do prisoners follow?

- We challenged the belief that prisons in England, France and Switzerland are wholesale incubators of Islamist Extremism because, of our characteristic sample of 279 Muslim prisoners:
  - **76 per cent** held the Worldview of **Mainstream Islam** of Unity-in-Diversity, reflecting an ethos of the basic equality of all humans before God and the need for universal justice and respect. In particular, the Worldview of **Mainstream Activist Islam** was significantly associated with a strong **Attitude to Rehabilitation** in the form of the avoidance of 'bad behaviour' and a commitment to work and education;
  - **19 per cent** held the Worldview of Islamism reflecting a Worldview of the exaggerated difference of 'Us'/Muslims versus 'Them'/ Non-Muslims;
  - **4 per cent** held the Worldview of **Islamist Extremism** of the absolute separation and antagonistic difference between 'Us'/Muslims

---

[1] Converts: 21 per cent; Intensifiers: 48 per cent; Reducers: 8 per cent.

versus 'Them'/Non-Muslims (including 'wrong Muslims') and which stripped non-Muslims of basic human attributes;
- **0.4 per cent** (1 prisoner) was committed to the Worldview of **Violent Islamist Extremism**.

Chapter 5: Mainstream Islam in prison

- We described how prisoners who held the Worldview of **Mainstream Islam** brought the core values of Islam to life in prison by:
  - caring for other prisoners through sharing material goods and advice and offering emotional support;
  - showing respect and politeness towards other people of all types;
  - returning to education;
  - developing a work ethic; and
  - aspiring to reconnect lawfully with family and society.

Chapter 6: Islamism and Islamist Extremism in prison

- We described the Worldview of **Islamist** prisoners and how they were likely to:
  - avoid (or pretend to avoid) non-Muslim prisoners;
  - reject democracy as un-Islamic; and
  - justify their crimes on spurious 'Islamic' grounds.
- We described the Worldview of the small number of **Islamist Extremist** prisoners:
  - who believed that Islam was violently opposed to Unbelief (*kufr*);
  - who supported terrorist groups; and
  - some of whom were prepared to conduct themselves violently against other prisoners in gangs, supposedly in the name of Islam.
- We described how **Islamist Extremist** prisoners, while representing only a small percentage (4 per cent) of our characteristic sample of Muslim prisoners, generated a degree of fear and disruption among other prisoners and prison staff that belied their minority status.

Chapter 7: The lives of Muslim prisoners: opportunities and risks

- We presented seven case studies of **Converts**, **Intensifiers**, **Shifters**, **Remainers** and **Reducers** to illustrate the:
  - diversity of the experience of conversion and religious change in prison with prisoners often experiencing multiple types of conversion within a single prison sentence;
  - real-life examples of the opportunities and risks presented by different types of conversion to Islam in prison.

Chapter 8: Caring for Muslim prisoners: Muslim prison chaplaincy

- We showed how a prisoner's engagement with Muslim prison chaplaincy significantly enhanced their likelihood of developing an Islamic Worldview in prison that would produce positive rehabilitative outcomes.
- We described the modalities and effects of the chaplains' provision of the Friday Congregational Prayer, Islamic Studies classes and pastoral duties, including the difficulties and challenges faced by chaplains.
- We offered some suggestions for improved chaplaincy practice, including:
  - avoiding exaggerating the difference between Muslims and non-Muslims;
  - the need for the development of a coherent between-faiths ethos; and
  - the need for a prison-appropriate Islamic Studies curriculum, especially for **Converts** into and **Intensifiers** in Islam.

Chapter 9: Managing Muslim prisoners: treading a middle path between naïvety and suspicion

- We showed how the quality of a prisoner's relationship with prison officers influenced their experience of their faith.
- We showed how the attitudes of prison staff towards Muslim prisoners ranged from an informed openness and appreciation of the potential rehabilitative impact of the practice of Islam upon prisoners, to suspicion about Islam and Muslims and a deep cynicism about conversion to Islam.
- We gave voice to prison officers who feel that the absence of religious training in the standard POELT has left them unprepared and ill-equipped to understand and manage the complexities of religion in prison.
- We highlighted typical flashpoints between Muslim prisoners and prison staff, and presented potential solutions that are guided by a balanced ethos which treads a Middle Way between an unrealistic naïvety towards or an unfair suspicion of Muslim prisoners.

Prison as a space of privation and enchantment

The prisons in which we researched were undoubtedly places of privation: they housed convicted criminals, many of whom had done terrible things to their victims; they were usually noisy places; sometimes grubby places; and occasionally violent places.

At the same time, our prisons were also 'enchanted' spaces (Taylor, 2007) in the sense that (usually young) men and women were afforded time and space to reflect on the meaning and purposes of their lives, to read, to return to education, to learn good manners and to receive a rudimentary spiritual instruction in Islam (and other faiths), often for the first time.

The 'pains of imprisonment' had often brought out the best in Islam and the best in Muslim prisoners. Our prisoner participants were usually poor; yet many often shared what little they possessed and they had tapped into the Islamic ethos to extend to other prisoners small acts of kindness and respect that generated genuine feelings of brotherhood.

In this 'enchanted' prison space, we discovered prisoners who had been brought to a place of repentance through striking dreams which they interpreted as God's guidance. Moreover, while many Muslim prisoners grappled with fierce inner demons and issues of mental health, the majority of the prisoners we encountered made consistent and genuine efforts to be decent to other people and to turn their lives around. Our data suggested that no Muslim prisoner was beyond redemption.

The Virtuous Cycle of Rehabilitation and the Vicious Cycle of Extremism

In this respect, we identified in prison a **Virtuous Cycle of Rehabilitation** which led to positive **Attitude to Rehabilitation** in the form of work, education and avoiding 'bad behaviour' (see Figure C.1).

The more a prisoner experienced this **Virtuous Cycle of Rehabilitation**, the less likely they were to be lured towards the **Vicious Cycle of Extremism** (see Figure C.2).

We have seen how skilled and sympathetic prison chaplains and informed and fair prison officers were critical agents of change in nudging a Muslim prisoner towards the **Virtuous Cycle of Rehabilitation**. Conversely, we have seen how ineffective prison chaplains – who exaggerated religious difference – an absence of chaplaincy – especially in France and Switzerland – and suspicious prison officers – who did not keep their word – could contribute to generating criminogenic 'Us' versus 'Them' Worldviews of Islamism and Islamist Extremism.

Learning from English, Swiss and French prisons

From the comparative element of our research in English, Swiss and French prisons, we learnt important lessons about prison chaplaincy.

- When compared with Muslim prison chaplaincy in England and France, Swiss Muslim prison chaplaincy was, to say the least, embryonic. The

Figure C.1: The Virtuous Cycle of Rehabilitation

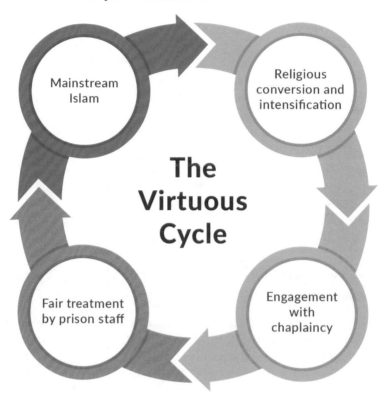

absence of professional Muslim chaplains in Switzerland left many prisoners vulnerable to reoffending. Yet in the single Swiss prison with a professional Muslim prison chaplain, the prison chaplaincy was imaginative and flexible and had instituted shared multi-faith events that drew on common faith values.

- In England, we witnessed the skilful and sensitive ministry of chaplains from a number of faiths and that Muslim prison chaplains were instrumental in generating hope and rehabilitative impetus in prisoners' lives. However, the different denominational structures were stoutly mono-faith and were resistant to shared religious events and exchange.
- In France a prevailing atmosphere of mutual suspicion between Muslim prisoners and prison staff hampered the ability of prison chaplains to engage with our participants and damaged Muslim prisoners' experiences of faith.

Figure C.2: The Vicious Cycle of Extremism

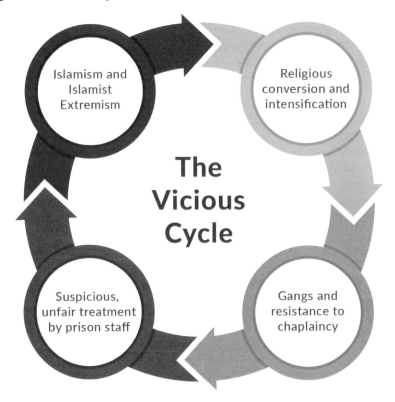

Gaps that need to be plugged

In order to build on the capacity of Islam to feed into values of rehabilitation and to reduce the criminogenic risk of this religious choice, we believe that there are five clear gaps that need to be filled:

1. Improving prisoners' understanding of Islam in a way that is relevant to life in prison

- Often the quality of Islamic education in English prisons depends too heavily on the Muslim prison chaplain's personal style and private knowledge.
- The current Tarbiya course, while containing strengths in its presentation of Mainstream Islam, is too long for the average time spent in a prison, is often boringly taught with no attention to pedagogy and does not connect strongly with the particular issues faced by Muslims in prison, such as dealing with feelings of guilt and repenting crime.

2. Raising the currently low 'prisons-literacy' of Muslim prison chaplains

- Many of our Muslim prison chaplains had been given little or no training in prison life before going on the wings.
- Despite the dedication most Muslim prison chaplains show to prisoners and the consequent life–changing effects that they can produce on prisoners' lives, many of our Muslim prison chaplains lamented their lack of Continuing Professional Development.
- This needs to be addressed since no one should underestimate the challenges faced by Muslim prison chaplains, who must work in the awkward intersection between the state and the religious community of prisoners: they are always vulnerable because they are often exposed to hostility from Islamist Extremist prisoners who accuse them of being 'Scholars for Dollars'.

3. Raising the low 'religious literacy' of prison officers

- While the Muslim prisoners who participated in our research were certainly no angels, Muslim prisoners were seen as 'doubly suspect' by some prison staff: both convicted criminals *and* Muslim 'hot potatoes' whose motives and behaviours were invariably negatively construed.
- Some prison officers described high stress levels when dealing with Muslim prisoners.
- Raising the 'Religious Literacy' of prison officers in their POELT would enable them to distinguish between Islam, Islamism and Islamist Extremism. This religious literacy would help prison officers make good decisions when dealing with the flashpoints identified in Chapter 9 and to tread that balanced Middle Way between naïvety and suspicion.

4. Improving the chaplaincy provision for female Muslim prisoners

- In Chapter 3, we saw how incarceration for male prisoners was often a religiously intensifying experience, but for female prisoners, prison was often a religiously reducing experience.
- To enable female prisoners also to tap into the rehabilitative potential of their faith, attention must be paid to the different psychological complexity of female prisoners, who, despite the fact that they are convicted criminals, often describe themselves feeling victims rather than criminals and therefore do not feel a need to repent.

5. Improving the legal process of changing religion in prison through the Prison Service Instruction

- The present process of changing religion in prison is not conducive to health and safety: a prisoner simply informs the Managing Chaplain in writing of their change of faith, which we found to be open to abuse.
- For example, conversion to Islam increases just before Ramadan and decreases just after Ramadan due to the reputedly better food in the thermos boxes Muslim prisoners are given before sunrise and at sunset.
- Prisoners often fill in other prisoners' change-of-faith forms, which can result in coercion.
- In the eyes of prison staff and other prisoners, the ease of the process of conversion in prison debases the currency of the faith of sincere prisoners (see Chapters 6 and 8).
- Most of our Muslim prison chaplains expressed their dissatisfaction with the process of conversion in prison because they could not ensure that prisoners were inducted safely and with legitimate knowledge into their new faith.
- Taking into account human rights legislation, the process of conversion in prison requires critical reflection and change.

Over the next four years, we are addressing these gaps in provision in our follow-up action research programme, PRIMO.

On the margins of European society, a new religious community is emerging

In prisons, on the margins of European society, a new religious community is emerging from which, if we address the five gaps identified earlier, prisoners can return to free society motivated by the values of human kindness, excellence and solidarity from which we all can learn.

APPENDIX 1

Theoretical framework

- UCIP brought together a multidisciplinary and diverse team, combining expertise in theology, criminology and the sociology of religion, which was integrated under one overarching theoretical umbrella.
- To accomplish this integration, the overarching theoretical framework for UCIP was drawn from an academic philosophy called critical realism and, in particular, from the contribution made by the Principal Investigator through the development of the philosophy and social theory of Islamic critical realism (Wilkinson 2015a; 2018) and its application by our Co-investigator (Quraishi, 2020).
- This critical realist framework provided a lens to make sense of the lives of Muslim prisoners in multiple, related 'knock-on' dimensions. For example, the dimensions of biology, sex-gender, the peer-group, education, employment and culture (Bhaskar, 2008; Irfan and Wilkinson, 2020) and, critically, included an evaluation of the religious Worldviews, religious practices and experiences of prison life.
- We provide a full technical account of our use of critical realist theory in other publications (Quraishi et al, 2021; Wilkinson et al, 2021).

Methodology

- Religious change among Muslims in prison exhibits not only individual depth, emotion and intensity, but also national and international patterns and breadth.
- This combination of breadth and depth called for a mixed-methods approach:
  - we used **quantitative questionnaires** to capture significant, broad patterns of belief, attitudes and behaviour across Muslims in different prisons and jurisdictions;
  - we used the **qualitative research tools of face-to-face interviews and observations of Islamic Studies classes and Friday Prayer** to plumb the depths of the experience of the individual Muslims and to explore the reasons behind the patterns that we had identified through our quantitative questionnaires.
- We applied our research methods in the following sequence:
  1. pilot semi-structured interviews to test our theoretical framework and identify suitable quantitative variables;
  2. quantitative attitudinal questionnaires;
  3. full semi-structured interviews coupled with
  4. observations of Friday Prayer and Islamic Studies classes.
- We conducted:
  - 279 attitudinal questionnaires with prisoners;
  - 158 interviews with prisoners, average length circa 45 minutes;
  - 19 interviews with Muslim prison chaplains, average length circa 60 minutes;
  - 41 interviews with prison officers, average length circa 40 minutes;
  - 15 interviews with prison governors, average length circa 40 minutes.
- In doing so, we looked at Islam in prison through the lenses of multiple methods and the perspectives of multiple types of people living and working in prison.

Ethics, recruitment, data analysis and data management

The gathering of our data was subject to robust social scientific procedures of ethics, recruitment of participants, data analysis and data management.

Ethics

- UCIP was subject to rigorous ethical evaluation prior to data collection.
- This comprised approval via the Principal Investigator's university Ethics Board to satisfy, inter alia, issues of informed consent, confidentiality, engaging with vulnerable respondents through sensitive questioning, data protection and risk assessments for prison-based research in line with the British Society of Criminology's *Statement of Ethics for Researchers*.

Recruitment and sampling

- Having identified prisons with diverse geographies in England, Switzerland and France with significant Muslim populations, the recruitment of participants was enabled through the research team spending intense induction periods of five research days in each establishment.
- Prisoner respondents were recruited through a combination of publicising the research via distributing leaflets and in-person invitations at congregational prayers, religious classes and various work, training or education-based activities in each site. This was a broad recruitment strategy. Nevertheless, we are aware that it is possible that religiously committed Muslims were more likely to engage with our research than those with little interest in their faith.
- Muslim chaplaincy teams and prison managers were instrumental in further publicising the research aims and encouraging prisoners and staff to participate.
- The social scientific reader might observe that our sampling was therefore self-selected and not randomised. This is true and an inevitable product of the ethical requirement to gain informed, consenting volunteers in the prison environment.
- Our sample of 279 prisoner respondents represents, to our knowledge, the largest body of Muslim prisoners who have yet engaged in academic research.

- Moreover, as we explain in Chapter 2, we believe that our sample is 'characteristic' of the general Muslim prison populations of England, Switzerland and France.
- Our sample also represents a large proportion (circa 35 per cent) of the available registered Muslim prisoner population of our sample of prisons.

Analysis

- The data from our questionnaires was analysed using a variety of statistical techniques including:
  - Descriptive Statistics
  - Correlations and Chi-squares
  - Principal Component Factor Analysis
  - Regressions
- Our semi-structured interviews were transcribed verbatim in the original languages (English, German, French and Urdu).
- Each semi-structured interview was first analysed with a focus on the respondents' own narratives. Then the semi-structured interviews were subjected to inductive, deductive and axial coding using software called NVivo.
- Our qualitative data – interviews, observation protocols and field notes – were compared, contrasted and integrated with the quantitative data.
- Observations of Friday Congregational Prayers and Islamic studies classes were particularly useful for understanding the institutional-level relationships between prisoners and prison chaplains.

Descriptions of our research prisons

- We researched in a variety of geographical settings, holding both sentenced and remand prisoners and covering all prison categories:
  - five English prisons
  - four Swiss prisons
  - one French prison
- Our research sample included all four security categories used in England (A, B, C, D); and to ease comparison, we used the same security categories in Switzerland and France, although we are aware that the equivalencies are not exact.
- According to the UK government (Ministry of Justice, 2021), male prisons are organised into four categories:

Category A

These are high security prisons. They house male prisoners who, if they were to escape, pose the greatest threat to the public, the police or national security.

Category B

These prisons are either local or training prisons. Local prisons house prisoners who are taken directly from court in the local area (sentenced or on remand), and training prisons hold long-term and high security prisoners.

Category C

These prisons are training and resettlement prisons; most prisoners are located in a Category C. They provide prisoners with the opportunity to develop their own skills so they can find work and resettle back into the community on release.

Category D – open prisons

These prisons have minimal security and allow eligible prisoners to spend most of their day away from the prison on licence to carry out work or education or for other resettlement purposes. Open prisons only house prisoners who have been risk assessed and deemed suitable for open conditions.

Women and young adults

Women and young adults are categorised and held in either closed conditions or open conditions, according to their risks and needs.

Females and young adults who are considered high risk are categorised as 'restricted status', meaning they can only be held in a closed prison. In exceptional cases, women and young adults may be held in a high security prison (Category A).

Our research prisons, all of which have been given pseudonyms, were:

HMP Cherwell

- Category C Medium Security
- male training prison
- run by HMPPS
- south England
- operational for over 50 years
- approximately 500 prisoners housed in five wings
- only one wing has in-cell sanitation
- showers are communal
- dedicated mosque with ablution area
- see Images 8.1 and 8.2

HMP Forth

- Category A Maximum Security
- male prison
- run by HMPPS
- north England
- approximately 600 prisoners
- prisoners are unlikely to have sentences of less than four years or to have been transferred here if they have less than 12 months of their sentence left
- shared multi-faith areas provided by the Chaplaincy Department

HMP Stour

- Category D Low Security prison
- adult male prison
- run by HMPPS
- south England
- approximately 300 prisoners
- resettlement institution for those in the last few months of their sentence

- small, dedicated mosque with ablution facilities and an Islamic library
- see Images 8.3 and 8.4

HMP Severn

- Category B High Security
- adult male prison
- run by HMPPS
- south-east England
- approximately 1,200 prisoners
- four residential wings plus a dedicated Drug Rehabilitation Unit
- one of the largest Muslim prisoner populations in England at the time the research was undertaken
- dedicated 'mosque' which can accommodate over 100 worshippers in congregation
- Friday Congregational Prayer is offered for Muslim prisoners in the main population and for Vulnerable prisoners separately
- see Images 8.5 and 8.6

HMP Parrett

- Category B High Security
- adult male and female prison
- privately run
- east England
- approximately 840 prisoners
- shared Multi-Faith Room operated by the Chaplaincy Unit
- see Image 8.7

Prison de la Citadelle

- Category A Maximum Security Prison
- female prison
- run by the Canton
- west Switzerland
- capacity for approximately 60 prisoners
- Pre-Trial Detention Unit
- Sentence Enforcement Unit
- ecumenical chapel also used for individual interviews with inmates, including Muslims
- as there are no dedicated congregational spaces for faith communities in Swiss prisons, Muslims gather for Friday Prayer in a classroom beside the ecumenical chapel

Prison de Doriath

- Category A Maximum Security Prison
- adult male prison
- run by the Canton
- west Switzerland
- capacity for approximately 80 prisoners
- intended for dangerous prisoners as well as for those serving long sentences and internments which require appropriate security measures
- ecumenical chapel, but the Muslim prisoners meet in the sports hall to do the Friday Prayer
- see Image 8.8

Prison de Fontgrise

- Category B High Security Prison
- adult male prison
- run by the Canton
- west Switzerland
- provides a closed and a semi-open prison environment
- capacity for approximately 100 prisoners at the end of their sentence or serving short sentences
- Muslims meet either in the ecumenical chapel or in a small classroom because there is no dedicated room for Muslims
- special occasions, such as religious festivals, take place in the sports hall
- see Image 8.9

Gefängniss Mitheilen

- Category A Maximum Security Prison
- adult male prison
- run by the Canton
- east Switzerland
- capacity for approximately 400 prisoners
- Multi-Faith Prayer Space operated by the Chaplaincy Unit, which is used for Friday Prayer as well as Christian and inter-religious celebrations
- see Image 8.10

Centre Pénitentiaire de Hauterive

- Category B High Security Prison
- adult male prison with two remand prisons for pre-trial detention and two detention centres

- run by the Ministry of Justice
- eastern France
- capacity for approximately 700 prisoners
- mainly houses prisoners coming to the end of their sentences or serving short sentences
- Inter-religious Room operated by Social Services
- Inter-religious Room serves for celebrations, the Friday Prayer, religious classes and discussion groups
- The six recognised chaplaincies have similar access to the Inter-religious Room: Catholic, Protestant, Jewish, Muslim, Buddhist and Jehovah's Witnesses

How UCIP ascertained the Worldviews of Muslim prisoners

Our calculation of prisoners' Worldviews was driven both by the theoretical categories and substantiated by the testimony of prisoners themselves.

First, we conducted 15 pilot interviews to check that our Worldview categories mapped onto Worldviews of Muslim prisoners, which broadly speaking they did.

Then, out of the interviews we constructed variables as part of our Attitudinal Questionnaires to test for and measure the categories. The following statements individually tested attitudes towards key traits associated with the different Worldviews:

- *It is part of Islam to treat Muslims more fairly than non-Muslims.*
  This was a test for a commitment to a Qur'anic belief in basic human equality as a core component of Mainstream Islam.
- *I avoid prisoners who are not Muslim.*
  This was a test for sympathy with Islamist Extremist Doctrines of Loyalty & Disavowal (see Chapter 6).
- *Islam teaches that wisdom can be found in many religions.*
  This was a test for religious pluralism and inclusivity as mandated in The Qur'an.
- *Islam teaches that I must follow the law of this country.*
  This was a test for an Islamic commitment to lawfulness.
- *Islam teaches that the laws of this country should be replaced by Sharia Law.*
  This was a test for Islamism and the desire to replace existing legal structures with Sharia Law.
- *Islam teaches me that human life is sacred.*
  This was a test for commitment to the sanctity of life as a core component of Mainstream Islam. Either to 'mainly disagree' or 'strongly disagree' with this variable was one indicator of extremism.

From answers to these questions, we combined the scores and calculated the mean response in order to develop a Worldview scale from 1 = Violent Islamist Extremism to 5 = Mainstream Islam.

No variable was used singularly to represent a Worldview, except

- *It is part of Islam to change things that are unfair in society.*

This was used as a test for Activist Islam.

The questions contained both negative and positive statements in order to avoid acquiescence bias.

Glossary of key terms and important names

Aaron a Prophet of the Abrahamic religions of Judaism, Christianity and Islam, known as Harun in Arabic.

Abbasid Caliphate (750–1258 CE) the second dynastic caliphate to succeed the Prophet Muhammad ruled by the family loosely related to the Prophet Muhammad's uncle, Abbas ibn Abd al-Muttalib.

Abraham a Prophet of the Abrahamic religions of Judaism, Christianity and Islam, known as Ibrahim in Arabic.

Abu Bakr al-Baghdadi (1971–2019 CE) the leader of the Islamic State of Iraq and the Levant (ISIL) or Daesh from 2014 until his death in 2019.

Abu Bakr as-Siddiq (573–634 CE) the intimate Companion of the Prophet Muhammad and the first Successor (Caliph) to him in leadership of the Muslim community. See Chapter 2.

Adam first Prophet of the Abrahamic religions of Judaism, Christianity and Islam.

Ahl al-Bayt the People of the Prophetic House, in other words the Prophet Muhammad's family.

Ahl as-Sunna wal Jama 'People of Prophetic Example and Consensus', in other words Sunni Muslims. See Chapter 1.

Akhira the Next World, in other words life-after-death.

Al-Banna, Hassan (1906–1949 CE) an influential Islamist thinker whose ideas have influenced both Activist Islam and Islamist Extremism.

Al-Qaeda translated as 'The Base', 'The Foundation', (alternatively spelled al-Qaida or al-Qa'ida) is a Violent Islamist Extremist multi-national organisation founded in 1988 during the Soviet–Afghan War.

Alhamdulillah   Arabic term meaning 'Praise belongs to God'.

Allah   the One God, literally the One Worthy of Worship. This word had been used in Arabic to denote God Almighty long before the coming of Islam in 610 CE.

Allahu Akbar   Arabic term meaning 'God is greater'. In other words, God is greater than anything that can be imagined by humans.

Amana   Arabic word meaning 'trust'.

Amir   a leader of a community or a commander of troops.

Anwar Sadat
(1918–1981 CE)   an Egyptian politician who served as the third President of Egypt, from 15 October 1970 until his assassination by Egyptian army officers on 6 October 1981.

Aqeeda   'belief', in other words what Muslims believe about God, Prophethood and related religious matters.

Ar-Raheem   Arabic word meaning 'the most Merciful', one of the 99 names of Allah in The Qur'an.

As-salamu 'alaykum   the Arabic greeting meaning 'Peace be upon you', is a standard Muslim greeting instituted by the Prophet Muhammad.

As-Salah   the Obligatory Prayer, which Muslims must perform five times every day: before sunrise, at midday, in the mid-afternoon, at sunset and in the first part of the night.

Ash-Shafi, Muhammad ibn Idris
(767–820 CE)   a Gazzan jurist who founded the influential Shafi School of Law.

Atatürk, Mustapha Kamal
(1881–1938 CE)   Secular Muslim leader and army colonel who founded the Grand National Assembly of Turkey and then the Turkish Republic in Anatolian heartland of the Ottoman Empire after the Ottoman defeat in the First World War.

Ayat	verse of The Qur'an, literally 'a sign'.
Babur (1483–1530 CE)	the founder of the Mughal Empire in the Indian sub-continent.
Bida'	religious innovation, usually with negative connotations.
Bismillahi Ar-Rahman, ir-Raheem	translated as 'In the name of God, the Compassionate, the Merciful.'
Boko Haram	a Violent Islamist Extremist organisation based in northeastern Nigeria.
Daesh/ISIS/ISIL	also called the 'Islamic State', is a Violent Islamist Extremist terrorist group that was founded in 1999 by Jordanian ideologue Abu Musab al-Zarqawi.
Dar al-Kufr	'The territory of Unbelief' in medieval times, this referred variously to territories in which Muslims were in the minority and/or which did not govern themselves according to Sharia Law. The concept has been revived by modern Islamist Extremists to refer to any country that does not govern by what they regard as pure Sharia Law, even if it is a country where Muslims can fulfill the obligations of their faith.
David	a Prophet of the Abrahamic religions of Judaism, Christianity and Islam, known as Daud in Arabic.
Deen	a religion or religious Life-Transaction or Covenant with God. Islam is often referred to as *Deen al-Islam*.
Deobandi	an Islamic revivalist movement within Sunni (primarily Hanafi) Islam that formed in the town of Deoband, India, during the late 19th century.
Dhikr	literally meaning 'remembrance', are Islamic devotional acts, in which phrases or prayers to God are ritually repeated.
Dua	a prayer of invocation, supplication or request asking for help or assistance from God.

Eid	literally means a 'festival' or 'feast' in Arabic. There are two major Eids in the Islamic calendar per year, Eid al-Fitr – which means 'festival of the breaking of the fast' – is celebrated at the end of Ramadan, which is a month when many adult Muslims fast. Eid al-Adha – which means 'feast of the sacrifice' – is celebrated just over two months later, at the end of the Hajj pilgrimage.
Fajr	'dawn prayer', one of the five Obligatory Daily Prayers. See Chapter 3.
Fatwa	a ruling or piece of advice on a point of Islamic law given by a recognised authority.
Fiqh	the rulings of Sharia Law, literally means 'understanding'.
Fitna	political oppression, rebellion, injustice and anarchy.
Fiy Sabilillah	'in the Path of God', usually connected with '*Jihad fiy sabilillah*' meaning 'Struggle in the Path of God'.
Gabriel	or *Jibrīl*, also spelled Jabrā'īl or *Jibreel* in Islam, the Archangel who acts as intermediary between God and humans and as bearer of revelation to the prophets, most notably to Muhammad.
Genghis Khan (c. 1158–August 18, 1227)	the first Great Emperor (Khan) of the Mongols, who united the tribes of Mongolia, and initiated a devastatingly violent conquest of much of the medieval Muslim world.
Ghusul	an Arabic term for the full-body ritual purification mandatory before the performance of Prayer.
Hadith	sayings and actions of the Prophet Muhammad. Authentic (Sahih) hadiths have highly reliable chains of transmission (isnad) through truthful and trustworthy Followers and Companions that stretched right back to the Prophet Muhammad. See Chapter 2.

Hajj	the Obligatory Pilgrimage to worship God in Mecca that a Muslim must perform once in a lifetime if s/he is able financially and physically to do so.
Halal	permitted by God in Islam. See Chapter 2.
Hanafi	someone who adheres to the Sunni School of Law founded by Imam Abu Hanifa (699–767 CE).
Hanbali	someone who adheres to the Sunni School of Law founded by Imam Ahmed ibn Hanbal (780–855 CE).
Haram	forbidden by God in Islam. See Chapter 2.
Hijab	a covering of the private parts in Islam which usually refers to a head covering worn in public by some Muslim women.
Hijra	'migration', which usually refers to the migration of the Prophet Muhammad and about 100 Companions from conditions of severe persecution in the town of Mecca to conditions of peace and recognition in the town of Yathrib, 200 miles to the north of Mecca, in July 622 CE. See Chapter 1.
Hudud	literally means 'limits' and refers to the penal code of Sharia Law.
Hulegu (1215–1265 CE)	a Mongol ruler and grandson of Genghis Khan who conducted the Siege and Sack of Baghdad in 1258. See Chapter 1.
Ibn Abdal Wahhab, Muhammad (1703–1792 CE)	the 18th century religious reformer and founder of Wahhabi Islam. See Chapter 2.
Ibn Abi Talib, Ali (599–661 CE)	the cousin and son-in-law of the Prophet Muhammad who was the fourth Successor (Caliph) to Muhammad in leadership of the Muslim Community until his assassination in Kufa, Iraq. See Chapter 2.

Ibn Affan, Uthman (577–656 CE)

the third 'Rightly-Guided' Successor to the Prophet Muhammad who was murdered in controversial circumstances. See Chapter 2.

Ibn Al-Khattab, Umar (579–644 CE)

the second 'Rightly Guided' Successor to the Prophet Muhammad, who is revered by Muslims as a great statesman and law-maker.

Ibn Ali, Hasan (624–670 CE)

a grandson of the Prophet Muhammad and a son of Ali ibn Abi Talib (the fourth Caliph of Sunni Muslims) and the Prophet Muhammad's daughter Fatimah. He was the second Imam of Shia Islam.

Ibn Ali, Hussain (626–668 CE)

a grandson of the Prophet Muhammad and a son of Ali ibn Abi Talib and Muhammad's daughter Fatimah. He was the third Imam of Shia Islam. He was killed in the Battle of Kerbala.

Ibn Hanbal, Ahmed (780–855 CE)

the founder of the hadith-based Sunni Hanbali School of Law.

Ibn Saud, Muhammad (d. 1765 CE)

considered the founder of the First Saudi State and the Saud dynasty.

Ihsan

'sincerity of worship', defined by the Prophet Muhammad as worshipping God as if you see see Him in the knowledge that, although you do not see Him, He sees you. It is the aspect of Islam that developed into Sufism.

Iman

traditional Islamic faith in God, His Books, His Prophets, His Angels, His Decree and His Final Judgement. See Chapter 2.

Imama

Shia Muslim principle that God has designated specific religious leaders to follow the Prophets in the guidance of mankind.

Imam

Arabic meaning 'leader', or 'model', in a general sense, one who leads Muslim worshippers in Prayer.

In sha Allah	Arabic language and Qur'anic expression meaning 'if God wills'.
Isaac	a Prophet of the Abrahamic religions of Judaism, Christianity and Islam, known as Ishaq in Arabic.
Islam	'submission to God in way that brings peace'. A Life-Transaction (*deen*) described by The Qur'an and the Sunna of Muhammad, that is traditionally constituted by the outer religious aspects of the worship of One God (*Islam*), inner belief (*iman*) and sincerity of worship (*ihsan*).
Ismael	a Prophet of the Abrahamic religions of Judaism, Christianity and Islam, known as Isma'il in Arabic.
Isnad	reliable chains of narrators for hadith.
Istishad	'seeking martyrdom'. The act of seeking to die for the faith of Islam. See Chapter 6.
Jacob	a Prophet of the Abrahamic religions of Judaism, Christianity and Islam, known as Yaqub in Arabic.
Ja'far as-Sadiq, Imam (702–765)	an early teacher of Islam and jurist whose followers founded the Shia Jafari School of Law.
Ja'fari school or Ja'fari fiqh	the school of jurisprudence in Twelver and Nizari Shia Islam, named after the sixth Imam, Ja'far al-Sadiq.
Jahiliyya	pre-Islamic ignorance. This concept was re-defined by the Islamist ideologue Sayyid Qutb to refer to anything or anyone that was not aligned with political Islam. See Chapter 1.
Jamat e-Islami	the Indian/Pakistani Islamist Party founded by Abul Ala Maududi.
Jannah	Arabic word for 'heaven', literally meaning 'Garden'.
Jesus	a Prophet of Islam, known as Isa in Arabic.

John (the Baptist)   a Prophet of the Abrahamic religions of Judaism, Christianity and Islam, known as Yahya in Arabic.

Joseph   a Prophet of the Abrahamic religions of Judaism, Christianity and Islam, known as Yusuf in Arabic.

Jihad   struggle, short for '*Jihad fiy sabilillah*' meaning 'Struggle in the Path of God'. Doctrines of different dimensions of 'Struggle in the Path of God', including armed Struggle in defence of Islam under strict regulations, were developed after the death of the Prophet Muhammad. See Chapters 5 and 6.

Jinn   supernatural unseen creatures made of smokeless fire in early pre-Islamic Arabian and later Islamic cosmology.

Jumu'a   Arabic word for 'Gathering' which is also Friday, the holiest day of the Muslim week on which special congregational prayers are offered. See Chapter 8.

Ka'aba   the Cube. The House of God in Mecca which Muslims believe was first erected by the Prophet Abraham to worship God. It is the focal point of the Hajj pilgrimage and the direction (*qibla*) of the Five Obligatory Daily Prayers.

Kafir, pl. *Kuffar / Kafirun*   an unbeliever, literally someone who covers up the reality of God's existence, in other words a proactive atheist. It was used by the original Muslim community to refer to Meccan pagans who actively rejected the message of Islam. It is used by Islamists to refer any non-Muslim, including believing Christians and Jews, and by Islamist Extremists to refer to anyone – Muslim or non-Muslim – who does not fight to establish an Islamic State. See Chapter 6.

Khadija bint Khuwaylid (556–619 CE)   first wife of the Prophet Muhammad and the first person after the Prophet Muhammad to accept Islam.

Khalifa   a Caliph. Either a political Successor to the Prophet Muhammad, or, in the theological sense, someone who deputises as a steward for God on Earth.

Kharijite, pl. Khawarij 'those who departed', in other words rebels who abandoned the army of the Caliph Ali ibn Abi Talib. See Chapter 1.

Khomeini, Ayatollah Ruhollah (1902–1989 CE) the revolutionary Islamist founder of the Islamic Republic of Iran. See Chapter 1.

Kufr Arabic term for 'Unbelief' or rejection of belief in God.

Lot a Prophet of the Abrahamic religions of Judaism, Christianity and Islam, known as Lut in Arabic.

Makruh Arabic word and category of Islamic law meaning 'disliked by God'.

Maliki one of the four major traditions of Islamic jurisprudence within Sunni Islam. Founded by Malik ibn Anas (711–795 CE).

Maqasid as-Sharia the Principles of the Sharia. The purposes underpinning Islamic Law such as the protection of human life, property, lineage and reputation. See Chapter 2.

Maryam Arabic name for Mary, the mother of Jesus.

Masha'Allah Arabic term meaning 'what God wills [happens]', used by Muslims to express contentment, joy, praise or resignation to the will of God.

Masjid mosque or place of worship for Muslims.

Maududi, Abul Ala (1903–1979 CE) a key Indian/Pakistani Islamist writer and activist. See Chapter 1.

Mecca is the birthplace of the Prophet Muhammad and the holiest city in Islam which houses the Ka'aba.

Medina short for 'Medinat an-Nabawiyya', which was called 'Yathrib' – the town in modern Saudi Arabia which welcomed the Prophet Muhammad and his Companions after migration in 622 CE and was re-named 'Medinat an-Nabawiyya', the Prophetic City.

Moses a Prophet of the Abrahamic religions of Judaism, Christianity and Islam, known as Musa in Arabic.

Mughal an early modern empire in South Asia, formally
(1526–1857 CE) dissolved by the British Raj after the Indian Rebellion of 1857 CE. See Chapter 1.

Muhammad ibn an Arab religious, social and political leader and the
Abdullah, founder of Islam. According to Islamic doctrine, he
Prophet of God was the last Prophet, sent to preach and confirm the
(570–632 CE) monotheistic teachings of Adam, Noah, Abraham, Moses, Jesus and other Prophets. See Chapter 1.

Mujahid, pl. someone who struggles in the path of God, who makes
Mujahideen jihad, often with the meaning of armed jihad.

Murtad an apostate, someone who officially abandons the Islamic religion and rebels against a Muslim state. The word is incorrectly used by Islamist Extremists to refer to Muslim states that deal with non-Muslim governments.

Muslim someone who has submitted to God by following Islam.

Noah a Prophet of the Abrahamic religions of Judaism, Christianity and Islam, known as Nuh in Arabic.

Ottoman a Muslim-led state that controlled much of Southeastern
(Empire) Europe, Western Asia, and Northern Africa between
(1299–1922 CE) the 14th and early 20th centuries. See Chapter 1.

Qur'an the central religious text of Islam, believed by Muslims to be a revelation of guidance from God (*Allah*). See Chapter 2.

Quraysh the powerful Meccan Arab tribe to which the Prophet Muhammad belonged. See Chapter 1.

Qutb, Sayyid a key Egyptian Islamist ideologue. See Chapter 2.
(1906–1966)

Rakat	a single iteration of prescribed movements and supplications performed by Muslims as part of the Obligatory Daily Prayer known as *As-Salah*. See Chapter 2.
Ramadan	the 9th month of the Islamic calendar, observed by Muslims worldwide as a month of fasting, prayer, reflection and community. The annual observance of Ramadan is regarded as one of the Pillars of Islam and lasts 29 to 30 days, from one sighting of the crescent moon to the next.
Rashidun, or 'Rightly Guided Successors' (632–662 CE)	the first four Successors (Caliphs) to the Prophet Muhammad in leadership of the Muslim community after his death.
Riba	Arabic word for usury/charging interest on loans and other financial malpractices.
Sabr	Arabic Islamic word for patience.
Sadaqa	charity given voluntarily in order to please God (Allah).
Salaf as–Salih	the Pious Predecessors, who were the first three generations of Muslims, that is the generations of the Prophet Muhammad and his Companions (the Sahabah), their Successors (the Tabi'un) and the Successors of the Successors (the Taba Tabi'in).
Salafi	followers of the Pious Predecessors. Salafi usually refers to those who follow the stripped-down reformed Hanbalism of Muhammad ibn Abal Wahhab in their aspiration to copy the Pious Predecessors as closely as possible in every detail.
Salal Allahu alayhi wa salim	'God bless him and grant him peace'. An honorific used in religious circumstances when the name of the Prophet Muhammad is mentioned.
Sawm	the Obligatory Fast of the month of Ramadan, the 9th month of the Islamic lunar calendar, when adult Muslims abstain from food, drink and sexual activity between dawn and dusk for 29–30 days.

Shah Muhammad Reza Pahlavi of Iran	the last Shah (King) of Iran from 16 September 1941 until his overthrow in the Iranian Revolution on 11 February 1979.
Shahada	the Witnessing. The first Individual Religious Obligation of Islam to witness that there is no god except the One God (*Allah*) and Muhammad is the Messenger of God.
Sharia	the Legal Pathway of Islam derived from The Qur'an and the Customary Prophetic Example of Muhammad (Sunna). See Chapter 2.
Shaytan	Arabic word for 'Satan'.
Shia t'ul Ali	the Party of Ali ibn Abi Talib. The faction which was loyal to the claims of Ali to be the first Successor to Muhammad which over generations developed into distinctively Shia Islam. See Chapter 2. Twelver Shia, Ismaili Shia, Zaydi Shia and Ibadi Shias are some of the subdivisions within Shia Islam.
Shirk	associating and/or worshipping partners with God in his Divinity.
Shura	counsel, usually in the political sense of taking counsel.
Solomon	a Prophet of the Abrahamic religions of Judaism, Christianity and Islam, known as Suleiman in Arabic.
Soviet–Afghan War (1979–1989 CE)	a conflict wherein insurgent groups (known collectively as the Mujahideen) fought a nine-year guerrilla war against the Soviet Army and the Democratic Republic of Afghanistan government throughout the 1980s. See Chapter 1.
Sufi	a follower of Sufism. See also *Tasawwuf*.
Sunna	the Normative Prophetic Example of Muhammad, which is the second primary source of Islam with The Qur'an. See Chapter 2.
Surah	a chapter of The Qur'an, which is comprised of 114 Surahs.

Tafsir	commentary on The Qur'an to explain its meanings.
Taghut	an Arabic term that is specifically used to denounce everything that is worshipped instead of or besides Allah. Can refer to idols or in the contemporary context is used by Islamists to refer to a tyrannical political regime.
Taqiyya	literally 'prudence, fear', is a precautionary denial of religious belief and practice in the face of persecution.
Tasbih	a set or string of 33, 66 or 99 prayer beads used by Muslims as a counting aid in reciting the 99 names of God and in other forms of Remembrance.
Tasawwuf	'Sufism', the sciences of purifying the heart to approach the Presence of God.
Tawba	Arabic Islamic word for Repentance.
Tawhid	the doctrine of the Unity of God: a core doctrine of Mainstream Islam that is abused by Islamist Extremists.
Thawb	a loose robe or cloak of a kind traditionally worn by Arabs.
Torah	the first five books of the Hebrew bible – Genesis, Exodus, Leviticus, Numbers and Deuteronomy.
Ulema, **sing.** *Alim*	literally 'those who know' how to make legal judgments, that is, jurists. Often in the past, the *Ulema* were adept in a whole range of knowledges including, for example, law, philosophy, mathematics, poetry and music theory.
Umayyad	the early Islamic ruling dynasty descended from Uthman ibn Affan whose capital was in Damascus, Syria. See Chapter 1.
Umma	the global faith-community of Muslim believers.
Umrah	Lesser pilgrimage to Mecca.

Urf

'custom', a category of legal decision-making in Sharia Law which takes account of the customs of a particular place.

Wudu

the Islamic procedure for cleansing parts of the body, a type of ritual purification or ablution. Consists of washing the face and arms, then wiping the head and finally washing the feet with water. See Chapter 2.

Zakah

the 'Poor Tax', an obligatory payment of 2.5 per cent of a Muslim's savings above a certain threshold paid annually for the upkeep of the poor and others in need. See Chapter 2.

References

Abulafia, D. 2012. *The Great Sea: A Human History of the Mediterranean.* Reprint edition. London: Penguin.

Aebi, M. F. and Tiago, M. M. 2020. *SPACE I-2019 – Council of Europe Annual Penal Statistics: Prison Populations.* Strasbourg: Council of Europe. https://wp.unil.ch/space/files/2021/02/200405_FinalReport_SPACE_I_2019.pdf

Al-Banna, H. 1975. *Five Tracts of Hassan Al-Banna (1906–1949): A Selection from the Majmu'at Rasa'il al-Imamal-Shahid Hasan al-Banna.* Berkeley, CA: University of California Press.

Al-Ghazali with Black, D. 2009. *Music and Singing.* Kuala Lumpur: Islamic Book Trust.

Ali, S. 2015. *British Muslims in Numbers.* Muslim Council of Britain. https://www.mcb.org.uk/wp-content/uploads/2015/02/MCBCensusReport_2015.pdf

Al-Khalili, J. 2012. *Pathfinders: The Golden Age of Arabic Science.* London: Penguin.

Allawi, A. A. 2009. *The Crisis of Islamic Civilization.* New Haven, CT: Yale University Press.

Al-Maghafi, N. 2019. *Undercover with the Clerics: Iraq's Secret Sex Trade.* Aired BBC 2, 23:15, 13 November.

Al-Oadah, S. 2014. 'Obeying the Law in Non-Muslim Countries'. *Islam Today.* 10 November. http://en.islamtoday.net/node/604

Al-Qaradawi, Y. 1994. *The Lawful and the Prohibited in Islam.* Plainfield, IN: American Trust Publications.

Archer, L. 2001. '"Muslim Brothers, Black Lads, Traditional Asians": British Muslim Young Men's Constructions of Race, Religion and Masculinity'. *Feminism & Psychology* 11: 79–105.

Azzam, A. Y. 1987. *Join the Caravan.* London: Azzam Publications.

Barr, J. 2012. *A Line in the Sand: Britain, France and the Struggle that Shaped the Middle East.* UK edition. London: Simon & Schuster.

Becci, I. and Schneuwly Purdie, M. 2012. 'Gendered Religion in Prison? Comparing Imprisoned Men and Women's Expressed Religiosity in Switzerland'. *Women's Studies* 41(6): 1–22.

Bhaskar, R. 2008. *Dialectic: The Pulse of Freedom.* 2nd edition. Abingdon: Routledge.

Bin Ali, M. 2015. *The Roots of Religious Extremism: Understanding the Salafi Doctrine of Al-Wala' Wal Bara'.* London: Imperial College Press.

Bonner, M. D. 2006. *Jihad in Islamic History.* Princeton, NJ: Princeton University Press.

Botterhill, D. and Gora, M. 2000. *Guidelines for the Preparation of Food for Muslim Prisoners and Procedures for Ramadan.* London: HMPS.

Bowen, I. 2013. *Medina in Birmingham, Najaf in Brent: Inside British Islam*. London: Hurst.

Brown, J. A. C. 2009. *Hadith: Muhammad's Legacy in the Medieval ad Modern World*. London: Oneworld Publications.

Buijs, F. J. and Rath, J. 2002. *Muslims in Europe: The State of Research*. New York, NY: Russell Sage Foundation.

Burke, J. 2003. *Al-Qaeda*. London: Penguin.

Clear, T., Clear, T. R., Hardyman, P. L., Stout, B., Lucken, K. and Dammer, H. R. 2000. 'The Value of Religion in Prison'. *Journal of Contemporary Criminal Justice* 16(1): 53–74.

Clear, T. and Sumter, M. T. 2002. 'Prisoners, Prison, and Religion'. *Journal of Offender Rehabilitation* 35(3–4): 125–56.

Coates, S. 2016. 'Unlocking Potential: A Review of Education in Prison'. *Ministry of Justice*. https://assets.publishing.ser-vice.gov.uk/government/uploads/system/uploads/attach-ment_data/file/524013/education-rev iew-report.pdf

Cook, S. and Griffiths, J. 2019. 'London Bridge Attack: "The Killer Sat Feet Away from Me. Now I Fear for the Scheme That Helped Me Go Straight."' *The Times Online*. https://www.thetimes.co.uk/article/london-bridge-att ack-the-killer-sat-feet-away-from-me-now-i-fear-for-the-scheme-that-hel ped-me-go-straight-3pxnmtgvc

De Galembert, C. 2020. *Islam et prison*. 1st edition. Paris: Éditions Amsterdam.

Desilver, D. and Masci, D. 2017. *World's Muslim Population More Widespread than You Might Think*. https://www.pewresearch.org/fact-tank/2017/01/31/worlds-muslim-population-more-widespread-than-you-might-think/

El-Menouar, Y. and Vopel, S. 2017. *Clear Progress for Integration of Muslims in Western Europe*. https://www.bertelsmann-stiftung.de/en/topics/lat-est-news/2017/august/clear-progress-for-integration-of-muslims-in-west ern-europe

Faraj, M. A. S. 1979. *The Absent Obligation*, ed. Umamah, A. Birmingham: Maktabah al-Ansar.

Fatsis, L. 2021. 'Who's Afraid of Critical Race Theory Today?' *thebscblog*. https://thebscblog.wordpress.com/2021/01/27/whos-afraid-of-critical-race-theory-today/

Fazel, S. and Wolf, A. 2015. 'A Systematic Review of Criminal Recidivism Rates Worldwide: Current Difficulties and Recommendations for Best Practice'. *PLoS ONE* 10(6). https://www.researchgate.net/publication/278714801_A_Systematic_Review_of_Criminal_Recidivism_Rates_Worldwide_Current_Difficulties_and_Recommenda-tions_for_Best_P ractice

Foucault, M. 1979. *Discipline and Punish*. Harmondsworth: Penguin.

Gilliat-Ray, S., Ali, M. and Pattison, S. 2013. *Understanding Muslim Chaplaincy*. Farnham: Ashgate.

Goffman, E. 1961. *Asylums: Essays on the Social Situation of Mental Patients and Other Inmates*. Garden City, NY: Anchor Books.

Graham, M. 2006. *How Islam Created the Modern World*. 1st edition. Beltsville, MD: Amana Publications.

Haleem, M. A. A. 2010. *The Quran English Translation and Parallel Text*. Oxford: Oxford World's Classics.

Haleem, M. A. A. 2016. *The Qur'an: A New Translation*. Oxford: Oxford University Press.

Hamm, M. 2009. 'Prison Islam in the Age of Sacred Terror'. *British Journal of Criminology* 49(5): 667–85.

Hamm, M. 2013. *The Spectacular Few: Prisoner Radicalization and the Evolving Terrorist Threat*. New York, NY: New York University Press.

Haq, I. and Khatib, H. A. 2012. 'Light through the Dark Ages: The Arabist Contribution to Western Ophthalmology'. *Oman Journal of Ophthalmology* 5(2): 75–8.

Head, J. 1999. *Understanding the Boys: Issues of Behaviour and Achievement*. London: Falmer Press.

Her Majesty's Prison & Probation Service. 2018. *Prison Officer Entry-Level Training Core Curriculum V3.2*. London: Her Majesty's Prison & Probation Service.

Her Majesty's Prison & Probation Service. 2020. *Prison Population Statistics December*. London: Her Majesty's Prison & Probation Service.

Hermansen, M. 2014. 'Conversion to Islam in Theological and Historical Perspectives'. In *Oxford Handbook of Religious Conversion*, eds. Rambo, L. and Farhadian, C. E. Oxford: Oxford University Press, 632–66.

Hourani, A. 2005. *Reason and Tradition in Islamic Ethics*. Cambridge: Cambridge University Press.

Huda 2020. 'Are There Special Rules for Handling the Quran?' *Learn Religions*, 26 August, learnreligions.com/when-handling-the-quran-2004549

Huntingdon, S. P. 1996. *The Clash of Civilizations*. New York, NY: Simon & Schuster.

Hussain, M. 2012. *The Five Pillars of Islam: Laying the Foundations of Divine Love and Service to Humanity*. Markfield: Kube Publishing Ltd.

Hussain, S. 2008. *Muslims on the Map*. London: Tauris Academic Studies.

Ignatieff, M. 1989. *A Just Measure of Pain: The Penitentiary in the Industrial Revolution, 1750–1850*. Harmondsworth: Penguin.

Iqbal, S. and Titheradge, N. 2016. 'Prison Islam Course "Could Turn Prisoners to Violence"'. *BBC News*. https://www.bbc.com/news/uk-36419430

Irfan, L. and Wilkinson, M. L. N. 2020. 'The Ontology of the Muslim Male Offender: A Critical Realist Framework'. *Journal of Critical Realism* 19(5): 481–99.

Irwin-Rogers, K. 2018. 'Racism and Racial Discrimination in the Criminal Justice System: Exploring the Experiences and Views of Men Serving Sentences of Imprisonment'. *Justice, Power and Resistance* 2(2): 243–66.

Ishaq I. 1955. *The Life of Muhammad*, trans. Guillaume, A. Oxford: Oxford University Press.

Kaiser, K. A. and Holtfreter, K. 2015. 'An Integrated Theory of Specialized Court Programs: Using Procedural Justice and Therapeutic Jurisprudence to Promote Offender Compliance and Rehabilitation'. *Criminal Justice and Behavior* 43(1): 45–62.

Kamali, M. H. 2003. *Principles of Islamic Jurisprudence*. Cambridge: Cambridge University Press.

Kamali, M. H. 2008. *Maqasid Al-Sharia'ah Made Simple*. London: International Institute of Islamic Thought.

Kamali, M. H. 2013. 'Introduction'. In *War and Peace in Islam*, eds. Prince Ghazi bin Muhammad, Kalin, I. and Kamali, M. H. Cambridge: The Islamic Texts Society.

Kamali, M. H. 2015. *The Middle Path of Moderation in Islam: The Qur'anic Principle of Wasatiyyah*. Oxford; New York, NY: Oxford University Press.

Kamali, M. H. 2017. *Shariah Law: Questions and Answers*. London: Oneworld Publications.

Kennedy, H. 2016. *The Caliphate*. London: Pelican.

Kerr, M. H. 1966. *Islamic Reform: The Political and Legal Theories of Muhammad 'Abduh and Rashid Rida*. Berkeley, CA: California University Press.

Khan, N., Chowdhury, S. and Alkiek, T. 2019. 'Women in Islamic Law: Examining Five Prevalent Myths'. *Yaqeen Institute for Islamic Research*. https://yaqeeninstitute.org/nazir-khan/women-in-islamic-law-examining-five-prevalent-myths

Lammy, D. 2017. *The Lammy Review: An Independent Review into the Treatment of, and Outcomes for, Black, Asian and Minority Ethnic Individuals in the Criminal Justice System*. https://www.gov.uk/government/publications/lammy-re-view-final-report

Lecker, M. 2004. *The 'Constitution of Medina': Muḥammad's First Legal Document*. Princeton: The Darwin Press.

Leghtas, I. 2016. 'Double Punishment: Inadequate Conditions for Prisoners with Psychosocial Disabilities in France'. *Human Rights Watch*. https://www.hrw.org/report/2016/04/05/double-punishment/inadequate-conditions-Prisoners-psychosocial-disabilities

Liebling, A., Arnold, H. and Straub, C. 2011. 'An Exploration of Staff–Prisoner Relationships at HMP Whitemoor: 12 Years on Revised Final Report'. Cambridge: Ministry of Justice National Offender Management Service & Cambridge Institute of Criminology, Prisons Research Centre.

Liebling, A. and Arnold, H. 2012. 'Social Relationships Between Prisoners in a Maximum Security Prison: Violence, Faith and the Declining Nature of Trust'. *Journal of Criminal Justice*, 40(5), Sep–Oct, 413–24.

Lings, M. 1983. *Muhammad: His Life Based on the Earliest Sources*. 3rd edition. New York, NY: The Islamic Texts Society.

Lipka, M. 2017. *Muslims and Islam: Key Findings in the US and around the World*. Pew Research Center. https://www.pewresearch.org/fact-tank/2017/08/09/muslims-and-islam-key-findings-in-the-u-s-and-around-the-world/

Luwayhiq, Abd Al-Rahman Ibn Mualla and l Rahmaan Ibn Mualaa Al-Luwaihiq Al-Mutairi 2001. *Religious Extremism in the Lives of Contemporary Muslims*. Bilingual edition. Denver, CO: Al-Basheer Publications & Translations.

Madelung, W. 1997. *The Succession to Muhammad: A Study of the Early Caliphate*. Cambridge: Cambridge University Press.

Makdisi, G. 2013. *The Rise of Colleges*. CreateSpace Independent Publishing Platform.

Martínez-Ariño, J. and Zwilling, A.-L., eds. 2020. *Religion and Prison: An Overview of Contemporary Europe*. Cham: Springer International Publishing.

Maruna, S., Wilson, L. and Curran, K. 2006. 'Why God Is Often Found Behind Bars: Prison Conversions and the Crisis of Self-Narrative'. *Research in Human Development* 3(2): 161–84.

Maududi, A. A. 1967. *The Process of Islamic Revolution*. Lahore: Islamic Publications.

Maududi, A. A. 1975. 'Political Theory of Islam'. In *Islam: Its Meaning and Message*. Leicester: The Islamic Foundation, 147–71.

Maududi, A. A. 1980. *Jihad in Islam*. Beirut: The Holy Koran Publishing House.

Mauer, M. 2017. 'Incarceration Rates in an International Perspective'. In *Oxford Encyclopedia of Criminology and Criminal Justice*. https://doi.org/10.1093/acre-fore/9780190264079.013.233

McCants, W. 2015. *The ISIS Apocalypse: The History, Strategy and Doomsday Vision of the Islamic State*. London: St. Martin's Press.

McCarthy, V. A. 1978. *The Phenomenology of Moods in Kierkegaard*. The Hague: Springer.

Mental Health in Prisons. 2017. House of Commons. https://publications.parliament.uk/pa/cm201719/cmse-lect/cmpubacc/400/400.pdf

Millie, A., Jacobson, J. and Hough, M. 2003. 'Understanding the Growth in the Prison Population in England and Wales'. *Criminal Justice* 3(4): 369–87.

Mills, A. and Kendall, K. 2016. 'Mental Health in Prisons'. In *Handbook on Prisons*, eds. Jewkes, Y., Crewe, B. and Bennett, J. London: Routledge, 187–204. https://www.taylorfrancis.com/books/9781317754558/chapters/10.4324/9781315797779-12

Ministry of Justice 2011. 'Prison Service Instruction 43/2011 Managing and Reporting Extremist Behaviour'.

Ministry of Justice 2014. *The Impact of Experience in Prison on the Employment Status of Longer-Sentenced Prisoners after Release.* https://www.gov.uk/gov ernment/publications/the-impact-of-ex-perience-in-prison-on-the-emp loyment-status-of-longer-sentenced-Prisoners-after-release

Ministry of Justice 2016. 'Prison Service Instruction 05/2016 Faith and Pastoral Care for Prisoners'.

Ministry of Justice 2017. *Freedom of Information Act (FOIA) Request 112352.* June.

Ministry of Justice 2020. *Offender Management Statistics Quarterly: April to June 2020.* https://www.gov.uk/govern-ment/statistics/offender-managem ent-statistics-quar-terly-april-to-june-2020/offender-management-statis-tics-quarterly-april-to-june-2020

Ministry of Justice 2021. *Security catergorisation policy framework.* London: Ministry of Justice.

Moore, D. L. 2007. 'Constructing a Learning Community'. In *Overcoming Religious Illiteracy: A Cultural Studies Approach to the Study of Religion in Secondary Education,* ed. Moore, D. L. New York, NY: Palgrave Macmillan, 111–38. https://doi.org/10.1057/9780230607002_5

Moore, D. L. 2016. *Teaching Understanding.* Harvard Divinity School. https://www.youtube.com/watch?v=2YOyW1-wTFI

Moorhouse, Geoffrey. 1984. *India Britannica.* New edition. London: Flamingo.

Mushtaq, G. 2011. *The Music Made Me Do It.* Riyadh: IIPH.

Newing, H. 2019. 'England and Wales Has Highest Imprisonment Rates in Western Europe'. *Thejusticegap.com.* https://www.thejusticegap.com/ england-and-wales-has-highest-imprisonment-rates-in-western-europe

van Nieuwkerk, K., ed. 2006. *Women Embracing Islam.* Austin, TX: University of Texas Press.

van Nieuwkerk, K. 2014. '"Conversion" to Islam and the Construction of a Pious Self'. *The Oxford Handbook of Religious Conversion.* http://www.oxfo rdhandbooks.com/view/10.1093/oxfordhb/9780195338522.001.0001/ ox-fordhb-9780195338522-e-028

Nyhagen, L. 2019. 'Mosques as Gendered Spaces: The Complexity of Women's Compliance with, and Resistance to, Dominant Gender Norms, and the Importance of Male Allies'. *Religions* 10(5): 321. https://doi. org/10.3390/rel10050321

Otto, R. 1958. *The Idea of the Holy: 14.* 2nd edition. New York, NY: Oxford University Press.

Pew Research Centre. 2017. 'Muslim Population Growth in Europe'. *Pew Research Center's Religion & Public Life Project.* https://www.pewforum.org/ 2017/11/29/eu-ropes-growing-muslim-population/

Philips, B. 2007. *The Clash of Civilisations*. Birmingham: Al-Hidaayah Publishing & Distribution.

Phillips, C. 2012. *The Multicultural Prison: Ethnicity, Masculinity, and Social Relations among Prisoners*. Oxford: Oxford University Press.

Phillips, C. and Bowling, B. 2017. 'Ethnicities, Racism, Crime and Criminal Justice'. In *The Oxford Handbook of Criminology*, eds. Liebling, A., Maruna, S. and McAra, L. Oxford: Oxford University Press.

Pina-Sánchez, J., Roberts, J. V. and Sferopoulos, D. 2019. 'Does the Crown Court Discriminate Against Muslim-Named Offenders? A Novel Investigation Based on Text Mining Techniques'. *The British Journal of Criminology* 59(3): 718–36.

Poushter, J. 2015. 'Most Dislike ISIS in Muslim Countries'. *Pew Research Center*. https://www.pewresearch.org/fact-tank/2015/11/17/in-nations-with-significant-muslim-populations-much-disdain-for-isis/

Prison Reform Trust. 2019. *Prison: The Facts*. http://www.prisonreformtrust.org.uk/portals/0/documents/bromley%20briefings/Winter%202019%20Factfile%20web.pdf

Quraishi, M. 2005. *Muslims and Crime: A Comparative Study*. Aldershot: Ashgate.

Quraishi, M. 2020. *Towards a Malaysian Criminology*. London: Palgrave Macmillan.

Quraishi, M., Irfan, L., Schneuwly Purdie, M. and Wilkinson, M. L. N. 2022. 'Doing "Judgemental Rationality" in Empirical Research: the Importance of Depth-Reflexivity when Researching in Prison'. *Journal of Critical Realism*, 21:1, 25-45. https://doi.org/10.1080/14767430.2021.1992735

Quraishi, M. and Wilkinson, M. L. N. 2022 forthcoming. '"Oh You're on Our Side, You're my Brother": Questions of Loyalty amongst Muslim Prison Officers in Europe, a New Occupational Ontology'. *Journal of Contemporary Islam*.

Qutb, S. 1964. *Milestones*. Karachi: International Islamic.

Rahnema, A. 1994. *Pioneers of Islamic Revival*. London: Zed Books Ltd.

Rambo, L. and Farhadian, C. E. 2014. *The Oxford Handbook of Religious Conversion*. Oxford: Oxford University Press.

Roy, O. 2016. *Le Jihad et la Mort*. Paris: Seuil.

Sarg, R. and Lamine, A.-S. 2011. 'La religion en prison'. *Archives de sciences sociales des religions* 153: 85–104.

Savage, M. 2015. *Social Class in the 21st Century*. London: Pelican.

Schneuwly Purdie, M. 2011. '"Silence ... Nous sommes en direct avec Allah". Réflexions sur l'émergence d'un nouveau type d'acteur en contexte carcéral'. *Archives de Sciences Sociales des Religions* 153: 105–21.

Schneuwly Purdie, M. 2020. 'Quand l'islam s'exprime en prison. Religiosités réhabilitatrice, résistante et subversive'. In eds. Desmette, P. and Martin, P. Paris: Hémisphères Editions, 83–99.

Schneuwly Purdie, M. and Tunger-Zanetti, A. 2020. 'Switzerland'. In *Yearbook of Muslims in Europe*, ed. Scharbrodt, O. Leiden & Boston: Brill, 614–30.

Schneuwly Purdie, M., Irfan, L., Quraishi, M. and Wilkinson, M. L. N. 2021. 'Living Islam in Prison: How Gender Affects the Religious Experiences of Female and Male Offenders'. *Religions* 12(5): 298. https://doi.org/10.3390/rel12050298

Sénat 2016. 'Number of Imams in French Prisons – Senate'. https://www.senat.fr/questions/base/2015/qSEQ150114581.html

Shain, F. 2011. *The New Folk Devils: Muslim Boys and Education in England*. Stoke on Trent: Trentham Books.

Shepard, W. 2004. 'The Diversity of Islamic Thought'. In *Islamic Thought in the Twentieth Century*, eds. Taji-Faouki, S. and Nafi, B. M. London: I.B. Tauris, 61–103.

Sherif, F. 1995. *A Guide to the Contents of The Qur'an*. Reading: Garnet Publishing Ltd.

Smith, D. A. 2002. *A History of the Lute from Antiquity to The Renaissance*. New York, NY: The Lute Society of America.

Smoyer, A. B. and Minke, L. K. 2015. *Food Systems in Correctional Settings: A Literature Review and Case Study*. Copenhagen: World Health Organization.

Snow, D. A. and Machalek, R. 1982. 'The Convert as a Social Type'. *Sociological Theory* 1(1): 259–89.

Spalek, B. and El-Hassan, S. 2007. 'Muslim Converts in Prison'. *The Howard Journal of Criminal Justice* 46(2): 99–114.

Statista 2021. *Religion of Prisoners in England and Wales 2020*. https://www.statista.com/statistics/872042/leading-religions-of-prisoners-in-england-and-wales

Strachan, H. 2014. *The First World War: A New History*. Reissue edition. London; Toronto: Simon & Schuster.

Sturge, G. 2019. *UK Prison Population Statistics*. London: House of Commons Library.

Sunnah.com 2022a. *Sunan An-Nasai*. Vol 3. Book 24. Hadith 3057.

Sunnah.com 2022b. *Hadith 34, 40 Hadith an-Nawawi*. Sunnah.com.

Sykes, G. 1958. *The Society of Captives: A Study of a Maximum Security Prison*. Princeton, NJ: Princeton University Press.

Tajfel, H. 1981. *Human Groups and Social Categories*. Cambridge: Cambridge University Press.

Taji-Farouki, S. and Basheer, M. N., eds. 2004. *Islamic Thought in the Twentieth Century*. London: I.B. Tauris.

Taylor, C. 2007. *A Secular Age*. Cambridge, MA: The Belknap Press of Harvard University Press.

TheyWorkForYou 2021. 'Prison Ministers of Religion. Ministry of Justice, written question from Crispin Blunt (MP) to Robert Buckland (Minister of State, Ministry of Justice) Answered 24 May 2019'. https://www.theywork-foryou.com/wrans/?id=2019-05-16.255249.h

Timani, H.S. 2008 *Modern Intellectual Readings of the Kharijites*. New York, NY: Peter Lang Publishing.

Tipton, L. and Todd, A. 2011. *The Role and Contribution of a Multi-Faith Prison Chaplaincy to the Contemporary Prison Service*. Cardiff: Cardiff Centre for Chaplaincy Studies. https://orca.cf.ac.uk/29120/1/Chaplaincy%20Report%20Final%20Draft%20(3).pdf

Trzebiatowska, M. and Bruce, S. 2012. *Why Are Women More Religious than Men?* Oxford: Oxford University Press.

Ugelvik, T. 2011. 'The Hidden Food: Mealtime Resistance and Identity Work in a Norwegian Prison'. *Punishment & Society* 13(1): 47–63.

UK Government 2016. *Summary of the Main Findings of the Review of Islamist Extremism in Prisons, Probation and Youth Justice*. https://www.gov.uk/government/publications/islamist-extremism-in-prisons-probation-and-youth-justice/summary-of-the-main-findings-of-the-review-of-islamist-extremism-in-prisons-probation-and-youth-justice

Webster, C. and Qasim, M. 2018. 'The Effects of Poverty and Prison on British Muslim Men Who Offend'. *Social Sciences* 7(10): 184. https://www.mdpi.com/2076-0760/7/10/184#cite

Welle, D. 2018. 'How Important Is Religion in the Daily Life of European Muslims?' *DW.COM*. https://www.dw.com/en/islam-shouldnt-culturally-shape-germany-alexan-der-dobrindt-claims/a-43335131

Wilkinson, M. L. N. 2014. 'The Concept of the Absent Curriculum: The Case of the Muslim Contribution and the English National Curriculum for History'. *Journal of Curriculum Studies* 46(4): 419–40.

Wilkinson, M. L. N. 2015a. *A Fresh Look at Islam in a Multi-Faith World: A Philosophy for Success Through Education*. Abingdon: Routledge.

Wilkinson, M. L. N. 2015b. 'The Metaphysics of a Contemporary Islamic Shari'a: A MetaRcalist Perspective'. *Journal of Critical Realism* 14(4): 350–65.

Wilkinson, M. L. N. 2019. *The Genealogy of Terror: How to Distinguish between Islam, Islamist and Islamist Extremism*. London; New York, NY: Routledge.

Wilkinson, M. L. N., Irfan, L., Schneuwly Purdie, M. and Quraishi, M. 2021. 'Prison as a Site of Intense Religious Change: The Example of Conversion to Islam'. *Religions* 12(3): 162.

Williams, R. J. 2018. 'Islamic Piety and Becoming Good in English Prisons'. *British Journal of Criminology* 58(3): 730–48.

Williams, R. J. and Liebling, A. 2018. 'Faith Provision, Institutional Power, and Meaning among Muslim Prisoners in Two English High-Security Prisons'. In *Finding Freedom in Confinement: The Role of Religion in Prison Life*, ed. Kerley, K. R. Santa Barbara, CA: Praeger, 269–91.

Wolff, H., Sebo, P., Haller, D. M., Eytan, A., Niveau, G., Bertrand, D., Gétaz, L. and Cerutti, B. 2011. 'Health Problems among Detainees in Switzerland: A Study Using the ICPC-2 Classification'. *BMC Public Health* 11: 245–258.

Woodhead, L. 2012. 'Gender Differences in Religious Practice and Significance'. *Travail, genre et société* 27(1): 33–54.

World Prison Brief. 2021a. *France | World Prison Brief.* https://www.prison studies.org/country/france

World Prison Brief. 2021c. 'Switzerland | World Prison Brief'. https://www.prisonstudies.org/country/switzerland

World Prison Brief. 2021d. *United Kingdom: England & Wales | World Prison Brief.* https://www.prisonstudies.org/country/united-kingdom-engl and-wales

Zwilling, A.-L. 2020. 'France'. In *Yearbook of Muslims in Europe*, eds. Raius, E., Egdūnas Račius, E., Müssig, S., Akgönül, S., Alibašić, A., Nielsen, J.S. and Scharbrodt, O. Leiden: Brill, 183–202.

Index

References to figures, images and infographics appear in *italic* type; those in **bold** type refer to tables. References to footnotes show both the page number and the note number (194n6).